MAHA-NATAKA,

A

DRAMATIC HISTORY

OF

KING RAMA

MAHA-NATAKA,

A

DRAMATIC HISTORY

OF

KING RAMA

TRANSLATOR

MAHA-RAJA KALI-KRISHNA BAHADUR

GYAN

Published by

Gyan Publishing House
5, Ansari Road
Daryaganj, New Delhi-110002
Phone: 011-47034999, 9811692060
E-mail: books@gyanbooks.com

Distribution Network
gyanbooks.com
India, USA, Canada, UK, Australia

ISBN: 978-93-6433-418-1 (HB)
First Published, 1840

2nd Impression 2024

Printed at: Gyan Press, Delhi.

MAHA-NATAKA, A DRAMATIC HISTORY OF KING RAMA
Transalator: MAHA-RAJA KALI-KRISHNA BAHADUR

MAHÁ-NÁTAKA,

A

DRAMATIC HISTORY

OF

KING RÁMA,

BY

HANÚMAT:

TRANSLATED INTO ENGLISH,

FROM THE

ORIGINAL SANSKRITA,

BY

MAHÁ-RÁJA KÁLÍ-KRISHNA BAHÁDUR,

C. M. R. A. S., &c. &c.

Calcutta:

PRINTED BY N. ROBERTSON AND CO. AT THE COLUMBIAN PRESS,
NO. 65, COSSITOLLAH.

1840.

TO

HER MOST GRACIOUS MAJESTY

VICTORIA,

QUEEN OF THE UNITED KINGDOM

OF

GREAT BRITAIN AND IRELAND,

&c. &c. &c. &c.

THIS TRANSLATION

OF A CELEBRATED DRAMATIC POEM OF THE HINDOOS,

THE

MAHA-NATAKA,

IS

(BY PERMISSION)

HUMBLY DEDICATED

BY

HER MAJESTY'S MOST DUTIFUL SUBJECT AND MOST DEVOTED SERVANT,

KALI-KRISHNA.

PREFACE.

Of the invention and antiquity of the "MAHÁ-NÁTAKA," the late Sir William Jones says in his preface to the "*Sakuntalá-Nátaka,*" that "the first *Sanskrit* verse ever heard by mortals was pronounced in a burst of resentment by the great VÁLMIC, who flourished in the *silver* age of the world, and was author of an epic poem on the wars of his cotemporary, RÁMA, a king of *Ayodhyá;* so that no drama in verse could have been represented before his time, and the *Indians* have a wild story, that the first regular play, on the same subject with *Rámáyana,* was composed by HANÚMUT or PÁVAN, who commanded an army of Satyrs or Mountaineers in *Ráma's* expedition against *Lanká:* they add, that he engraved it on a smooth rock, which, being dissatisfied with his composition, he hurled into the sea; and that, many years after, a learned prince ordered expert divers to take impressions of the poem on wax, by which means the drama was in great measure restored. By whomsoever or in whatever age this species of entertainment was invented, it is very certain, that it was carried to great perfection in its kind, when VICRAMÁDITYA, who reigned in the first century before CHRIST, gave encouragement to poets, philologers, and mathematicians."

According to the "*Adbhuta-Rámáyana,*" the history of king RÁMA contains *a hundred millions* of *slokas* or stanzas, which had been predicted by the great Hindu sage VÁLMIC *sixty thousand years* before Ráma came into existence, and which used constantly to be read to Brahmá, when surrounded by sapient and devout beings. From among the whole number of stanzas *twenty five thousand*, in *seven* cantos, are known to mortals on earth.

This *play*, the "Mahá-Nátaka," is highly approved of for its composition, and very popular among Pandits or learned men, and generally read by such pupils of theirs as are advanced in learning. It is written with such conciseness, that it comprises, in nine acts, the principal subjects of the voluminous *Rámáyana*, and includes descriptions of the supernatural actions of Ráma, whom the Hindus acknowledge to have been the incarnate Vishnu, and of Hanúmána, the progeny of the wind, besides numerous allusions to other parts of Hindu mythology.

I have my Pandit's authority, though he states it as a tradition, for saying, that Kálidása, the brightest gem in the court of Vikramáditya, has given lustre to this work, and displayed his genius, by changing some words or adding some *slokas*, with a view to render it a perfect drama. He adds, that when Vikramáditya had gone by desire of Mihir, a well-known astronomer, to the shores of the ocean in company of his nine courtiers, and there pitched his tent, Hanúmána coming to the knowledge of Kálidása's enterprise, hid himself behind a cloud, and caused it to appear as a mountain from a distance, in order to frighten Kálidása, who at this time thought, that if any misapplication of words and phrases had crept into the Nátaka, the mountain would fall upon the tent, and crush all that were in it, to death. He therefore spared no pains to complete the task in the best manner practicable. And HANÚMÁNA threw a garland upon KÁLIDÁSA's head as a reward and a mark of satisfaction.

Some time after, MADHUSÚDANA MISSARA, an up-country Pandit, edited the "MAHÁ-NÁTAKA" and arranged the *slokas*. Since which time, his examplar has been universally received.

In the "*Adbhuta Rámáyana*" I find there are, independent of the *twenty-five thousand* stanzas above alluded to, *a thousand slokas* which VÁLMIC pronounced in honour of SÍTÁ and RÁMA.

There is another kind of *Rámáyana* entitled the "*Adhyatma Rámáyana*" which was uttered by SHIVA in an address to PÁRVATÍ his consort; the work consists of *four thousand* and *two hundred slokas*, and is intended for the benefit of the people.

The Pandit KÍRTIVÁSA of Bengál, and TULSIDÁSA of Upper Hindusthán, have translated the *seven Cantos* of the *Rámáyana* into their own dialects; the former into *Bháshá* or *Bengáli*, and the latter in *Brija-Bhákhá*, and these have been widely circulated for many years.

I undertook to publish an English translation of the "MAHÁ-NÁTAKA," in compliance with the wish of my learned friend Captain A. Troyer, formerly Secretary to the Government Sanskrit College of Calcutta, and now a resident in Paris, that a correct edition of the original *Nátaka* should be published for the use of my countrymen and of foreigners. To fulfill this intention I have made a collection of a dozen manuscript copies both ancient and modern, and a printed copy in the Bengálí character, to compare them with one another; and I have not been wanting in my endeavours, aided by my Pandit, to present the reader with a correct edition of the work in *Dévanágara*, and with a translation in every respect faithful to the original, except in the omission of a few passages which would appear exceptionable to modern taste and refinement.

I perfectly coincide with Professor H. H. Wilson, "that it does not seem probable the Hindus ever knew what *scenes* were, and that they substituted curtains for them." But to avoid obscurity, I have, with reference to the subject of each act, indicated in the *headings* both in *English* and *Sanskrita*, the scenes where the transactions are supposed to occur. I have interspersed some annotations, to facilitate the perusal of the author by English readers.

The difficulties attendant on the translation of a dramatic work from one language into another, will, I trust, be deemed a sufficient apology for any mistakes which may have crept into this version, especially when it is taken into consideration, that this is my first attempt in translating plays into a tongue which is foreign to me.

KÁLÍ-KRISHNA.

Sobhá-Bázár,
June 5*th*, 1840.

PRINCIPAL CHARACTERS OF THE DRAMA.

MALES.

DASHARATHA, *the king of Ayodhyá.*
RÁMA, *the eldest son of Dasharatha.*
LAKSHMANA, *the second son of Dasharatha.*
SHATRUGHANA, *the third son of Dasharatha.*
BHARATA, *the fourth son of Dasharatha.*
PARASHURÁMA, *a Brahman.*
JANAKA, *the king of Mithilá,* (in Tirhoot.)
MÁRÍCHA, *in the shape of a golden deer.*
RÁVANA, *the ten-headed king of Lanká.*
VÁLÍ, *the king of Vánaras.*
SUGRÍVA, *the king of Kiskindá, and the Ally of Ráma.*
HANÚMÁNA, *the destroyer of Lanká.*
ANGADA, *the son of Válí.*
VIBHÍSHANA, *the brother of Rávana.*
THE MANAGER *of the play.*

FEMALES.

SÍTÁ, *the wife of Ráma.*
KÉKAÍ, SUMITRÁ, } *the wives of Dasharatha.*
TÁRÁ, *the wife of Sugríva.*
MANDODARÍ, *the wife of Rávana.*
SARAMÁ, *the wife of Vibhíshana.*

Besides these, Bards, Sages, Charioteers, Female Attendants and Travellers, Citizens, Generals, Male and Female Rákshasas, Courtiers, Ministers, Porters, the Regent of Death, Physicians, Messengers, &c.

*** All the proper names and Sanskrita words introduced in the translation and notes, are spelt according to the Romanized system.

MAHÁ-NÁTAKA,

OR

THE GRAND DRAMA.

THE BENEDICTION.

May the Lord of the universe, the self-existent omnipresent Being, whose ministers are the three primitive qualities* through which He of his own will creates, protects and destroys the world at times, whose glory is illimitable, and who without the organs of sense is skilled in all their operations, bless you!

2. May the remover of obstacles, who by the tip of his trunk † emptied the ocean and scattered its waters abroad to the astonishment of the heavenly divinities, who seeing it exclaimed, where is Vishnu, where is Brahmá, where is Ananta, where is Lakshamí, where is the submarine fire, where are the mountains, where are the gems, where are the crocodiles, and where is the *chakra?*‡ protect you!

3. May the head of the tribe of Raghu, the promoter of the happiness of Koushalyá, that is, Ráma, the destroyer of the ten-headed Rávana, the son of Dasharatha, he whose eyes are like the water-lily, be ever glorified!

4. I acknowledge the deity resembling the *kalpa* § tree; the archer; of an azure-colored body, the sight of which is

* Pleasure, benevolence, and irascibility.

† Ganésha or the god of wisdom.

‡ A discus or sharp circular missile weapon, used by Vishnu, who is otherwise called *Chakra-páni* or one who wields the discus.

§ A fabled tree growing in Indra's paradise and yielding any fruit that one may desire, (figuratively a very generous man.)

pleasing to mankind ; whose face is like the lotus ; whose abode the goddess of fortune never quits.

5. Ráma, who was born before Lakshmana, and is the chief of the Raghus, and the husband of Sítá; the excellent, the descendant of Kukutsa, the merciful, the gem of virtue, the lover of Bráhmans, the pious, the great king, the resolute, the son of Dasharatha, the azure-colored, the peaceful, I acknowledge as the glory of men, as the prince of the Raghu-tribe, the descendant of Raghu, and the enemy of Rávana.

6. The delight of the heart, eye, tongue, ear, ever pleasant and ever joyous, the son of Dasharatha, him I acknowledge.

7. The fame of Rámchandra, whose brilliancy like the moon's is diffused throughout the world, whose smiling face is like the moon, the delightful moon, the moon of the ocean* of the Raghu-tribe, the charming moon of the lily-like heart of Sítá, I acknowledge and respect.

8. May the name of Ráma, the causer of prosperity, and the hater of crimes, the life of virtuous men, the provision of travellers in the way to beatitude, the asylum of ease, the purifier of the pure words of the poets, the root of the tree of piety, be propitious to you !

9. May the arms of the head of the Raghu-tribe, the destroyers of the pride of the ten-headed Rávana,† tinted with red saffron from the chaste breasts of the daughter of Vidéha (Sítá,) like sacrificial posts to those commencing a sacrifice for the preservation of mankind, and unequalled in valour, pour upon you all their choicest blessings !

10. May his youthful actions, his breaking the bow of Shiva, his obedience to paternal authority in retiring into a wilderness, his intimacy with Sugríva,‡ his command to construct a bridge over the ocean, his high renown for killing the

---

* According to the Hindu theology, when the ocean was churned by the deities and monsters to obtain *nectar* therefrom, the moon was produced, and she showered the water of life through her beams. The moon is personified by Hindu authors as *masculine.*

† A monster, the sovereign of Lanká.

‡ The chief of monkeys.

lord of Lanká,* and his disregard even of Janaka's daughter (Sítá,) sanctify you !

Enter the Manager. †

11. *Man.* They who drink in daily the words of Válmíki‡ which issued from his pure moon-like mouth, which are most agreeable, excellent, pure, worthy to be heard, and ambrosia-like, which are contained in the Rámáyana, § exhibiting the superior qualities of Vishnu|| the teacher of the world, will obtain illustrious fame and be daily preserved from their enemies.

12. Hanúmána¶ himself being instructed by Válmíki has wondrously delineated, in this act, the achievements of Ráma, the glory of the Raghu-tribe,—of which achievements we are the actors before an assembly of wise men. O ye learned men ! be now entertained with the representation of the Rámáyana, which I mean to set before you.

ACT I.

SCENE, *a Palace in Ayodhyá.*

Enter Dasharatha, Ráma, Lakshmana, Bharata *and* Shatrughana.

13. *Man.* Dasharatha was a king and a great warrior, and the immediate descendant of the Sun ; he had three consorts, who were objects of delight and admiration. He had four sons, who were heroic and valorous, viz. Ráma, Lakshmana, Shatrughana and Bharata, the incarnate portions of the foe of Kytabha.**

14. Shatrughana was a prince and the destroyer of his enemies he was beloved of Bharata, the son of Kékaí ; Lakshmana, was the associate of Ráma, and a remakable devotee.—

* A city in Ceylon under the equinoctial line.

† It is to be observed that the manager is present during the whole of the play.

‡ A great sage. §The great epic poem of the Hindus, or the life of Ráma.

|| The second of the Hindu deities, to whom the office of preserver is ascribed by the Hindu religion.

¶ The deified monkey, who was the ally of Ráma, and the progeny of Pavana, the wind, and otherwise named Vánara.

** The name of a monster killed by Vishnu.

These were the children of Dasharatha, and the incarnate portions of the enemy of the giant Mura.*

Enter Vishwámitra.

15. *Man.* Among these, Ráma, who was invited by the son of Kushika,† was conspicuous for the performance of a certain religious ceremony, and his obedience to his father. He accompanied Lakshmana, who was the admiration of all the females of the city, and the destroyer of R ákshasas, (monsters); and he honored the place of ceremony with his presence. [*Exeunt.*

SCENE, *a Hermitage in a grove, called Shidhya-áshrama, near Buxar.*

Enter Rámchandra *with* Lakshmana.

Bards ‡ *address the assembly from behind the scene.*

16. *Bards.*—Rámchandra who had learnt from the son of Gádhi, § the good art of slaying the Rákshasas ‖ called Vijayá and Jayá, and who is the friend of devotees, enters.

[*They point to* Ráma.

(After the conclusion of the ceremony.)

17. *Bards (again.)*—Márícha, the general of the troop of the Rákshasas, being defeated by Rághava, ¶ and the rest being slain by the arrows of Lakshmana, have gone to the abode of Death.—All persons, particularly Bráhmans, together with the chief sage,** being herewith gratified, blessed them with hands uplifted, and the religious performances were concluded with magnificence.

18. *Man.* When the host of Rákshasas were thus slaugh-

---

* A name of Vishnu.

† Vishwámitra, a Hindu sage, his father Kushika was the king of Kalinga, a place near or between Cuttack and Madras.

‡ According to the custom of Hindus yet prevalent, bards on any occasion mingle in an assembly.

§ Vishwámitra.

‖ Giants.

¶ A descendant of the Raghu-tribe.

** Vishwámitra.

tered by Ráma, the ceremony terminated. And Koushika* in company with Ráma returned to the city of Janaka.

[*Exeunt.*

SCENE, *Palace of Janaka in Mithilá.*

Enter Ráma *and* Janaka.

19. *Bards (behind the scene.)* He who was sent by his father to the son of Kushika, the sage, in order to remove all obstructions to the ceremony, who in his journey to the forest had slaughtered Táraká, the famous Rákshasí, † who had received instructions in the use of arms from the sage, who had witnessed the ceremony, and who had with pleasure followed that sage, was this Rághava, who now comes in company with his brothers into the city of the head of the Nimi family. ‡

20. *Jan. (pointing to the bow.)* Whoever from among demons, gods, serpents, monkeys, or men, *kinnaras,* § demigods, or *cháranas,* ‖ is able to bend this bow, shall be rewarded with the gift of my daughter in marriage.

Enter Shoushkala.

21. *Shoush.* (*irritated.*) What severe trial would the bending of the bow be to the strong arms of him, who possesses ten-heads, who raised up Kailása,¶ which is surrounded by Hara and his consort, by Héramba (Ganésha,) by Sharánana, ** the bull, and others ?

22. *Jan.* Whoever can bend the bow of Mahéshwara †† with a string, shall have her.

Shoush.—Should not the bow belong to his Guru,‡‡ the Shambhu,§§ it will in a moment be turned and bent down.

[*Exit Shoushkala.*

* The name of the hermit Kushika, whose family is distinguished by that appellation ; here Vishwámitra is meant.

† The feminine of Rákshasa.

‡ Janaka.

§ A kind of beings with horses' heads.

‖ The choristers of heaven.

¶ The chief of all mountains.

** The god of war, represented as having six faces.

†† The name of the third or the last Hindu deity, who is represented as the destroyer of the world.

‡‡ A spiritual guide.

§§ One of the names of Shiva.

Enter Shatánanda.

23. *Man.* Hear the words of Shatánanda, the priest of Janaka, which he declared in the assembly of nobles.

24. *Shatá.* Mark, O ye chiefs! Ye children of Kshétri,* the challenge of Janaka, to which even the strength of the several arms of the ten-headed is unequal, that is, to bend the bow with its arrow and to marry the heroine of the three worlds,† the illustrious Maithilí.‡

All the chiefs strive, but are unable to bend the bow.

25. *Jan.* All the rulers have assembled here even from distant continents, to obtain my daughter, who resembles polished gold, and who is delicate and beautiful. What more can be said of her? But it is strange that none can draw, bend or raise from the ground the GREAT BOW; strange that there should be no powerful hero on the surface of the earth!

Enter Sítá *and Female Attendants.*

26. *Attend.* (*in surprise.*) Ráma is like a green herb and Jánakí is like a golden creeper. These two would be fit companions for each other; but the fulfilment of the conditions of the challenge regarding Mahádéva's bow, is a matter very difficult of achievement!

27. The bow is as hard as the shell of the tortoise, and the son of Raghu is of a delicate make; it is therefore doubtful how the conditions of the extraordinary challenge of your father can be fulfilled! [*To* Sítá.

Sítá's *looks excite* Ráma *to attempt it, and* Lakshmana *thus prompts his eagerness.*

28. *Lak.* O! dread lord of the Raghu-tribe, Lakshmana thy beloved fears not in the least the Suméru§ or other rocks, or even the Pináka.‖

* The warrior caste among Hindoos.

† Heaven, earth, and the subterraneous regions, according to the Hindu theology.

‡ Mithilá is the name of a city in the Western Provinces, the ruler of which was Janaka, whose daughter Sítá is thence termed Maithilí.

§ A celebrated mountain in the north pole according to Hindu ideas.

‖ The name of Mahádéva's bow.

29. O hero ! command me, and I will with pleasure raise, exercise, bend and break the bow.

30. *Man.* When Ráma held it, then was the auspicious moment of their happy union, and the left eye of Jánakí* as well as Jámadagna† began to flutter.

Ráma *holds the bow.*

31. *Lak.* Firm be thou, O earth, and thou, O serpent, support her ! O thou, the head of the tortoise, support them both ! Ye elephants‡ also, that at various points support the globe, while the hero attempts to string the bow.

32. The world will enter into the inferior region, the heads of the serpent will be humbled, the tortoise with the earth-bearing elephants be in agony, the *Dikpáls*§ and all the mountains will tremble, when the head of the Raghu-tribe strings the bow.

All the kings endeavour to raise the bow.

33. *Man.* When Ráma raised up the *rudra-bow,* the other lords‖ smiled; when he stringed, they laughed and clapped their hands ; but when he broke it, they fainted away and fell upon the earth.

34. When the bow was raised up, it delighted Koushika, and put the kings to shame ; and it removed the doubt of Janaka ; when the bow was drawn, it attracted the attention of Vaidéhí ; and when it was struck, it caused the fall of Bhárgava's¶ pride.

35. The powerful sound of the bow, when pressed by the nervous arms of Ráma, caused the deafness of Vidhi** and

---

* The fluttering of a woman's left-eye, is considered as a good omen, and that of a man, the reverse.

† Parashurám, the master of arms.

‡ These are eight in number.

§ Deities who superintend the several quarters of the world. They are Indra, Agni, Yama, Nirriti, Varuna, Maruta, Kuvèra, Isha, Brahmhá and Ananta.

‖ Those who were present at the assembly of Janaka.

¶ Parashuráma, who at twenty-one periods destroyed the whole race of Khsétris.

** One of the names of Brahmá, the first of the Hindu deities, who is the creator of the world.

confused the eight quarters of the world ; it shrivelled up the eight united bodies of Mahéshwara ;* and occasioned the trembling of the eight remarkable mountains ;† it deafened snakes of eight different kinds.‡

36. The great sound of the bow when broken by Shrí§ Rághava, shook the seven *lokes*,‖ and dispersed the seven horses.¶ It interrupted the meditation of the seven sages ;** it caused the seven oceans to overflow ;†† and loosened the foundations of the earth, which entered into the seven inferior regions. ‡‡

37. The terrible noise caused by the breaking of Mahádéva's bow, created such confusion that the horses were scattered ; the head of Shambhu trembled ; the supporting elephants of the globe fell ; the mountains oscillated ; the seven oceans were vehemently agitated, and the passion of Vaidéhí became like the inflamed Madana (Cupid,) whereby the three worlds had been fascinated.

38. I revere him, who in breaking the bow became the accepted and the worthy bridegroom of the daughter of Janaka ; him, who has broken the *bow* which others could not bend, and is renowned throughout the world.

SCENE, *the preparations for the marriage of* Sítá *with* Ráma.

Dasharatha *enters attended by* Shatánanda.

39. *Bards (behind the scene.)* Shrí Shatánanda declares the words of Dasharatha, regarding the marriage of his sons, which

---

* *Kshiti*, (earth) *Jala*, (water) *Agni*, (fire) *Váyu*, (wind) *Akásha* (ether) *Yajamána*, (for whom sacrifice is made) *Soma*, (the moon) and *Súrya*, (the sun).

† Namely :—Níla, Shevéta, Shringaván, Nishadha, Hémakúta, Himálaya, Mályavána, and Gandhamádana, according to the *Bhágavat Purána*.

‡ Ananta, Vásuki, Padma, Mahá-Padma, Takshaka, Kulíra, Karkata, and Shankha.

§ This word signifies auspicious, and is prefixed to the names of the Hindu gods or of men, to denote respect.

‖ Bhú, Bhuva, Su, Maha, Jana, Tapa and Satya.

¶ According to the Hindu mythology, the Sun has a car of one wheel drawn by seven grey horses.

** Maríchi, Atri, Angira, Pulastya, Pulaha, Kratu and Vashishtha.

†† The oceans of salt, of the juice of sugar-cane, of spirituous liquors, of clarified-butter, of curds, of milk, and of water.

‡‡ Atala, Vitala, Sutala, Tala, Talátala. Rasátala and Pátála.

he had learnt in private. Dasharatha being greatly delighted, is accompanied by his two other sons, the lord of the Raghu-tribe and the descendant of the Sun, all as wealthy as Indra* himself.

40. *Man.* Dasharatha, the supporter of strangers, the head of Mithilá, remarkably hospitable, has solemnized the nuptials of his sons with the daughters of Kushadhwaja.

41. A mixture of musical sounds, *Mádalas*,† *Rasálas*,‡ long trumpets, large drums and tabors, filled the atmosphere with joy when the head of the Raghu tribe obtained the hand of the daughter of Janaka (Sítá) in marriage.

42. When these great kings solemnized the auspicious marriage of their respective children, their subjects were overjoyed.

43. Sítá was married to the lord of the Raghu tribe; Bharata to Mándaví, the daughter of Kushadhwaja; Shoumitri,§ the younger brother of Ráma, to the moon-like and beautiful Unmilá; and Shatrughana to the virtuous Shrutakírti. At the happy conclusion of these marriages, each returned to his own capital with his wife.

[*Exeunt.*

ACT II.

SCENE, *a street.*

[Parashuráma *seen on the road by* Ráma *and* Lakshmana *who are riding in a car.*]

44. *Man.* The GREAT BOW of Pashupati|| has been broken by Rághava for the daughter of Janaka. On hearing this, Jámadagnya,¶ the sage, was enraged, and instantly made his appearance.

* One of the Hindu gods, he presides over the atmosphere, and is esteemed as the chief of deities.

† A kind of tabor.

‡ A sort of musical instrument.

§ From the name Shumitra is derived Shoumitri, one of the consorts of Dasharatha, whose son is Lakshmana, who is otherwise so called.

|| One of the names of Shiva.

¶ Jamadagnya was a celebrated sage, whose son is Jámadagnya, otherwise called Parashuráma.

Enter Parashuráma.

45. *Lak.* Jámadagnya, who has conquered the three worlds, is coming in a rage, his eyes flaming like the rising sun, and his axe besmeared with blood, that flows as a river from the throats of Kshétris ; while by his high and quick respirations and by the agitation of his bow, he seems as if he intended again to disturb the world.

46. This is he, who has applied to his crest the leaves of kankas;* to his back a pair of quivers; to his breast, pure ashes; who has put on deer's skin, and whose waist is bound with a girdle of the *elephant grass;* whose robes are dyed with madder; whose hand bears a bow; on whose wrists are rosaries made of the seeds of the rudráksha, † and whose staff is of the ashwatha ‡ tree.

47. This is he, who liberated the earth when covered with the seven oceans by Arjuna; who severed Arjuna's neck, in a dreadful combat, with the edge of his axe; and at once cut into pieces his thousand arms, which had covered the waters of the river called Révá; the same Arjuna being his inveterate enemy, on account of having killed his father.

48. This is he, who distinguished himself in the field of battle, which was incessantly flowing with blood, and of which the dust was washed in the gore of the young Kshétris. Such heroes ascending to heaven, look like bridegrooms before heavenly maidens, their hands being filled with lotus flowers, the odour of which is diffused through paradise.

[*To* Ráma.

[Jámadagnya *in wrath thrice utters the following sentences.*]

49. *Jáma.* Who is it that has broken the *ajagava*§ and wishes to draw punishment on himself from the Regent of death

50. That weapon which belonged to Párvatí's husband, and was held in esteem by Párvatí, and which Nandi || used to cover with the slough of Vásuki (a serpent,) that excellent

---

* An ornament of war. † Elæocarpus ganitrus.

‡ Ficus religiosa. § Shiva's bow.

|| One of Shiva's attendants.

weapon before which the demon Tripurá appears but a withered branch, which belongs to him who consumed Cupid; shall I, who am living on the earth, see it broken?

51. I, who had a conference with Arjuna, though he has a thousand arms, and I but two; though he is a sovereign, and I stood alone; now ask, who, save the Sun, is to witness our conflict? [*Looking upwards.*

52. I who have frequently, yea twenty-one times, killed in my anger all the descendants of the Kshétri kings, even their newly-born ones, and filled a cistern with their blood for the offering up of oblations to our ancestors, and thus extinguished the fire of my anger; what! have not you heard of my well known power?

53. The blood that issued from the throats of the youthful and irascible Kshétris flowing like a river, I offered up as a libation. I have made the hair of the Kshétris' heads like *kusha*.* I have poured out oblations† of blood without regarding whether they were accepted with satisfaction or rejected with disdain, whether they excited pleasure or wrath.

54. And this axe *(pointing to it)* is well adapted for cutting down the arms (resembling bushes,) of Kárta-víryárjuna; it is decorated with kéyúra,‡ knobs and strings set with precious stones; it causes fear, and is as brilliant as the twelve suns,§ and the destruction of Kshétris. It is strange, that you, who broke that bow of the enemy of Pura,|| have not heard of this axe.

55. The worshippers of fire, and hermits, and Shrotris,¶ as well as renowned kings, have not only heard, but borne testimony to Jamadagnya and me. The *pinda*** either of the tribe of Ikshuka, or of the prophet Bhrigu, shall be extinct.

* A species of *grass* held in high estimation. (*Poa cynosuroides.*)

† Oblations to the manes of one's ancestors were usually made of water.

‡ The plate of metal worn as an ornament, on the small part of the arm.

§ It is stated in Hindu books that when a general dissolution of nature takes place, the *twelve suns* will roll over the earth, and cause an universal conflagration.

|| The name of the demon killed by Shiva, who is hence called *Purári.*

¶ A Bráhman versed in the study of the Védas.

** A funeral cake, that is offered by the legal heirs of the deceased: here the speaker means either that the whole race of Dasharatha or his own, shall be annihilated.

This, I now swear by the Védas,* by my axe, and by the lord of the creation.†

(Ráma *with his hands joined out of respect.)*

56. *Ráma.* I know not the strength of thy arms, nor that of the bow of the three-eyed,‡ hence my folly; O Parashuráma, pardon the feebleness of my arms, in which my superiors naturally take delight.

57. *Parashu. (angrily, and disregarding* Ráma.*)* Where is that Ráma, who has eclipsed my fame, and resembles the moon by breaking Purári's bow, while the descendant of Bhrigu is living.§

58. *Ráma (respectfully,)* O sage, no sooner did I touch the *bow* of Purári, than it broke; what could I do?

59. Whether we have a necklace or an axe on our necks; whether there be antimony‖ in the eyes of our wives or tears; whether we see the incomparable countenance of our consorts, or behold the king of the deceased (the Regent of death); yet would we not be heroes when compared with Bráhmans.

60. Alas! we the descendants of Rághava are not heroes in killing cows and Bráhmans. O Parashuráma! do as you please with this axe.

(Upon Parashuráma's *assuming a position for a conflict, the son of* Dasharatha *begs of the sage to be excused.)*

61. O Bráhman! I cannot challenge you to fight; for we are weak, whereas you are superior to all champions. The power of all the sovereigns (Kshétris) depends upon the bow, which has only one string, but you, who are a twice-born¶ personage, have the strength of the sacred thread of nine strings.

---

* The sacred books of the Hindus, namely, *Rik, Yaju, Shám*, and *Atharva*, which are esteemed as the fountain of all real knowledge.

† A *title* of Shiva.

‡ A name of Shiva, who is represented as having three eyes; those on the two sides were receptacles of the *sun* and *moon*, and the one on the forehead, of *fire*.

§ That is Parashuráma.

‖ A black substance used by the Hindus to paint the eye-lids to beautify the countenance.

¶ The second class of Bráhmans, when they are consecrated with the sacerdotal threads.

62. *Lak.* My Ráma was born in an unknown age, and not at a certain time, and he is sole-existing. I also am the same, and not the son or grandson of the king of the Raghu tribe. Let the people pronounce me either learned or ignorant, I have afforded instruction for the punishment of all twice-born wicked persons. [*To* Parashuráma.

63. *Ráma.* I am he whose origin is from the sun. I have learnt the arts of fighting from Kshétris and Shrotrias, and also from the sapient Vishwámitra. Let the world speak either well or ill of me, I am backward in committing the crime of bearing arms against a Bráhman.

64. *Parash.* The bow which you have broken belonged to Isha;* it was already worn out by the use of Ráma's arms; and you have been merely an agent in the operation. Hold this bow of mine, which was once in the possession of that being (Vishnu) who had on his flag Garura† which is destined to kill the Kshétri kings. [*To* Ráma.

65. *Man.* Ráma held the bow with ease, and fixing an arrow drew it; at this time, he looked like Makaradhaja‡ and who, by the letting off of an arrow, caused an obstacle in the way§ of Bhárgava.

66. When the destroyer of Táraka (Ráma,) drew the bow, the daughter of Vidéha being secreted,‖ cast a jealous eye on Ráma lest he ally himself in marriage with another woman.

67. *Parashu.* I am the hero Jámadagnya, who cut off the thousand arms of Kártavírya, but I say submissively to Ráma, I am a Bráhman.

68. This is Ráma, who was ushered in the world by the blood of the Kshétri race, who have been killed with the axe of the disciple of Shiva. If he (Ráma) whose hand was engaged in saving the three worlds, and who is an eminent per-

---

* One of the names of Shiva.

† The regent of birds.

‡ One of the names of the Indian Cupid, who had the sign of a marine-monster on his flag.

§ In heaven.

‖ In a chariot.

son, and the chief among the children of the Sun, had not been born, how would the people have been protected?

69. ***Ráma*** *(to* Jámadagnya.*)* Your descent is from Jamadagnya; your preceptor is the lord of the Pináka;* your valour is indescribable, and known by your actions; your generosity is unlimited, you have made a bestowal of the whole world, surrounded by seven oceans; your chief theme is rectitude; your property is worship; what would your actions be if they were not superior to those of others?

[*He falls at his feet.*

70. ***Man.*** Ráma hears from the son of Jamadagnya of the valour of Rámchandra, and they both embrace each other cordially; the former makes over to the latter all his splendour, enabling him thereby to destroy the Kshétris.

71. Parashuráma having separated, returned to his own habitation. The king (Dasharatha) along with his sons Ráma and others, returned to Utra-koshala (Oudh).

72. Ráma having obstructed the path of Parashuráma, the sage, and having invited all the members of his family, both paternal and maternal individually, he saluted the respected Bráhmans and others of his own rank, and then retired with his father.

73. Afterwards, the sun, finding that both the daughter of Janaka and Raghu-nandana were being pierced by the arrow of Madana,† went down the Astáchala‡ and with delight immerged himself in the last ocean.

74. When the friend of the lotus§ and the sun of the ocean|| cheerfully appeared in the east, of the color of a ripe orange, Ráma, at the suggestion of his elder relatives, stepped into his bedchamber, and the daughter of Janaka with her person full of attraction, followed him so gracefully that she delighted his soul. [*She walks gently.*

* Shiva.

† The Indian Cupid.

‡ The western mountains, behind which the Hindus suppose the sun retires when he sets.

§ In rhetoric the sun is called the friend of the lotus: because when he rises its petals are opened.

|| The moon, because it originated from the ocean; it is personified of the masculine gender.

75. *Man.* Shrí Ráma was much gratified by the welcome* of the senior members of his family consisting of Koushalyá, Sumitrá and Kékaí, when he entered into the chamber.

76. The queens and other ladies of the palace, also warmly received Ráma's wife, the fortunate Sítá, and the renowned Unmilá (the wife of Lakshmana).

77. The royal families then, clad in linen dresses, performed the ceremony of oblations of fire,† and supplicated hearty blessings upon them, as well as upon the two daughters of Kushadhwaja (the respective consorts of Bharata and Shatrughana,) who were also received by them.

78. They then took the young princesses into the palace temples, and desired them to prostrate themselves before the deities and to salute the respected women of the family.

79. Afterwards, the sons of the king Dasharatha, performed other duties which their father had instructed them to do.

80. When Dasharatha spoke to Bharata, that the son of the king Kékaya (Judhájit) was sitting near him,

81. And added, "Your uncle Judhájit has himself come to receive you,"—Bharata, the son of Kékaí, on hearing this, went accordingly.

82. Shatrughana, having obtained his father's permission and that of Ráma, the merciful, accompanied the valiant Bharata.

---

* With wreaths of flowers, sandal, &c.

† It is customary among Hindus to offer clarified butter on fire, pronouncing certain passages of the Vêdas, to propitiate ceremonial observances. This is generally done through priests.

83. He at the same time took leave of his own mother.—Judhájit, receiving Bharata and Shatrughana, was highly delighted.

84. He (Judhájit) then conducted them into his house, when Judhájit's father was elated with joy.—After their departure, Ráma and Lakshmana served their most excellent father.

85. And by command of the father, they conducted their domestic affairs in a suitable manner.

86. They also executed several other virtuous actions, and attended upon their mothers.

87. And at times, waited on their spiritual guides, whereby Dasharatha, the Bráhmans and the traders were greatly pleased.

88. All the royal officers observed with satisfaction the mild disposition and bravery of Ráma, who acquired also the esteem of the other sons of Dasharatha.

89. Amongst all, Ráma, like Shiva, was accomplished in virtues, and remained at home for a certain time.*

[*Exeunt.*

---

* Shri Rám Sharman, the commentator, says, on the authority of the *Padma-Purána*, about twelve years, and adds, that the marriage of Ráma took place when he was sixteen years of age.

NOTE.—*Slokas* 75 to 89 of this Act, appearing unsuitable for publication, the Translator has expunged them, and substituted in their place the same number of *Slokas* on the same subject from the "Rámáyana" of Válmíki, to correspond with the number of pages and *Slokas*, in the language of the Manager, the work having been printed before the omission was decided upon.

ACT III.

SCENE, *a palace in Ayodhyá.*

Enter Dasharatha, *attended by* Sumantra *and other Courtiers.*

90. *Man.* When Rághava had been for some time in the agreeable company of his wife, the period arrived when the curse* which Shravana, the sage, had pronounced upon his father, was destined to be fulfilled; for bad omens presented themselves at this time, viz. the sudden waving of the sun's rays, the occurrence of a great tumult, the falling of meteors from the sky, and the quaking of the earth.

91. Clouds of dust arose from every side, brilliant stars were visible, the sun appeared as if eclipsed, a rain of blood fell, and in the middle of the day, a great howling of jackals and boars, and croaking of ravens, were repeatedly heard.

92. Dasharatha, noticing the good policy and manly conduct of Rámchandra, and resolving to make him sovereign

* It is stated in Válmíki's "Rámáyana," that once on a time, in the rainy season, the king Dasharatha, while young, went a hunting in the wilderness, and spent the whole day in search of game. In the evening being greatly fatigued and the night being very dark, he proceeded towards the river *Sarayú.* Meanwhile, the son of the sage Shravana was taking water from the river. The gurgling sound of his flaggon, induced the king to think it proceeded from an elephant or some other animal drinking water, and forthwith he discharged his *Sabda-bhédi-bána* (or an arrow which pierces a person by its sound,) towards the quarter the sound came from, and hit the boy. Soon as the young hermit fell on the ground, the cries of other anchorites reached the ear of the king, who, coming to the spot, bitterly lamented the consequences of his mistake.—The boy however could make no effort beyond requesting the king to carry the flaggon filled with water to his father, for which purpose he directed him the way to his residence. No sooner did the king withdraw the dart from the wound, than the young hermit expired. While the king was drawing near the hermitage, the sound of his feet was heard by the sage, who being blind, imagined it was his son, and chid him for his unusual delay in bringing water, as his parents were very thirsty, and urgently demanded water. The king then, with unfeigned sorrow and in a submissive tone, informed him, that it was *not* his son but the king Dasharatha, and presenting to him the water in a respectful manner, related the sad occurrence unreservedly. The sage on listening to the heart-rending circumstance, was overwhelmed with grief and cursed the king thus: "Thou also shalt lose thy life with affliction for the separation of thy son." The hermit and his wife immediately breathed their last.

of his empire, commanded Nishchika to make the necessary preparation. Sumantra, afterwards, made this declaration before all the citizens.

93. *Sum.* The king, aware of his being advanced in years, as well as of Ráma's capacity for governing a kingdom, has resolved to anoint Ráma as his successor. Now therefore rejoice, ye citizens, on the happy occasion of Ráma's being enthroned.

[Sumantra *goes out of the palace.*

94. *Man.* To anoint Ráma, the maidens of the palace had gone for water, but being overjoyed, they became absent-minded near the bank, and the golden pots which they carried on their waists, fell upon the stairs,* and occasioned a jingling sound.

Enter Kékaí *from the female apartments, presenting herself before* Dasharatha.

95. *Man.* Kékaí,† whose eyes are like the blue-lotus, the brilliancy of whose person is like polished gold, appeared before Dasharatha, who was surrounded by the learned, and spoke thus to him:

Kékaí. "You, O king! are weak minded, though your origin is from an unblemished tribe; desist from your intention to enthrone Rámchandra; for how can he be the lord of the earth, while his wife is the daughter of the earth?"‡

King. O Kékaí! approach me.

Kékaí. (approaching.) Since this unlucky woman (Sítá) came here, several bad omens have been observed; expel her

---

* *Eleven* in number.

† One of the consorts of Dasharatha.

‡ According to Hindu mythology, Sítá was the daughter of the earth. It was therefore inconsistent, by the Hindu law, that Ráma should rule the earth which was to him *quasi* mother-in-law.

therefore, and fulfil now the two promises you have made, the one, to send Sítá, Ráma, and Lakshmana to a desert; and the other, to anoint my son Bharata as king.

King. (*aside.*) O Ráma! the joy of the good, your wife being the daughter of the earth, your becoming lord of the earth is improper, as Kékaí has declared.

Enter Rámchandra.

Sum. (*knowing the king's inclination, aside to Ráma.*) Here comes Sumantra to represent something to you.

96. The daughter of the king Kékaí, having heard of the joy expressed by distinguished women, on your approaching enthroning, reminded the king, your royal father, who is the friend of Indra, of his two former promises with a view to his fulfilling them.

97. Namely: "That Ráma with his hair matted proceed into a wilderness for the period of fourteen years, in company of his younger brother (Lakshmana,) and in that of Sítá; and that the king make over charge of his whole kingdom and his royal offices to her son."

98. *Ráma (going up to* Kékaí.) If by Ráma's proceeding to the wilderness, according to the command of his father and your wish, the empire should descend to his dear brother Bharata; what, O mother, can be more pleasing to him!

[Ráma *prostrates himself at the feet of* Kékaí.

Ráma. Go, my beloved brother, and conduct your brother's wife, the princess, to this place, whilst I prostrate myself before my father. [*To* Lakshmana.

99. *Man.* Ráma, having saluted his father, Dasharatha, his two stepmothers, and his own mother, prepared to set out for the wilderness accompanied by Maithilí and his brother.

100. Sítá, finding Rághava obedient to the order of his father, went first to Koushalyá,* and then to Sumitrá, to salute them both; which being done, she stroked the birds Shuka,† Sáriká, and black cuckoo, and followed Ráma.

* Rámá's own mother.

† A parrot.

Enter Sumitrá.

101. *Sumit.* Look upon Ráma as Dasharatha, and upon Sítá as myself; and consider Ayodhyá as a desert. Now O my son, may thy departure be prosperous! [*To* Lakshmana.

102. You and Sítá are but young children, do not therefore go to the southward; for there is the abode of the Rákshasas. [*To* Ráma.

103. *Man.* When Ráma proceeded towards the new world (a wilderness,) all good people were immerged in an ocean of grief; and though the immovable earth appeared as if moved with affliction, yet the hard heart of Kékaí was not affected.

The citizens bewail the departure of RAMA. [*Omnes exeunt.*

SCENE, *a forest.*

Enter Sítá.

104. *Ráma (aside, sighing.)* O Sítá! you are like the tender flower shirísha:* having proceeded but a few paces from the capital, you have repeatedly asked what the distance is to the wilderness, your present abode. You are the chief occasion of my lamentation.

105. Are you so soon disturbed by the flowery ornaments, and the rays of the rising sun? I know not, O Vidéhí! how you will reach yon wilderness?

[*Pointing to it with his hand.*

Enter Hermits.

106. *Herm.* (*looking at* Ráma.) This perhaps is a mendicant? No, for he has a young woman beside him! An ascetic? No, for he holds a bow! A prince? No, for he has matted hair! A hunter? No, for he has quite new bow-strings! Whence has this azure-colored person so suddenly made his appearance here?

[*They gaze at each other.*

107. *Ráma* (*to the earth.*) O earth! forsake thy hardness, while Jánakí thy daughter, unaccustomed to toil, proceeds

* *Acacia sirisa.*

with her tender and lotus-like feet, as red in color as the rising sun, on her way to the wilderness.

Enter female travellers.

108. *Fem. (to Sítá.)* Pray tell us, O lady! who this azure-colored person is?

[*Pointing to* Ráma.

(Sítá, *smiling, looks downwards through modesty, by which they understand that he is her husband.*)

109. *Fem.* O daughter of Janaka, walk a little slowly, as this field is full of darbha,* and cover your head with the hem of your garment, as the sun is powerful, and his rays affect you.

[*They leave her after giving this advice.*

110. *Man.* Sítá followed the footsteps of Ráma, the chief, and the new traveller; bnt she was unable to reach him. Being alone, she began to roam in all directions for Ráma as Rohiní† had done in search of the new moon.

[*Exeunt.*

SCENE, *the palace of Dasharatha.*

(Sumantra, *having conducted* Shrí Ráma *into the wilderness, returns to* Dasharátha.)

Enter Sumantra *and* Dasharatha.

111. *Sum.* At your command, Ráma, the chief warrior of the Raghu tribe, has retired to a wilderness with a bow in his hand and arrows on his back, Lakshmana and Sítá following him. [*To* Dasharatha.

112. *Dasha.* I did not perceive that he was sad at his departure for the desert, although he was in expectation of a crown.

113. (*Aside, sighing.*) O Ráma, thou art not far from my heart; I view thee on all sides! O my son Ráma, thou art gone from me; this is a great shock to my heart!

* The name of a species of grass held in such veneration by Hindus, that no religious act can be rightly performed without it. (*Poa cynosuroides.*)

† The *fourth mansion* or *an asterism*, according to Hindu astronomy. In Hindu mythology, this mansion is personified as one of the daughters of Daksha and the wife of the moon.

114. Dasharatha, hearing from Sumantra of his son's retirement into a wilderness, began to reflect that the time had arrived for the fulfilment of the curse once pronounced. Thus reflecting he exclaimed : " Ah Rághava !" and, sighing deeply, breathed his last.

Enter Citizens.

115. *Cit.* Ráma, who is a descendant of the sun, and the son of Dasharatha ; who is a great king, the consort of Sítá, and a lover of truth ; and whose younger brother is Lakshmana ; whose valour is unequalled, and who is renowned through the world, is suffering under the wrath of the great Creator.

116. Though Ráma be the son-in-law of Janaka, and the chief of men, and though his marriage with Janaka's daughter, had been negotiated by Vishwá-mitra himself, and the matrimonial ceremonies performed by Vashishtha, the priest, and though the planets at his birth were in the eleventh mansion, yet is he gone to the desert: what more need be said of the vicissitudes of earthly things !

Enter Bharata *and* Kékaí.

117. *Bhara.* O mother, where is my father ? *Ké.* He is gone to the paradise of Indra. *Bhara.* Why ? *Ké.* Because of his separation from his son. *Bhara.* Who is that son ? *Ké.* It is he to whom you are the next. *Bhara.* What has happened to him ? *Ké.* He is gone to a wilderness. *Bhara.* Why? *Ké.* By order of the king. *Bhara.* Why so ? *Ké.* Because of his promise to me, whereby you were to obtain the sovereignty. *Bhara.* What a pity !

118. *Bhara.* (*loudly.*) O Ráma! in obedience to the command of thy father, thou art gone in company with Lakshmana to a desert, forsaking us all. O! Shrí Shrí Ráma, it is proper for you to live in a wilderness with me, who am your next born (brother) ; as Shoumitra* is but an infant ; and the king has departed this life merely because of your separation.

---

* Lakshmana.

119. *Again aside, sadly.*) O Kékaí, how have such nefarious and wicked thoughts entered your mind, and why has your birth been in the family of Kékaya, whilst there are inferior tribes such as those of the Rákshasas? You are like a poisonous plant in a garden of sweet mangoes.

120. O Kékaí! you have been instrumental in sending Ráma, who was most agreeable and pleasant to the sight of men, into a wilderness; and made him leave his splendid robes, and put on the habit of self-denying devotees.

He grieves much.
[*Exeunt.*

Scene, *the forest of Chitrakúta.*

Enter Bharata *and* Ráma.

121. *Ráma.* Brother Bharata, look upon others' wives as you would upon your mother, covet not others' wealth, disregard not respectable persons, and associate not with menials; be strong to the wicked; patient in adversity, and humble when fortunate; these are the good ways in which you are required to walk.

122. I respect those who associate with the learned, who appreciate others' virtues, who are submissive to respectable individuals, who are possessed of learning, and happy in their consorts, who fear calumnies, who have faith in Shiva, who have subdued their passions, and who never keep company with envious persons.

123. I often pay attention to future kings,* and request them generally to preserve good conduct in all times to come, and in all ages.

124. *Bhara.* (*aside.*) Though I can easily endure the burning of fire, and bear the tortures of Indra's weapon, of hills, and scimitars, and arrows; yet I cannot bear a separation from Ráma's feet. [*He looks upwards.*

125. *Ráma.* I could put up with the inconvenience of residing in a wilderness, but I cannot refrain from noticing the

* Though the expression here is general, it is to be understood as limited to Bharata, who was to succeed Dasharatha in the kingdom.

fatigue which my beloved Jánakí endures in walking. Notwithstanding that, I am unwilling to possess the sovereignty.

126. *Man.* Bharata, whose hair was matted, and who wore the bark of trees, fell prostrate at the feet of Sítá, and she cried so loud, that all the birds that were on the trees, were terrified at it, and the beasts were alarmed; the chief hill Chitrakúta echoed with the loud cry, and Sítá's tears flowed like a stream of water descending from that mountain.

127. *Bhara. (to Ráma.)* You, Ráma, are worthy to have the sway. Let me reside in the wilderness, that thereby the command of our father may be obeyed.

He falls at Ráma's *feet.*

[Ráma *not accepting the offer, Bharata takes* Ráma's *sandals, and returns to the Capital.*]

128. *Man.* Bharata placing the sandals on the throne, returned to the village called *Nandi**, and assumed the sway of the kingdom until the return of Rághava.

[*Exeunt.*

Scene, *a desert called Panchavati, or Dandakáranya: with a river adjacent.*

Enter Sítá, Ráma, *and* Lakshmana.

129. *Man.* Ráma, having for a long while continued in several hermitages, proceeded farther from Chitrakúta, where he had slain the Rákshasa Viradhá, in consultation with the son of Kumbha, a sage, and he made the wilderness called Panchavati, his abode.

130. Some young peacocks mistaking the azure colored body of Rámchandra for a cloud and flashes of lightning, began to dance in the forest called Dandaka.

131. Lakshmana, on intimation from Raghu-nátha, brought the gold colored parts of the lotus, with which Jánakí decked her ears.

132. *Sítá.* My lord, since by the dust of your lotus-like feet the virtuous wife of Goutama, the sage, (who had been trans-

---

* The birth place of Bharata's maternal grandfather.

formed into a block of stone,) was restored to him, I know not how many women will be raised by your present travelling, out of the stones of the Vindahya mountain, and restored to the fond caresses of the affectionate devotees.

[*To* Ráma *when travelling.*

Lakshmana *calls to a* Boatman.

Enter a Boatman.

133. *Boatman.* Good Sir, as it is said, that by the dust of your feet, men have been produced from stones, I beg permission to wash your feet before you get into my boat, which is constructed of wood only.

134. Goutama's wife having been doomed by a curse from her husband to be transformed into a stone, what doubt can there be that some other woman also, having incurred her husband's displeasure, has been doomed to transformation, and thereby converted into this boat,—(*pointing to his own boat,*) and may quickly spring into life by the touch of your feet.

135. *Man.* Observing how great were the sufferings of Janaka's daughter, Ráma and Lakshmana made up their minds to live near the banks of the Godávarí ; they therefore prepared a hovel of leaves for their abode.

136. Lakshmana, to keep himself from the enchantments of Súrpanakha,* drew his sword and chopped off her nose. But she, being the sister of Rávana, and feeling highly insulted at such treatment, raised a strong body of men to revenge herself on him.

137. Ráma, being engaged in a conflict, slew by a single arrow an army of fourteen thousand hardy Rákshasas ; and stretched his bloody hands over Khara and his younger brother Dúshana, who, though hideous in appearance from having three heads, were soon destroyed.—Rághava's bow then flourished.

* A celebrated giantess, the sister of Rávana, who was so named from the length of her nails, *Súrpa* (a fan for winnowing corn) *nakha* (nails).

138. Rávana having heard from Súrpanakha of the exquisite beauty of Sítá, sent Márícha to Ráma to seduce his wife.

[*Exeunt.*

SCENE, *a forest.*

Enter Márícha.*

139. *Márí.* (*aside.*) Ráma holds a great rod like the Regent of Death, he being the offspring of the sun. The lord of Lanká is no less courageous, for by him Indra was defeated. I come this day doomed as it were to die.

140. What therefore is to be done had better be done ; for I am doomed to die. At whose hands would it be nobler to meet with death—Rághava's or Rávana's ? Better far to die by the hand of Rághava !

[*Exit* Márícha.

SCENE, *a hovel in a forest.*

Enter Ráma, Lakshmana *and* Sítá, *and* Márícha *in the shape of a golden antelope grazing at a distance.*

141. *Man.* Ráma, who is the head of the Dasharatha tribe, passed some time in the company of Sítá and Lakshmana in a forest, and lived upon sweet fruits and roots. When Jánakí viewed the beautiful male golden antelope, which had been sent by the ten-headed Rávana, she was enchanted with its beauty.

142. *Sítá.* My love, be so kind as to bring me that strange and yet beautiful antelope, for you possess the strength of a lion. [*To* Ráma.

[Ráma *going in quest of the golden antelope.*]

143. *Ráma.* Dear Lakshmana, keep a watchful eye over this princess, until I return with the golden antelope.

[*Exit* Ráma.

144. *Man.* Ráma with his arrow in one hand, and his great bow in another, and with a wreath of flowers on his matted head, went to look for the antelope in the wilderness.

* The maternal uncle of Rávana.

145. The magical antelope now began to lick the grass, which Ráma held out to it on the palms of his hands. It was not however easy to touch it, for at times it used to lie concealed between some shrubs; and at times it used to smell the shooting herbs, and then look around and run about; sometimes it rubbed its body against objects, and ran at a distance; sometimes it stopped and then moved about.

146. *Sítá.* Lakshmana, what think you of your elder brother, my dear lord's delay? He has been some time now in quest of the antelope in the wilderness. As the place is infested by night-haunters or Rákshasas, why do you not proceed to look after him, since I desire it so earnestly of you?

[*To* Lakshmana.

147. *Man.* Shoumitra, dejected at the harsh expressions of the king of Mithilá's daughter, encircled her with three lines, which he drew on the earth with the end of his bow, and then followed the footsteps of his brother Ráma.

148. The magical golden antelope had at this time led Ráma to a great distance. His brother Lakshmana, however, followed him at a quick pace. Meanwhile Rávana, though touched with a degree of fear, entered in the disguise of a beggar, where the noble hermits lived. Shame! Shame!

149. No sooner was the golden antelope pierced in the breast with the shaft of Ráma, than it resumed the original shape of Márícha all over bloody; and the disguised beggar was transformed and appeared as the ten-headed Rávana, decorated with precious stones, which shed a lustre upon his cheeks.

150. There in that forest, Raghu, the great warrior, pierced the antelope through the breast with his sharp arrow. There the ten-headed Rávana appeared before the hovel disguised as a beggar.

151. *Beg.* O! chaste princess Vidéhí, the ornament of the descendants of the sun, give me some alms, and receive this garland of flowers, which is dusted with the dust of Hari's feet, in order to ensure every prosperity.

[*He then shews some Tulasí or sacred basil.*

152. *Sítá.* From thy peculiar looks, it appears that thou seekest unlawful pleasure; and that thou art therefore disguised as a beggar. I entreat thee, O unfortunate person, to excuse me for not granting thy request.

153. *Man.* Rávana persisted in begging: "Virtuous lady, give me some alms, after overstepping the circle marked by Lakshmana on the earth." No sooner had Sítá done so, than Rávana got hold of her, when she thus cried out for help: "Where are the children of Raghu?"

154. There (in yon forest) Ráma, the pursuer of the antelope, is proceeding on his way, and Lakshmana following his (Ráma's) course with uneasiness. And here (in the hovel) Rávana carries away the daughter of Janaka, almost lifeless, to the pleasant city of Lanká.

155. Sítá was surreptitiously carried away by Rávana during the fortnight of the waning moon, when Saturn (in her horoscope) was in the eighth mansion;* and she had hardly bestowed the half of what she had in her hand, when she was carried away. It was then mid-day, but the sun appeared less bright than usual, the moon being in her fourth lunar day.

156. When the gold-like Sítá was carried away, she cried out: "O Rámchandra, son of Raghu!"

157. When the lord of the Rákshasas flew upwards, the daughter of Vidéha mourned and exclaimed: "O Ráma! my love, thou chief of heroes, hast thou forsaken me?"

158. When Sítá entered Rávana's car, she began to throw away in all directions her nupúra, her upper garment, her bracelet, and her beautiful necklace.

Jatáyu‡ *is observed in the forest.*

159. *Man.* Jatáyu witnessed these three occurrences; the discharge of Ráma's arrow against the antelope, the sudden de-

---

* Hindu astrologers have it, that when the planet *Saturn* comes into this mansion, it indicates mishaps.

† An ornament for the ankles and feet.

‡ A bird of a huge size, the offspring of Garura, and the favorite of Dasharatha.

parture of Shoumitra to his friend Ráma; and the bestowal of alms by Sítá herself.

160. *Jatá.* (*seeing* Sítá *in* Rávana's *car, aside.*) Ráma and Lakshmana seem to be intent upon deer hunting; but it is strange to find her, whose eyes are like the antelope's, in Rávana's car.

161. *Káva.* (*aside.*) Perhaps it is the hill *Maináka,* which obstructs my passage? No, it has not the power to do so, for it dreads Indra's weapon. Perhaps it is Garura?* No, for it knows me and its lord (Vishnu) well. It must therefore be the old Jatáyú, that seeks death at my hands.

162. *Jatá.* Are not you ashamed of yourself for carrying off the wife of Raghu? You, who have sprung from the family of Bráhma, and are signalized as a worshipper of Hara by cutting off your own heads, whose arms are enough to overcome Indra, since you with great facility raised the mountain *Kailasha* like a ball.

163. O malignant monster, thou and thy kinsmen shall perish at once through thy own folly in carrying off Sítá, though your progenitor has sprung from the family of Bráhma, and is the great worshipper, the bravest among living creatures, the most wealthy, and the husband of some heavenly women.

164. O Rávaná! stop your car from proceeding further and liberate the hero's wife. I have overlooked your faults, because of your ignorance. Know me to be the protector of Sítá, since I am Dasharatha's ally.

(Rávana *contemning the bird, proceeded on eagerly.*)

165. *Jatá.* O thou infernal beast, thou robber of another's wife, art thou yet proceeding on? halt, for I am that Játáyú who resides near the hill *Gandha-mádana,* and liberate this chaste woman; (*looking at Sítá,*) or I shall fix my long goad-like beak into your chest, and cause blood to flow therefrom, to be drunk by vultures.

* This in Hindu mythology is the regent of birds, a gigantic crane.

(Jatáyú *encourages Sitá and manifests his anger towards* Rávana.)

166. Be not dismayed, dearest Sítá, as this vile creature cannot proceed further. Whither art thou proceeding with the wife of the great Rághava? I shall with my extended bill tear you into pieces, and throw your intestines in all directions for a repast to Dikpáls, and break your head.

167. O thou sinful wretch, I see thou hast kidnapped Sitá, who is compared to the crescent of the moon, that is on the forehead* of Shiva, and thou art running away:—look, these sharp claws of mine shall serve to lacerate your heads, which are adorned with jewels, in the same way as Gurura killed snakes. [*To* Rávana.

[*A fight between* Jatáyú *and* Rávana.]

168. *Man.* This bird having wounded the lord of the Rákshasas on the eye, broke the flag and the yoke, as well as the wheels of the car, and hurting the steeds, it made a noise, and by the fluttering of its wings drew and shook the car to the amazement of Rávana.

[*The bird then flew upwards.*

169. Rávana being highly enraged, struck the king of the birds which was then soaring in the sky, apparently fatigued, and felled it to the ground half dead. The bird then called out to Ráma repeatedly for help.

170. The bird which had broken the car, fell to the ground motionless. Rávana suspected that it was counterfeiting death; he however hastened on to Lanká, having kept the daughter of king Janaka in the delightful park called *Ashoka*.

171. *Jatá.* Alas! I am unable to serve either the king Dasharatha, or Vidéhí, and I am unable to destroy any thing with my foot; alas! the moon-eyed Ráma sees me not; I am the unsuccesful Jatáyú, whose birth has been inauspicious.

[*Thus regretting, he falls to the ground.*

---

* In the Hindu mythology, it is said that Shiva bears the disc of the moon on his head, and is therefore termed *chandra-churá*, from *chandra*, the moon, and *churá* a crest.

[Ráma *and* Lakshmana, *in conversation in the way.*]

172. *Ráma.* Why, my beloved Lakshmana, art thou come to me, leaving Sítá? *Lak.* The respectable Sítá, finding you long in returning, censured me bitterly; I could not therefore help coming here.

173. *Man.* Rághava, who had by a single arrow slain the wonderful Rákshasa Márichi, suddenly became pensive at finding his hermitage not graced with Sítá's presence.

174. Ráma, after slaying the magical antelope, returned to the hovel with his brother, and looked into the three corners of the place; but into the fourth, he was unable.

[*Exeunt.*

ACT IV.

SCENE, *the hermitage in the forest.*

Enter Ráma.

175. *Ráma (bewailing.)* I looked after Sítá within and without the hovel; but strange to say, I could find no mark of her footsteps: perhaps it is not the same hovel, or perhaps I am not the very person. Ah! I cannot endure to be bereft of her.

176. O Vidéhí, who wert a prop to the hovel, and comparable to moons,* and the solace of my life, whither hast thou gone?

177. *Man.* Ráma's whole body was at this time besmeared with the dust of the earth; his mind was perturbed with grief; he was burning with the fire of Sítá's love at her separation; and he seemed as if he were embraced by the earth.

Enter a Hermit.

178. *Her.* These four events have happened to Rama, viz. the loss of his crown, his retirement to a wilderness, his deprivation of Sítá, and the demise of his father.

179. At the approach of such calamities men become destitute of reason; as for instance, although it be unreasonable

---

* This is an pyperbole, in allusion to the brightness of the moon.

to believe in the existence of a golden antelope, yet Ráma believing such a thing went in pursuit of it.

180. Fate opposes or overcomes the understanding; but the understanding never overcomes fate; for Ráma, though sound in intellect, pursued the golden antelope.

181. The ill fate of Ráma obliged him to forsake his kingdom; to retire into a wilderness; to attack Rákshasas; and has caused the loss of his sound judgment at the appearance of a magical antelope; the loss of his wife; and his roaming in a forest under different shady trees.

182. *Ráma (rising from the ground.)* O my love, the glory of the Janaka race, to my eyes thou wert the moon, and the resemblance of the bird *Chakora.*

183. *Ráma. (looking at the hovel again.)* Whither art thou gone, O my dear wife, with thy lovely eyebrows? This is the place at which I kissed thy lotus-like eyes: here I drank nectar out of thy honeyed lips. *(Seeing some flowers scattered.)* Here lie the flowers that once pleased us both. Ah! whither hast thou flown, my love?

(Ráma *in search of Sítá by the side of the* Godávarí.)

184. *Ráma.* Tell me, O Godávarí! who art rich with transparent streams, if my loving Jánakí has come to you to gather lilies. Tell me, ye trees, ye peacocks, ye passages and passengers, tell me whichever of you can, where Maithilí is.

185. Ye trees that stand on mountains and are laden with blossoms, and that bend at every blast of wind, satisfy me, Ráma, the distressed son of Dasharatha, by saying whether you know where Sítá, my lovely Sítá is, with lips like the *Vimba** and with charming eyes, who moves as gently as the stately elephant, who has long dishevelled hair and a beautiful waist.

186. I see this is the same river Révá, the same forest, the same bower, the same mountain: here the wind blows as gently as it blew from the *Malayá,*† this is the same rivulet, but alas! here the darling Jánakí is not.

---

*The name of the red fruit of the *Momordica monodelpha.*

† The name of the Malabar range of mountains.

187. *Man.* Ráma looks after his wife, roaming over hills and in caves and forests; and he eyes the thick creepers with incessant thoughts of her and her ornaments.

188. *Ráma (not finding Sítá.)* Perhaps the lion has robbed her of her thin waist, the blossoms of her smiling countenance, and the antelopė of her eyes. The champaka* while yet in blossom has perhaps robbed her of her fair color, and th e black cuckoo of her agreeable voice. The loveliness of her person has returned to its native creeper, the elephants have imitated her in her gait, and the remainder of her beauty has been stolen by such in the forest as needed it.

·189. *Ráma (finding the nupúra.)* Lakshmana, this *nupúra* delights me as did that of Sítá: examine Shoumittra, if it be the same, go in search of her other ornaments.

190. *Lak.* To identify her other ornaments would be a difficult task for Lakshmana. But he is the best judge of her *nupŭra,* from the care he always took of her feet.

[*At a short distance,* Ráma *discovers her upper garment.*]

191. *Râma.* This is Sítá's upper garment which was laid as a wager when we were engaged in playing at chess. This once served me for a fan, and this was that cloth she lay upon, when she was offended.

192. *Ráma (seeing the moon.)* O Shoumitra! repose thyself under the shadow of trees, as the burning sun has now appeared. *Lak.* Ráma, this is the moon appearing, why talk you of the sun? *Ráma.* My beloved, how do you know this? *Lak.* Because she has dark spots. *Ráma.* Ah! my darling Jánakí, whose eyes are like the deer's and whose face is as bright as the moon, whither hast thou gone?

193. *Ráma (to the moon.)* It is known that thou possessest cooling beams; but why art thou scorching me with thy fiery radiance? I would have cut thee into bits with my arrow, hadst not thou resembled my Jánakí.

---

*Michelia champaca.

194. *Ráma.* Who are you that reside here? *Lak.* I am the same person, your servant and brother Lakshmana. *Râma.* My lad, tell me who am I? *Lak.* You are the reverend and inspired being Rághava. *Ráma.* What brought us into this wilderness? *Lak.* We came in search of the lady. *Ráma,* What lady? *Lak.* The daughter of the mighty king Janaka. —— *Ráma.* Alas! my dear Jánakí.

195. *Ráma (still musing.)* For fear of a separation, I did not allow Sítá to put on her necklace; but ah! we are at last separated, and it seems to me as if rivers, oceans, and mountains had divided us.

196. Although I have submitted to the death of my father, and the abandonment of my empire, and am content to reside in the wilderness, yet am I unable to bear separation from Jánakí.

197. She is like the goddess of fortune in a house, and a pretty painting brush for the eyes; her body is like the sandal when touched, and her arms are like snow, and resemble a necklace of pearls when placed round the neck; she has all praiseworthy virtues, therefore her loss is painful.

198. O wind, that blowest gently, touch once the comely body of Sítá, and then me, for I cannot live without her.

199. Her absence is as poignant as wounds caused by Cupid's fiery darts, which are inflamed with grief, and which burn my body.

200. The wind is gently blowing on my right side, the bees are humming on my left, the wide waste of the forest is before me, the bird *chakraváka* is weeping behind me, and the moon appears above. Amidst these five torments of the mind, I sit musing on Jánakí, and how I am to pass this long night!

201. The moon now acts the part of the sun; the gentle breeze is no better than the thunder itself; the necklace pricks me like a needle; the light is made darkness to me, my life hangs heavily under the shocks of fate; and oh! the loss of Jánakí is death to me.

202. Cruel and unconquerable Cupid, I entreat thee not to let fly thy shafts, which resemble a full blown lotus, at me. Thine is no proud achievement to slay me, I am already melted in fire at my Jánakí's separation. Sages do not deem it an act of heroism to strike one that is pining to death.

203. All thy arrows, five in number, have pierced my body; they are about to be turned into ashes since my body is consumed by fire at its separation from its fond object. Thou, Madana, art therefore unarmed from this day, and though I fall a victim at thy hand, I shall have the satisfaction of seeing others freed from thy oppression.

[*At sunset,* Ráma *looking eastward, which was full of radiance, speaks* to Lakshmana.]

204. *Ráma.* O Shoumittra, put out the fire of the forest with the water that issues from the mountain. *Lak.* Brother, what say you? It is the moon appearing from the eastern chain of mountains. *Ráma.* Why then is she smoky? *Lak.* It is not smoke, but the shadow of the earth. *Ráma.* Where art thou gone, O Síta, daughter of the earth!

205. I apprehend Maithilí is where I have not been; for wherever beggars go not, there victuals are in abundance.

206. *Man.* Whilst in search of Vidéha's daughter, Ráma met Jatáyú in a dying state, who expired immediately after having uttered these words: "Your Sítá has been carried away by the ten-headed Rávana."

207. *Ráma (turning towards the bird.)* You that are an ally of Dasharatha, and the destroyer of his enemies, can you, revered king of birds, say what is the matter?

208. *Ráma (after performing the funeral rites of the bird.)* O revered bird, ascend thou into heaven by thy merits. What more need I say to thee except this, that thou shalt conceal from my father the fact of my wife's having been decoyed. But if I be Ráma indeed, the ten-headed Rávana, who has defeated Indra, shall in a few days reach thither* with ignominy, and be made to confess all the circumstances.

---

* The place of the departed.

209. Leaving my empire, resorting into the wilderness, being bereft of Sítá, and losing my father, are so many afflictions, each of which appears to me as if calculated to cause an ocean of tears.

210. I see no limit to my affliction, I find no shore to the boundless ocean of my grief; one bad omen brings in its train many others.

211. Kékaí has certainly acted right in enthroning Bharata, for how could I, who am unable to protect a wife, have governed a kingdom?

212. My father has prudently sent me into the wilderness, for I am devoid even of common sense, so as not judge of the impossiblity of there existing such a thing as a golden antelope.

213. Sagara has acquired fame from the ocean *Ságara*,* Bhágíratha from the river Ganges;† but what have I acquired! I could not even keep possession of a wife!

214. Wealth, when once destined for a man, can never afterwards be kept back, even from unforeseen circumstances. So, man ought not to grieve or be amazed at his destiny; for, it can never be set aside.

215. Where is that dear wife of mine, both young and delicate; of noble extraction and fair color; the most delightful and talented; and the cause of my happiness? By thy separation, we can walk no further. O devotee, is such a female thy consort; no! no! she is thy helping stick.

216. Jánakí, you on the one hand distress my mind, and the lord of Lanká on the other burns me in the fire of Madana, whilst anger preys upon me. I am consumed as it were by the fire of the chaff and of dry cow dung.‡

217. I mourn not at the separation or taking away of my beloved; but I mourn at the possession of this bow.

---

* The ocean *Ságara* is named after the king Sagara.

† Otherwise called *Bágiratha*, after king Bhágiratha, according to the *Bhágvata Purana* and *Rhámáyana*.

‡ Such fires are known to be very heating and not easily extinguished.

218. *Ráma.* My beloved, I went to a distance for the golden antelope, little imagining that I would thereby be deprived of Jánakí. Alas! I am deeply grieved to think that my wife has been taken away; for none of the Kshétri race is yet known to have lost his wife even up to his last gasp.

219. What else can be more tormenting to me? my actions are already known. It would therefore be better for me to die than re-assume the reins of a kingdom, that has been the occasion of such calamities. [*To* Lakshmana.

Ráma *sees a serpent.*

220. *Man.* The serpent following Ráma, and preceding Lakshmana, said: "Praised be Ráma, and this large forest." The serpent then proceeded on.

Lakshmana *meets a* Kavandha.*

221. *Lak. (seeing him.)* Who is this Kavandha with extended arms of *four kroshas,*† by which he blocks up the way? Is not this he whom Ráma slew with as much ease as a plantain tree covered with fruit is cut down?

[*To* Ráma.

222. *Man.* Kavandha having been slain by the arrow of Ráma, is purified and transformed into a comely person, whose friend's life, the husband of Sítá gained at Shravana's hermitage, through the medium of Hanúmána and Sugríva, who promised him such assistance as he might need in searching after Sítá. Rághava also has made a declaration to the chief of the Vánaras to slay Válí, Ráma's enemy.

223. Ráma, being helpless, began to ramble upon the hill *Rhishya-muka,* where he found Sugríva also, as a friend in affliction.

224. The active Ráma, on the promise held out to him by the king of the Vánaras to help him in destroying Válí, threw at a distance the bones of Dundubhi (a demon,) which were as heavy as a great mountain, and dashed his arrow as a

---

* A headless trunk. In Hindu history, it is the name of a demon, whose head was forced down his body by a stroke of Indra's thunderbolt.

† Eight English miles.

thunderbolt on the ground, which penetrated the seven subterraneous regions, and caused a deafening noise to all persons.

225. *Ráma (to his arrow.)* If I have always been known to venerate Kushika's son, and if I have also respected the *twice-born* Bráhmans, and ever looked upon others' wives with singleness of eye, then may this arrow penetrate the seven unfathomable lower regions.

226. *Man.* When the son of Dasharatha darted his arrow, it went through seven palm-trees, and then penetrated the seven regions, as if one had by a single stroke perforated a number of plantain trees; and the sound thereof was so great, that it echoed through the atmosphere, and filled with consternation seven mountains, seven elephants, seven sages, seven oceans, and seven subterraneous regions.

[*A field of battle, forming part of the Scene.*]
Enter Válí.

227. *Man.* Válí, hearing that Ráma, who was naturally kind, had without provocation driven his arrow through seven palm-trees, grew wrathful, and, setting out from his mountainous caves, appeared in the field of war.

[*Exhibition of a mountainous cave.*]
Enter Tárá.

228. *Man.* Being overjoyed she mused thus: "This day, I who have been long deserted, shall through Rámchandra's kind instrumentality, lie on the bosom of my husband."

[*She pronounces a benediction upon* Sugríva.]

229. *Man.* Tárá, the wife of Sugríva, put by her necklace, and sat in the mountainous cave, with her hair dishevelled from affliction; and she was nigh unto the shore of the ocean of grief, having been pierced with the arrow of Madana; she raised her hands and prayed that the life of Válí, who was an oppressor, and a sinful and quarrelsome person, might be forfeited.

230. *Lak. (with signs betokening caution.)* Válí is unequalled in power within the four boundaries of the wide world.

231. *Ráma (smiling.)* O Shoumittra, be not amazed at Rághava's stringing his bow: he has done it to slay that sinful wretch, by whose destruction all honest people shall be delivered from the bondage of fear.

232. *Válí* O son of king Raghu, hold this arrow, you know me to be a son of Indra, and to have a weapon with which I cut off the demon Dundhuvi, and have sent him to inhabit the dominions of the regent of Death.

[*Both of them appear in the field of battle.*]

233. *Lak.* Válí, being slain by the famous Ráma, fell down wallowing on the ground. At this time, the deities showered flowers over the head of the enemy.

234. *Válí.* Rághava, was I not capable of doing that which Sugríva is deemed competent to do? Why have you killed me without a fault.? [*To* Sugríva.

235. *Ráma* (*complaisantly.*) O son of Purandra,* your body is now purified, though you condemn my act by pleading your innocence: I tell you however, that for this wrong perpetrated by me, merely to please a friend, I shall have again to suffer the absence of Janaka's daughter.

236. *Válí.* Let the great warrior, by his favor, come to me, O fortunate root of the Raghu tribe, and leader to heaven; and make my son Angada your slave, and support him.

237. *Man.* Rámchandra, having in the field of battle, put Válí to death with his arrow, has committed the kingdom of Kiskinda to Sugríva; and passed the gloomy rainy season in the caves upon the hill *Málayavána.*

[*Exeunt.*

ACT V.

SCENE, *the hill Málayavána.*

Enter Ráma and Lakshmana.

238. *Man.* Although *Shri* Ráma is unequalled in power, yet being ashamed at the loss of his wife, he has passed the autumnal weather in caves.

* One of the names of Indra.

[Ráma *being dejected in mind, pines on the hill Mályavatí.*]

239. *Ráma.* My beloved, the lilies which resemble your eyes, have sunk under water; the moon which looks like your mouth, is clouded; and the ganders which resemble you in their gait, have disappeared. When these things, which you resemble in some measure, are from the change of season not to be seen, to what may you be compared when I reflect upon your person?

240. *Lak.* The gentle zephyr is blowing, the clouds are thickening, the lightning is flashing, the peacocks are singing. All these must be grievous to Raghu's son and cause his heart to fail him.

241. *Ráma (thinking on the former condition of* Sítá.) I am invariably reflecting upon that daughter of the king of *Mithilá,* who witnessed the sage Ráma or (Parasharuma) once enraged at the sound of *Purári's* bow, and in a fighting attitude with me; which sight so terrified her, as to change her moon and lotus like complexion, and make her appear irritated.

242. Though the appearance of the pleasing black aquatic birds and that of the cloud, and the blowing of the breeze, the drizzling of rain, and the sound of peacocks, be endurable to a saddened heart, as the earth endures all her burdens; yet ah! I am unable to endure the loss of Vidéhí!

243. How can you, my beloved, be still amidst the swarm of bees, which annoy you, and, taking your eyes for blue lilies, your hands for lotuses, your cheeks for the flower of the *Madhuka,** buz around you and sit upon you?

244. *Ráma.* My dear wife is to me a minister in business; a servant in service; a chaste woman in religious matters. And I would compare her to the earth in forbearance, a mother in affection, and a welcome companion in merriment.

245. Tell me Shoumittra, whither is she gone, the object of my fondest regard, and as dear to me as Cupid who wears a flowery bow, as a valuable jewel on a head ornament for

---

* *Bassia latifolia.*

women; who is a charm to gay persons; whose graceful walk is like that of the elephant; and whose looks are like the flower of a hundred petals.* [*To* Lakshmana.

246. (*Aside.*) Ráma has often heard, that there is none so wretched among the race of the sun as Shoumitra, whose wife has been decoyed by a lustful monster. Such an event may perhaps reach his father's ears, and grieve him though he be seated with Indra on his throne.

[*Ráma perceives that* Sugríva *had not returned at the close of the rains.*]

247. *Man.* The powerful Ráma desired Lakshmana to invite Sugríva, that he might fix a cantonment.

SCENE, *a part of the kingdom of Kiskinda.*

Enter Sugríva.

248. *Lak.* Hark, thou chief of the Vánaras! The renowned king Ráma is in the wilderness, and Lakshmana, who has been deputed by him, is now arrived at your city-gate to relate all about the king of the Raghu tribe. The head of the Vánaras laughed at this, and asked:—"What about Ráma?" The Vánara felt surprised for a moment.

249. Ráma, who by desire of Koushika, slew Táraká, and defended his religious ceremonies; and in order to gain Sítá, broke Hara's bow, defeated Parashuráma, and killed Máricha in the chase, and lately destroyed Válí, is now roaring like a lion.

(Sugríva *then enquires after* Shrí Ráma's *health.*)

250. *Lak.* Rámchandra has said, that the arrow with which he killed Válí, is not yet blunt; let Sugríva therefore be careful lest in time he share Válí's fate.

[*To* Sugríva.

251. *Sug.* O excellent man, what is said by you relates to the Vánaras; though I wish to be freed from such qualities, yet I cannot.

* The lotus.

252. (*now entreating.*) Excellent people never change their good qualities, not even till death; as the lustre of gold fadeth not though it be often thrown into fire; sugar-cane, though cut into pieces, retains its sweetness; and sandal-wood though rubbed incessantly, loses not its fragrance.

253. *Ráma* (*aside.*) My father has given the kingdom to Bharata, and Rávana has decoyed Sítá. *So saying, he flung his bow and cried aloud.*

[*Seeing* Sugríva.

254. *Sug.* Pray, tell me, lord of the Raghu tribe, the cause of your flinging away your bow; Jánaki must be within this small world, encircled as it is by seven oceans, ten ends, seven principal mountains, and fourteen spheres with one sky.

255. *Ráma.* The mind of man is not at rest when calamities befal him. I see the residents of Lanká are undaunted, who then is able to go thither?

Enter Jámbuvána.

256. *Jám.* Ráma, send for the son of Pavana, Hanúmána, who is of the race of the Vánaras, for he is capable of proceeding thither.

Enter Hanúmána.

257. *Hanú.* (*saluting* Ráma.) My liege, permit me either to uproot the city of Lanká, which is well secured by strong walls and gates, and bring it here, or to destroy the whole army living there; or let me make a bridge over the ocean, by breaking the summits of mountains, as these are to me slight undertakings; or favor me with your commands, for I am skilled in every operation.

258. *Ráma* (*looking at* Hanúmána.) I am sensible of your capability in any of these undertakings; but it would be vain to attempt any thing of the kind, if Sítá be no longer alive. First enquire if she is living.

259. *Hanú.* My lord, to me this atmosphere appears a tree, which has the crocodile for its root, the oceans for its bed,

the clouds for its leaves, the stars for its buds and flowers, and the sun and moon for its fruits.—All these are under my control; command me therefore without hesitation to look after Sítá.

[Ráma *hearing these words of* Hanúmána *smiled.*

260. *Hanú.* (*aside, not knowing where Sítá was.*) O hard fate, it is thou that art the cause of these events, viz. Ráma's being at Ayodhyá, and going thence into the wilderness, called Dandakáranya, at the instigation of Dasharatha; the appearance of Márícha in the shape of a golden deer; the missing of Sítá; the friendship of Sugríva with Ráma; and my going in search of Janaka's daughter.

261. *Man.* Hanúmána, calling upon Ráma, fell prostrate at the feet of Jámbuvána, and embraced all the men of the army, giving them, at the same time, hopes of his return to his friends, who were then crying with their heads bowed down. After this, Hanúmána left orders with his servants, and jumped into the ocean from the summit of the *Mahéndra* mountain.

Enter Sampátí.*

262. *Man.* Sampátí viewed the city of Lanká which was situate on the other side of the ocean, and at the distance of a hundred *Yojana*† from the abode of Sítá. And Hanúmána thinking that a diminutive body would not be able to leap over the ocean, stretched himself perpendicularly to such a degree as to reach the sky with his head.

263. When the progeny of the wind leaped so furiously as to resemble the *Garura* whilst flying, the ocean appeared still, and the aquatic animals were motionless and kept gazing in all directions and making a great noise.

264. A confusion was then occasionrd in the camp of the Vánaras, who were thinking how Hanúmána could approach Rávana alone.

---

* The elder brother of Játayu.

† *Yojana* is equal to 800 English miles.

Enter Surasá.*

265. *Man.* Hanúmána, who had been devoured by Surasá, came out of her, and standing on the mountain *Mainákat*† slew Singhiká the female Rákshasa, who had obstructed his way: he then entered the city of Lanká.

SCENE, *the city of Lanká.*

266. *Man.* At night, Hanúmána, the chief among the children of Pavana, entered Lanká, and began strictly to look after Sítá every where, on the brink of the water and the land; under shrubs, near walls and on trees; and in the palaces of Kumbhakarna‡ and Indra, on the summit and in the caves of hills; but not being able to find Vidéha's daughter, he became pensive, and thought thus.

267. Though I have looked after Sítá in the apartments of Rávana's mother, brother, wife, minister, and courtiers, and in the dwellings of renowned personages; in palaces, and other secret places; yet have I been foiled in my attempt to trace her out. Perhaps, being fearful of Rávana, she has plunged into the ocean.

268. The progeny of the wind, contracting himself, looked at Lanká and the palaces there, which appeared as clear as the rays of the full-moon, and then getting into the garden of Asoka clandestinely climbed the Asoka tree‖, whence he espied Jánakí surrounded by a number of female Rákshasas.

Enter a female Messenger deputed by Rávana.

269. *Fem.* Rávana is he whose orders are obeyed even by Indra, who has conquered the three worlds, who is Shiva's captive, and has his abode in this Lanká; who has sprung from Bráhma, and has none to equal him. If however there be any other as conspicuous, yet none possesses such qualities.

---

* A magical woman.

† Which sprang from the Himálayá or snowy mountain, that divides India from the Chinese Tartary.

‡ Brother of Rávana.

‖ Jonesia.

Enter Rávana.

270. *Ráva.* O Maithilí! you who have a moon-like face, and afford cooling beams, save my life; you who have deer-like eyes, my soul, be kind to me.

271. O daughter of Janaka! Is it he who is but a devotee and an ignoramus that has occasioned such ill treatment to you? he is but a worm of the earth, alienate therefore your affections from him, and love me, I beseech you.

272. O Sítá, compose yourself and accept the king's regards. Look at the golden city of Lanká, and at its king. He will employ his ninety-nine queens in your service; Mandodari only shall be excepted. Rest assured that the king will do this for you.

273. O Sítá, look at my heads, which Mahésha himself puts upon his head,* and which are *now* at you feet; and despise me not. — Sítá hearing such expressions from the libertine spoke thus: "Fie upon thee, for bearing the heads that were once offered up!" May such words of Sítá ever be auspicious!

274. *Sítá.* Know, thou wretch, that he who conquered Shiva, is he from whom Kártavíryárjuna, (in whose custody thou wast,) learned the skill of arms, and by whom he has been subdued, and the same is my husband.

275. *Man.* The ten-headed Rávana fell at the lotus-like feet of Jánakí, and looking at her, addressed her thus:— "If you are not pleased even at Indra, the king of the deities, prostrate at your feet from fear, what then may I do? O instruct me how to act."

276. Sítá, in reply to the king, gave utterance to the following words which flowed gently, though angrily, from her sweet lips. "I shall be pleased when Ráma shall have slain Rávana with his arrow, and when vultures shall put their claws upon the head of the deceased."

---

* It is said, that when Rávana was in the act of worshipping, he severed his ten heads, and offered them to Shiva in order to gain his favor.

277. *Sítá* As there is a difference between a crow and Garura; between a jackal and a lion; between a fire-fly and the sun; such is the difference between you and the son of Raghu.

278. *Ráva.* You shall lament for the destruction of Ráma by me. *Sítá.* Not of Ráma, but of Áráma,* to a certainty. *Ráva.* Why are you mortifying your comely person from self-esteem? *Sítá.* Certainly, because of your unpleasant words.

[Hanúmána *laughing at their conversation.* Rávana, *being reproached by* Sítá, *withdraws.*]

Enter Trijatá.

279. *Sítá.* Pray, tell me how Rávana, who is strict in his duties, could have been guilty of decoying such a woman as I who am another's wife?

280. *Trij.* Sítá, he who is once pierced with the love shafts of Manamatea (Cupid,) never regards either morality or sobriety.

281 For the breast of Rávana even Indra's weapon was blunt; the circular weapon of Hari was bent when it struck such a breast; the rod of the regent of death was broken into a hundred pieces; and the rope of Varuna† was torn; but the arrow of him who holds the arrow of love, has pierced through that breast. Now I, who am a female messenger, ask where is your love for that arrow, and of what tree has it been made?

282. *Hanú. (seeing Sítá.)* Pray, who are you, whose eyes are like the petals of the lotus, who wear yellow silken cloth, and who hold fast the branches of trees, and are eminent for beauty?

283. Why are tears of grief gushing like a stream from your lotus-like eyes, or water flowing from petals?

284. *Sítá.* I am the daughter of Janaka, the mighty king of Vidéha, and the wife of the wise Ráma: my name is Sítá.

---

* She means the destruction of Rávana's garden, which is signified by áráma.

† The Indian Neptune.

285. *Hanú.* What are Ráma's valiant deeds? *Sítá.* He has saved the Raghu tribe, and fulfilled his contract* with Janaka: he has also defended his subjects, and maintained his faith.

286. He is skilled in arms, and versed in the Védas and all the other sciences pertaining to them; and he is strong in his faith: he is renowned in arms, and has a shell-like neck,† and a noble mind.

287. *Hanú.* (*shewing a ring.*) Ráma, of noble descent, of fair complexion, and of a pleasing appearanee, has sent this gold ring of chaste work.

288. O mother Jánakí! *Jan.* Who are you? *Hanú.* I am Hanúmána. *Jan.* Who has sent you? *Hanú.* The respected Raghu, as a messenger. *Jan.* What is that in your hand? *Hanú.* A gold ring.

[*She takes it in her hand, and presses it; crying at the same time aloud for* Ráma, *who had induced* Hanúmána *to come to her.*

289. *Man.* Sítá, on looking attentively at the ring, on which was the picture of Ráma, and which was ornamented with precious stones, exclaimed:—"I see he participates in my grief." So saying, she fainted away. On recovering her senses, she asked:—"Is Ráma so very weak and reduced?"

290. *Hanú.* Shrí Ráma, from want of your presence, is sad upon the mountain, and finds nothing to please him: his body is as hard as a mountain gem while it is yet entire. The *earth*‡ which is named after him is not yet cleft. *Sítá.* Pray, how have you crossed the ocean?

291. *Hanú.* Under your auspices, a favourable wind, and the complaisance of your husband, I have crossed it; and I have from these three favors, had strength to overleap the ocean, which I considered as the mere print of a cow's foot.

[Sítá *recovers her senses a second time.*

---

* Of bending the bow.

† In allusion to the *convexity* and *thickness* of a turbinate univalve shell.

‡ The *first* of the five elements, the names of which are *earth*, *water*, *air*, *ether*, and *light*, or energy; these make up the corporeal frame.

292. Where* the moon appears like the sun, scattering his beams as sparks of fire, and where he exhibits himself though he is camphor colored, like Indra's thunderbolt, where his disc appears as if in alarm, and where the wind is as the submarine-fire, and the sandal wood† thereof as the conflagration of a forest. *Sítá.* Take these fruits‡ as a token from me, and go quickly to Ráma.

293. Lay one of these fruits at the lotus-like feet of Ráma; distribute two of them to the army; give the best one to Sugríva; and one to Lakshmana with my blessings. After this, you, the promoter of happiness to the army, shall take it.

294. *Hanú.* O moon-faced! I am Ráma's messenger, what can be insurmountable to me, the head of the Vánaras, who are apt to kill their offspring !§ It appears that Providence is now favorable to you, but Lakshmana is grieved on your account.

SCENE, *a mangoe garden in Lanká.*

295. *Man.* When Sítá had concluded her kind expressions, the mighty son of Pavana resolved to destroy the garden; he therefore instantly disguised himself as an old Bráhman, toothless, with red eyes and grey hairs, and in that shape reached the garden gate, where he humbly addressed the porters as follows :—"Brothers, favor me with some of the fruits that are lying at the foot of the trees."

296. *Porters (to* Rávana.) The garden, where the wind blows gently; the sun is terrific and warm; the clouds are ready; and Vishwákarma|| is always in waiting to repair old delapidated walls; has just been destroyed by a single monkey.

[*Exeunt Porters.*

---

* The ocean. † This wood possesses the quality of cooling when it is rubbed with water and applied to the body; it denotes therefore, a cooling substance. ‡ Mangoes.

§ It is natural with the male of monkeys to destroy their cubs (particularly the male ones). The females therefore take all possible care to remove them as soon as they are born.

|| The architect of the deities, declared to be the son of Bráhmá.

Enter a wounded Porter of the Garden.

297. *Wound. Por.* Listen to me, my lord! A cruel Hanúmána has in sport uprooted all the trees, and in anger destroyed all the porters, except one who has been providentially spared to bring you the news.

[Rávana, *hearing this resolves to encounter* Hanúmána, and *sends an army of* Rákshasas *for the purpose.*]

298. *Man.* Rávana, affected at such news, asked: "Is it a Hanúmána that has so easily crossed the mighty ocean?" And being ashamed he bent down his head, by which his ear-rings dropped, and he began to reflect that this envious beast must be for Ráma, and must have come to Lanká to shew its prowess. The progeny of the wind thus gave much trouble to the ten-headed Rávana.

299. *Trij.* Hanúmána, having been deputed by Ráma, complimented Sítá with a ring.—"What, what?" exclaimed the courtiers, all of whom were standing about the throne, with a commission to Akshaya, the eldest son of Rávana, to catch the beast.

Enter Askhaya.

[*When* Akshaya, *by command of* Rávana, *prepared to set out, the courtiers thus addressed him.*]

300. *Cour.* An undaunted Hanúmána, having jumped over the wall and city-gate of Lanká, bids open defiance to all. Think on this, O prince Akshaya, before you meet him.

[Akshaya *opposes* Hanúmána *and falls;* Shakrajit *permitted by* Rávana, *goes against* Hanúmána.]

301. *Cour.* The king, being informed of the death of Akshaya, sends Shakrajit in arms to bring you down, O Hanúmána: whither have you fled?

302. *Shakra.* O Máruta! (Hanúmána,) you have given some hopes to Sítá by intelligence from Ráma and others, and have taken from her the most valuable jewel as a sure token for the lord of the Raghu tribe; and you have spoiled the garden *Ashoka,* and destroyed Akshaya and other Rá-

kshasas without hesitation. You have now made yourself a captive to see Rávana.

[*To* Hanú.

303. *Ráva.* O Hanúmána, vile messenger, how have you overleaped the insurmountable ocean, which is filled with aquatic animals, and which has terrible waves? How have you come hither without a car?* Tell me who sent you, and what is your name? fear not: I shall never kill you.

[*To* Hanú.

304. *Hanú.* I have been deputed by Shri Ráma and Lakshmana, who are of renown, and who reside on the hill *Chitrakúta,* to go on a strict search after Sítá. I have long obtained a boon from Shiva, which enables me to go from place to place. Know, Rávana, that I am the son of the wind, and that my name is Shrí Hanúmána.

305. Shrí Ráma, who has destroyed the powerful Válí, and strengthened the troop of the Vánaras, and who has made Sugríva a great king, and is always happy with his companion, who is sorrowful at the words† of all the deities, now shines like the Regent of death, at the loss of Janaka's daughter.

306. *Ráva.* Who are you, Hanúmána? *Hanú.* I am the son of the wind, and the messenger of him who holds a sharp weapon, and is the master of arms in the world, whose strength is such that the mountains *Trikúta* and *Suméru* are but trifles in estimation, and in whose presence many Rávanas like yourself are but as insects.

307. *Hanú.* Know, Rávana, that though I, the son of the wind, am alone, and you possess ten heads and are the king of millions of subjects, yet am I able to succeed in battle and get Síta back. But Ráma seems resolved to touch the earth‡ with his right hand, and, as he declared to Sugríva, to kill you himself.

---

* Meaning the car of Rávana, which has the power of passing through air.

† Complaints of the deities for Rávana's oppression towards them.

‡ An ancient Hindu custom of swearing.

308. O Rávana, who art inferior to all Rákshasas, and a beast, ignorant wretch! I advise you to leave off your vain boasting, to present the daughter of Janaka to Ráma, and to lie prostrate before him, if you seek the enjoyment of your kingdom and desire to leave it to your sons and grandsons after you.

309. If you mean to preserve your life, and the lives of your sons and grandsons, your brothers, relatives, and friends, as well as your generals and subjects, go then with all your hearts' desire to Ráma, the great and glorious, and restore Maithilí (Sítá) to him.

310. You are to be the king of Lanká, until you have seen the son of Dasharatha's face, the embankment of the ocean, and the destruction of Lanká; and until you witness the death of your friends, sons, relatives; or until you have yielded yourself up to Ráma, the lord of men.

311. Although you may be the ruling king of Lanká until you see Rághava, yet, when he arrives, where will you and Lanká be?

Enter Vibhíshaua.

312. *Vibhí. (to* Rávana *on finding him incensed.)* I find no mention made in our religion of destroying a messenger; but it is said, that if such a one use indecent language, he should be punished either by disfiguring or chastising him, or shaving his hair, or inflicting some marks on his body.

313. It is advisable soon to burn the long tail of Hanúmána, which is his only ornament, and then to let him depart.

314. The king was about to kill the messenger, but being enraged at hearing Vibhíshana, he tied Hanúmána's tail with a cloth, and set fire to it to disfigure the beast.

315. *Ráva.* Now a fire has broken out. *Hanú.* Desire the clouds to shower rain. *Ráva.* The wind is too high. *Hanú.* It shall cease, for all the inferior deities are subject to you.—By such expressions of Hanúmána, the heart of the ruler of Lanká was as much in a flame as the city itself.

[*At this time, the inhabitants began to deliberate thus.*]

316. Is it the sub-marine fire of the ocean that we see, or the sun appearing in its fiery orbit? It is either the lightning flashing in the sky, or Shiva exhibiting his fiery forehead; it is either the fire of dissolution or the rainbow in the clouds; or the mountain Suméru, or the polar star visible in its orbit, or the same Hanúmána with its long tail.

317. *Hanú.* I am now consuming the city of Lanká, which is well peopled and ornamented with crystals and precious stones, for your crime of stealing Sítá in the absence of Ráma and Lakshmana.

318. *Man.* At this time, several Rákshasas named *Agni-mukha* being alarmed, cried out incessantly for water. But the fire not being extinguishable, Lanká was consumed.

319. *Háva.* Be quick in securing the stables of horses and elephants, my bed-room, the rooms of my wives, the cabinet of my jewels, and my treasury; for the wind is blowing hard and the fire is blazing: the eyes of damsels appear to be hurt by the smoke, and their breasts are beaten by them with violence: the young as well as the old cry bitterly from fear, and the shrieks of women are heard from all quarters.

320. *Man.* When the lord of Lanká saw that Lanká was in flames, he cried out incessantly for water, from the neighbouring ocean and river, to quench the fire.

321. *Háva.* None of the Nikumbha,* Kumbhodara,* and Kumbhakarna, were able to put out the fire, that had broken out in the room of Mandodarí,† by means of water. Hence, their having the names to which is prefixed the word *kumbha* (pot) is useless.

322. *Man.* After the destruction of Lánká, the son of the wind presented himself before Sítá in the garden of *Ashoka*, and said:—"I have consumed *Lanká;* pray, lady, now give me leave."

323. Sítá, like a deadly female serpent against her enemies, gave Hanúmána her head-jewel as a memorial for her husband.

* The sons of Kumbhakarna, who is the brother of Rávana. † Rávana's wife.

324. *Sítá.* Convey this news to Ráma, (who upon one occasion, decorated my cheeks with red arsenic by applying it first to his hands,) that I shall endure this life only a month longer.

325. *Man.* The son of the wind, after destroying Lanká, unhesitatingly returned and joined Jambuvána, the general, to whom he gave a narration of his exploits; by which the general was much delighted: Hanúmána then went in company of other Vánaras to the garden named *Madhu-vana,* which was Sugríva's choicest place of resort for relaxation.

326. In that garden was a porter named Dadhi-mukha; the Vánaras overpowered him, and by that means went into the garden, where they indulged themselves in pleasure: the defeated porter at this time went to Sugríva.

[*Exeunt.*

ACT VI.

SCENE, *the Vindhya hill.*

Enter Dadhi-mukha *and* Ráma.

327. *Dadhi.* Be prosperous, O Sugríva, at whose command the Vánaras have got upon the mountain *Vindhya,* (to meditate upon Vidéhí,) where there was a garden which they entered with the intention of destroying it. The Vánaras then saluted the deities that were on the mountain, and, having obtained fruits in return, eat them with relish.

328. *Ráma (to* Sugríva, *not knowing of* Hanúmána's *arrival.)* It is a month now and Hanúmána has not yet returned from Lanká; may he be prosperous! I fear, however, that he has been ensnared.

329. Hear me, O Sugríva! how strange it is, that no intelligence has been received regarding Hanúmána! I fear because of the dangerous ocean and the strong citadel of Lanká, as well as the ten-headed Rávana, who is both wicked and dangerous. Perhaps Hanúmána has been destroyed in his hazardous enterprise, particularly from using such language as may have caused Rávana's displeasure.

330. *Sug. (to* Ráma *on* Hanúmána's *return from* Dadhimukha.) We have a garden on this mountain called *Madhuvana* into which Hanúmána, being successful in his undertaking, has entered, and which he has destroyed. We believe therefore that Hanúmána is succesful, and that his return is not untrue.

Enter Hanúmána.

[*While such conversation was going on,* Hanúmána *appeared with a smiling countenance.*]

331. When Hanúmána, the chief general and the greatest warrior, presented himself before the distracted Rama, it was cheering to him like the return of the spring.*

332. *Ráma.* Hear me, O Hanúmána. *Hanú.* What is your command, my lord? *Ráma.* Have you seen Jánakí? *H.* I have. *R.* Is she alive? *H.* She is. *R.* Does my beloved think of me? *H.* She does. *R.* Is she emaciated? *H.* She is. R. What does she utter? *H.* The names of Ráma and Lakshmana. *R.* What proof have you of all this being true? *H.* Here is her chief ornament.

[Hanúmána *then gives the jewel of the head, as the first taken of her.*]

333. *Man.* Rághava, on receiving the jewel, put it round his neck, and now and then on his breast and back, and addressed it in a fit of deep love, to know the welfare of its possessor: he then bathed it with his tears, and looked at it attentively.

334. *Hanú.* You once decorated the cheeks of Jánakí with red arsenic by first rubbing it with your hands; this is the second proof I have of my visit to Sítá.

[Ráma *attempts to embrace* Hanúmána.]

335. *Hanú.* O Rághava, I am not worthy of your embrace, for I have not been able either to drink the ocean,

---

* One of the six seasons of the Hindus, each of which continues two months; viz. cold, dewy, vernal, hot, rainy, and autumnal.

or destroy at once Rávana's mansion; or bring his heads; or convey Sítá to you.

[*At saying this the son of the wind felt much ashamed of himself.*]

Ráma. What more remains to be done by you when you have consumed Lanká?

336. *Hanú.* O Raghu-nandana! Lanká has been consumed by the fire of your anger; as for me, I have been but a mere agent in applying the fire. *Ráma.* You have done every thing by overleaping the ocean.

337. *Hanú.* My lord, your lustre is like the sun's, and it is that which has dried the ocean, so I fearlessly walked through it as through dry land. As to the water with which it appears filled up, it is the tears of the female Rákshasas; hence vain would be my boasting of having overleaped such an ocean.

[Ráma *and* Hanúmána *sitting together begin to converse with one another.*]

338. *Ráma.* Where does Sítá reside? *Hanú.* In the secret garden of Rávana. *R.* What kind of passage is there which leads to it? *H.* Dreary, but I fortunately made my way through it.

[*When the son of the wind spoke thus,* Ráma *became senseless from fear and joy, which his eyes betokened.*]

When Ráma recovered from his trance, he asked;—"How is Sítá?"

339. *Hanú.* The moon-like Sítá is darkened in her complexion; her eyes are the deer's; the tips of her fingers look greenish like tender leaves; her sweet voice is like that of the female cuckoo, by which the good looking plume of the peacock appears shorn of its beauty.

[Ráma *inquires into the present state of* Sítá.]

340. *Hanú.* She is as weak as the moon on the first day of her appearance; her color is pale, and she looks like the blue stalk of the lotus; her tears are shed as copiously as the

current of the ocean; her grief is more ardent than fire. I have given you but a faint description of her appearance and suffering; she lives notwithstanding, and repeats your name constantly.

341. Naturally she is of a delicate make, but her separation from you has thinned her a good deal, even as learning is diminished when read on the first day of the waning moon,* and is therefore seemingly lessened.

[Ráma *then questioned* Hanúmána *as to how he had gone over the ocean.*]

342. *Hanú.* Our movements are merely from one branch to another; but in overleaping the ocean, I have done it merely by your favor.

343. Should a sinful person pronounce the word Ráma, he would overcome worldly fascinations, which are compared to the ocean; and can it be a strange thing for me to overstep the ocean, when in possession of your ring?

344. *Ráma.* What! overstep Lanká, which is a square city, encompassed with seven strong walls, and guarded by four hundred thousand generals and three millions of cars.

345. A city surrounded by three millions of edifices, and nine millions of holy places. Pray, how did you get through such difficulties, the ten-headed Rávana being yet living;

346. And how did you set fire to the great Lanká which can hardly be approached even by the deities?

347. *Hanú.* Sítá's strong breathing and your fierce anger, O king, caused the destruction of Lanká; I was but an agent in the work. *Ráma.* How have you defeated Rávana?

348. *Hanú.* That Rávana, with his several necks, arms, and mouths, and a set of large teeth, frightened me much. Seeing him I was inclined to do mischief, for whoever respects you can do much harm; but on second thoughts I declined as a mere servant to do that which properly is the province of

* It is still the practice of the Pandits not to teach their pupils on such days.

349. O Hanúmána, as a reward for yout late services to me, I have only to give myself up to you as yours for ever, and for any services you may render me in future, we shall both be beholden to you.

350. *Hanú.* O Rághava, you have many servants like me; I have not yet found a master possessed of so many good qualities as you.

[*Exeunt.*

SCENE, *the ocean and Lanká.*

351. *Man.* On the fifteenth day of the moon's increase, in the month of September, and on the tenth lunar day or *Vijayá*,* Rámchandra proceeded to kill the ten-headed Rávana, in company of Dwivida and Gaya,† and the numerous Vánaras, as well as their generals.

352. The Vánaras appearing delighted, reached Lanká, the frontiers of which seemed to be thrown into confusion by their heavy jumping and noisy chattering; the mountainous gardens and the whole city at the same time appearing shakened.

353. At the sight of Ráma, the city quaked, and the mountains oscillated; the tortoise and the serpent under water, as well as the deities, felt terrified. Moreover, Vibhíshana from fear thought of fleeing into some secret place.

354. *Ráma (on the brink of the ocean, aside.)* Lanká appears situate on the shore of the ocean, and blockaded by strong walls, within which are troops capable of doing mischief even to lions; among these, are the valorous Vibhíshana and others, who guard the place. Add to all this, there is the ten-headed king, my worst enemy, who is himself a renowned warrior. Amidst such difficulties, I find my brother but a babe, and my friends are the Vánaras; but the only help I have is in my bow.

[Ráma *then looks at it, and calls upon it to exercise its own power.*]

355. *Hanú.* Command me, my lord, one way or other, whether I am to root up Lanká in an instant and bring it

* The last day of the Durgá festival, or the day fixed for throwing the image into the river.

† The names of the Vánaras.

here; or I am to bring *Jambudípa*;* or I am to drink the water of the ocean and dry it, or overthrow the mountains *Vindhya* and *Mandara*; or make a bridge over the ocean with the stones of *Suméru* and *Trikúta.*

356. *Man.* Rávana, thinking Lanká to be in a dangerous condition, summoned all his old and skilful warriors, and asked several of those champions, as well as the inspired devotees, if they had heard any thing relative to that city, and what they thought of it.

357. The mother of Rávana, named Nikasha, advised Vibhíshana to refrain from mischief. And Vibhíshana, saluting the lord of Lanká, said; "O king, forsake Sítá, whose life is endangered by the Rákshasas; for if one single Hanúmána has committed such depredations in this city, what man of common sense would dare to face such a Hanúmána?"

358. *Vibhí.* Subdue passion, which destroys, by the root, a whole race, and sullies fame, and think of Ráma, by whom one's family renown is preserved: abandon the thought of going to war without a cause; and return Maithilí to the son of Dasharatha.

359. If a messenger of Ráma could consume Lanká, destroy a well-known garden, and overleap an ocean; consider what may not Ráma himself do.

360 None among Rávana, Mahodara, Kumbhakarna, Atikáya, and Indrajit, is able to compete with the son of Dasharatha in valour: he has the strength of a hundred Indras.

361. His arrows, which have golden wings, and are very sharp, are like Indra's weapon. They are discharged as swiftly as the wind, until your heads are blown off. Return therefore, Maithilí, to the son of Dasharatha.

[*To* Rávana.

---

* By the geography of the *Puránas*, this is the central division of the earth, including the whole of Hindusthán.

Enter the son of Kumbhakarna.

362. *Son of Kum.* Rávana is by no means less powerful, for he has raised *Kailásha,* the summit of which is as white as quartz, and which is so very heavy, that it stops the motion of the earth, and is not shaken even by the skipping of Tripura-hara (Shiva,) and he has uprooted other hills.

[*Pointing to* Rávana.

363. *Ráva.* There are many able champions, who have fixed upon a place in Lanká for battle, at which place the most powerful warriors are quartered; and so valorous am I, that from fear of being crushed under my arms, the mountain *Kailásha* discharges arsenic and bloody substances till now.

364. In my house Indra is the maker of flowery garlands, the Sun is the porter, the Moon is the umbrella holder, the Wind and Varuna are the sweepers, and Fire is the cook. Have not you found them doing service? Moreover, Rágha-va, though of human kind, is food for Rákshasas, how then does he deserve praise?

365. *Vibhi.* Ráma is noted for courage among the brave; his fame is always sung by bards: his arrows pass through a range of seven palm trees.

366. I dreamt last night, as if I were beholding the sun and the rainbow without any appearance of clouds, and, strange to say, as if I were eying Ráma, to whom you should give up the daughter of Janaka, and with whom you should contract friendship.

367. How can you pronounce Ráma to be of human kind, when a messenger of his, a young Hanúmána, has over-leaped a terrific ocean, and entered Lanká (which had not been even approached by the deities,) and slain all the keepers of the garden at Lanká; nay, destroyed the garden, and had a sight of Janaká's daughter? Furthermore, he has put to death Akshaya, and destroyed Lanká, and returned to Ráma.

368. You seem to me as if on the point of dying. I may add, that I entertain no doubt as to that, for you are void of judgment, since you do not attend to my advice, given you publicly before courageous Rákshasas.

369. *Man.* When Vibhíshana, the minister, was kicked by Rávana, he appeared senseless, and ready to fly instantly to Ráma.

370. *Vibhí. (while goinng away.)* Rávana, I entreat you yet to give up Sítá to Ráma, with some valuable presents and ornaments of precious stones, as well as costly apparel, and then you may fearlessly reside at Lan ká.

371. *Ráva.* I know Sítá to be the daughter of Janaká, and Ráma the incarnated deity himself, and though I am sure to be slain by Ráma, I am not inclined to give up Sitá to him.

372. *Man.* Vibhíshana, in company of four descendants of ministers, flew in the air as meteors in the Rakshasa family to cause disturbance at Lanká, and then he reached Rághava.

[*Exit* Vibhíshana.

SCENE, *the ocean and Lanká again.*

373 *Man.* When Vibhíshana, appearing as millions of suns in splendour, approached the gate, every one took him at a distance for Rávana, and therefore the Vánaras were dispersed.

374. Hanúmána then ascertained, that it was Vibhíshana and not Rávana. Vibhíshaná was now so eager, that he meant to fall at the feet of Ráma as black bees upon lotuses.

Enter Porters.

375. *Porters.* My lord, there are five Rákshasas at the gate, of whom Vibhíshana, the brother of Rávana, is one; and the others are the descendants of ministers, who seem to expect refuge under your lordship, in order to be freed from all fears. We however are ignorant of the cause of their arrival.

[*To* Ráma.

[Ráma *looking at* Hanúmána.]

376. *Hanú.* O son of Dasharatha! True it is, that Rávana has a brother named Vibhíshana, whose younger brother is the ever-sleeping Kumbhakarna. The former possesses all the virtues of his ancestors, and by him Lanká is secured.

377. *Ráma.* If this man be honest, why has he been dismissed by Rávana ? *Lak.* True ; an honest person is under no difficulty, as for example let us refer to the case of Sugríva and Válí.

378. This is the brother of the chief of Rákshasas, which I perceive by his gait ; pray tell me what is to be done : it is inconsistent with the doctrines of the Kshétris to wrong one who seeks refuge.

[*Pointing to* Vibhíshana.

379. *Vibhí.* (*to* Ráma, *approaching him.*) O Ráma ! your fame as the chastiser of the ten-headed Rávana, is like that of the goose, which whilst soaring in the air was impregnated by Brahmá's gander,* and flying horizontally laid an egg like the moon's orbit. Such fame is whiter than the jasmine produced on the banks of the celestial Ganges.

[*Referring to the Moon.*

380. O hero, your fame is brighter than the waves of the milky ocean, and even the moon is unworthy to be compared to you in renown ; for he has black spots, but he would be worthy of such a comparison if the deer† which is in his lap, come upon the terrace to feed on the grass which covers your enemy's palaces.

381. You can sever the arms of the ten-headed Rávana, with the sharp arrows which are in your quiver, and your scimitar is sharp enough to decapitate Indrajit, if you, the husband of Jánakí, be bent upon it.

382. You are he (Hari,) who once rescued the earth from the desolating ocean by assuming the shape of a boar, and using your assumed teeth on the occasion. The earth is so very mighty, that it is supported by a tortoise, a serpent, an elephant, and *Suméru,* at whose disturbance the earth shakes.

---

* By the Hindu mythology, Bráhmá is said to be mounted on a gander.

† This, according to Hindu *Puráns* or histories, took place, when the moon was subject to a pulmonary consumption, and finding no relief, he had recourse to Shiva for advice ; upon which, he was told to keep always a *deer* in his bosom for the cure of his malady.

383. O sire! chief of the Raghu tribe, the tortoise is like a pedestal, the serpents are like sticks, the earth is like a lamp, the water of the ocean like oil, the mountain *Suméru* like a wick, the rays of the sun like flame, the gloomy atmosphere like lamp-black, and the troop of your enemies like grass-hoppers. These are the apparatus of your ardour, which is like a torch.

384. Though Brahmá himself were the holder of the scales; and the earth, the balance; the serpent, the string; the mountain *Suméru* the weighing stones on one side; and the famous club of Dámodara,* the prop; yet your high virtues would overbalance them.

385. O warrior, your army is bent upon defeating your enemies, troubling the tortoise, and causing devastation in every part of the world, by breaking mountains, drying up the ocean, and overwhelming the sun (with the dust of their feet,) and by overcoming your enemies, and causing thereby a tumultuous sound.

386. If you take my words for true, I should add, that poets aggrandize you by mentioning your good qualities. O my lord, the oceans are already dried by the heat of your anger; but the waters with which they are filled, are the tears of your enemies' wives.

387. My lord, your Hanúmána has consumed Lanká by means of the following things, viz. a car as swift as the eye-sight, a bow which is like the head of the serpents, Hanúmána himself being like Shiva, and the chariocteer like Brahmá, the arrow like Vishnu, and the other materials like those with which Shiva once consumed the abode of Tripúra.†

388. *Sug. (pointing to* Vibhíshana.) How can he, who has no intimacy with his own relations, have any with a

---

* One of the names of Krishna, who being excessively unruly and mischievous, was bound by the waist with a rope by Yashodá his foster mother.

† The name of a demon.

stranger? Hence Shoumitra being fearful exclaims :—" Let Vibhíshana keep at a distance."

[*To* Lakshmana.

389. *Man.* Vibhíshana, hearing a great noise issuing from the Vánaras, feared awhile, though he was valorous, and looking at Ráma's countenance, as full of attraction as that of the protector of refugees, was stunned and could not proceed onward or go backward.

390. Ráma *(seeing him.)* My arrow never flew *twice* in one direction; I never took any one *twice* under my protection; I never extended my favour *twice* to the needy; nor has a word proceeded *twice* out of my lips.

391. *Hanú.* *(guesses the secret intention of* Vibhíshana.) Perceiving Sugríva's prosperity and Lakshmana's fraternal affection, Vibhíshana thinks in himself what course he is to follow.

392. *Sug.* My lord, Vibhíshana has an elder brother, who is the chieftain of Lanká, but Hanúmána has already spoken of the former's great virtues.

[*To* Ráma.

393. *Ráma.* O younger brother of the king of Rákshasas, are you well?—*Vibhí.* Very well, and gratified at seeing you and Lakshmana.—R*áma.* We have guessed your object in coming to us; you are therefore proclaimed this day the ruler of Lanká.

394. *Man.* Lakshmana, finding how attached Vibhíshana was, anointed him king of the capital of Rákshasas, *(Lanká,)* it being usual with the great among the Raghu family, to afford protection to those who seek it.

395. *The Vánaras.* We have this day observed the lord of the Raghu tribe perform the rite of anointing Vibhíshana with his own hands: we are therefore witnesses of the fact of Sugríva being made a king, which is known in *three* worlds;—we hope he may be successful in his business; for we are witnesses of the fact.

396. *Ráma (aside.)* O reverend ocean, let thy waves subside and make way for me, I beseech thee and pray to thee with joined hands, for Sítá has been decoyed by Rávana; by such means wash away the stain on my character.

[Ráma, *after fasting three days and being vexed with the ocean, thus addresses* Lakshmana.]

397. To beg a favor of another indicates poverty and defeat; and although none of the *Ikshuka* family has been accustomed to do that which I have done, yet the ocean has not complied with my request, I am therefore induced to hold out my hand to you for my bow.

[*He stretches his hand.*

(*The* Ocean *and the* Sun *in conversation, at sunrise.*)

398. *Sun.* O Ocean!—*Ocean.* I salute thee. *Sun.* Why art thou retreating? *O.* From fear of Shrí Ráma's arrows which are let off. *S.* What fear is there so long as your *sons** are in your favor, for Ráma has the word *Chandra** (moon) prefixed to his name; and *Lakshmí** in his house; he has *nectar** in his word; his hands are as the *kalpa** tree; and the points of his arrows are *poisoned.**

399. *Ráma (in anger.)* O Shoumitra! give me my bow and arrows, which are like a destructive fire; and I shall dry the ocean to facilitate a passage to the Vánaras.

400. By the discharge of my thunder-like arrows, I shall dry the ocean and fill it with dust, or make a land of it, or a barren field, or a heap of ashes, or I shall make it appear like a sheet of water at a distance.

401. *Man.* Shrí Rámchandra was much irritated on going to the abode of the ten-headed Rávana, and therefore he took his fiery weapon to discharge it at the ocean, upon which the mountains *Ména* and *Himálaya* shook.

402. When the chief of the Raghu tribe had discharged his arrow, it was smoky all over; the crocodiles were frightened, and the shells of oysters and other shell-fish burst.

403. *The Ocean (submissively.)* My lord, your arrows have an unlimited and piercing quality to cause dissolution.

---

* These are found in the ocean, according to Hindu mythology; they are therefore figuratively termed the offspring of the ocean.

As for my water, it is of little consequence; therefore, be so good as to cool your anger, and have a bridge constructed over me with the mountain-stones that have been brought by the Vánaras, and then you shall have an easy and free passage.

404. *Nala* (eulogising* Ráma *upon commencing the bridge.)* I praise Ráma who is comparable to a very valuable pearl, and to the mountain *Chitrakúta* as a casket; and to Kaushalyá as a pearl-oyster, which is an ornament for Jánakí's neck.

[*The Commencement of the Ocean embankment.*]

405. *Man.* The mountains which were deep rooted having sunk, and their summits which reached the sky having been scattered on all sides, by Hanúmána and the other Vánara menssengers pulling them down, they were brought with great difficulty, and with them a floating bridge was made over the ocean by Nala.

406. *Sug. (eulogising* Ráma.) The chief of the Vánaras being somewhat experienced, removed the most formidable hill upon which the ordinary elephants had an opportunity of drinking the water of *Mandákiní*†, which had been destined for *Airávata*‡ to drink.

407. *Vibhí.* The stones that have ever been under water are now floating, evidently to terrify Rávana, and further your design. It is not, my lord, owing to the qualities of the stone, or the attraction of the water, or the abilities of the Vánaras; but it is evidently owing to you, that they thus swim on the surface of the water.

[*To* Ráma.

408. *Sug.* To associate with the wicked is to put honest people to trouble; as for instance, Rávana's having carried away the wife of Dasharath's son has been the cause of *this ocean* being bound as it were by a bridge.

---

* A name of Vánara. † The celestial Ganges.

‡ The name of Indra's elephant, the same that is the guardian of the northern quarter.

409. Knavish persons are harmful to honest individuals; for example, Rávana having decoyed Sítá, the great ocean is made a sufferer by it.

SCENE, *Lanká, on the other side of the ocean.*
Enter Prahasta.*

410. *Pra. (hearing of the embankment of the ocean.)* For Ráma to erect a bridge over the ocean, and slay the king of Rákshasas (Rávana) with his arrows, and for him to get Sítá back, would be as impossible as it would be for elephants to get into the nostrils of mosquitos.

411. *Man.* When the bridge was commenced upon, Rávana laughed; when half the ocean was embanked, he was surprised; when it was finished, he perspired and shook like a mountain by the wind at the time of universal destruction.

412. *Háva. (hearing of the bridge of stones under water.)* Fie unto thee, that bearest the *names*† ocean, the main, the great sea, &c.

413. *(Again hearing of the embankment, and being terrified, asks the minister abruptly.)* Is it a fact, that a bridge has been constructed over the ocean?

414. Though the sage‡ that was born in a pitcher had drunk thee up; and the deities, as well as demons, had churned, and Ráma has now bound thee; yea a Vánara has overleaped thee; yet the people speak of thy greatness as the chief thing and of the fountains of thy waters.

[*To the ocean.*

415. *Man. (regarding Lanká.)* The inhabitants of Lanká fearfully said:—"This Hanúmána is the only gem in the army of the Vánaras: his tail was so long that it used to touch the sky, and resemble a flag-staff: strange, that the great Hanúmána should return here!"

* One of the ministers of Rávana.

† A commentator has it, that Rávana pronounced the ten synonymous names of the ocean with his ten mouths.

‡ Agasta, who is frequently named in the Hindu writings.

416. Eighteen hundred thousand millions of Rághava's generals prepared to proceed by the bridge.

417. Rávana, hearing the tremendous noise of the Vánaras at Lanká, commanded Kumbha, Nikumbha, Sárana, and Suka, to prepare themselves for combat.

418. All the people were frightened by the brawling noise of Sugríva's army (the Vánaras) on the bridge; and Ráma fixed a camp on the hill *Subéla* (which was in the forest,) with a view to destroy the lord of Lanká.

Enter Suka *and* Sárana.

419. *Man.* By desire of Rávana, Suka and Sárana disguised themselves in the shape of Vánaras, and came to Ráma's camp as spies to number his army. Vibhíshana coming to the knowledge of this, arrested them; but Ráma, seeing them in that plight, rescued them instantly, and they went their way with Ráma's leave.

420. *Suk. and Sár.* We see there is no room for a mustard, what then are we to say as to the number of Ráma's army? Every quarter, every forest, as well as the ocean and the caves of mountains, is full of them. Even your brother, who confined us, is in the army. But the noble-minded Shrí Ráma has set us at liberty at once. Now you may act your part in all haste as may be deemed necessary.

[Rávana *from the terrace of his palace, inquires of* Suka *and* Sárana, *which among the enemy's force was* Ráma, *and they point him out.*]

421. Where *Mandara** the flower, which is full of honey, drops; where all sorts of music are heard; and where the birds sing; there the azure-colored Ráma, with his lotus-like eyes, holds a bow in his left hand, and in anger looks to Lanká, whilst he turns his arrow with his right hand.

422. Ráma lies down with his head in the bosom of Sugríva, his feet in the lap of Hanúmána, and his hands on the thighs of Angada,† and he makes his bed of the golden deer skin; moreover, he surveys the counting of arrows by his

* One of the five trees in the Hindu paradise.

† The sun of Tárá, the envoy, a minister of Ráma.

younger brother (Lakshmana,) and eyeing Lanká lends an ear to the words of your brother.

[*To* Rávana.

423. *Ráva.* These are the arms* that have defeated those of Indra; and I am he who has conquered the universe; I am the governor of Lanká, and my name is Rávana. But alas! I hear of the embankment of the ocean, and find that Lanká has been besieged by the Vánaras; to behold which, whilst I breathe, is insufferable. What then may I say, I have never so much as heard of these evils!

424. Strange it is, that the profligate Ráma, who is a devotee, should be aided by the Vánaras (whose abode is in caves,) and attempt to take back Janaka's daughter, whom I have carried away. To attempt this, is like attempting to extract the teeth of a lion, which by his sharp nails scratch the frontal globes on the elephant's head, and taste the bloody liquid which is converted into pearls.†

425. Ah! it is the Lanká of Rávana, on entering into which, the wind, the moon, the sun, Indra, and others, fearfully render daily service, that is now invaded by the timid and cowardly Vánaras.

[Rávana *expressing the above, abused* Suka *and* Sárana.]
Enter Nikumbha.

426. *Man.* Nikumbha, who is skilled in the art of transformation, having a letter from the ten-headed Rávana, appears before the chief of the Raghu family, and presents it.

(The following are the contents of the letter.)

427. "*May good attend thee! Shrí Rávana's fame extends to the three worlds, and his letter is like Indra's weapon: it is addressed to thee, O Ráma, who residest in a wilderness. Rávana has, it is true, carried away the daughter of Janaka; but dost thou, O ignoramus, mean to get her back with the help*

---

* Twenty in number.

† It is said, that pearls are produced in the head of elephants, when it rains on the fifteenth lunar asterism: the rain water by penetrating the pores of the head, is changed into pearls.

of Sugríva's force? if so thou shalt trifle with thy own life."

(Rávana *further authorized* Nikumbha *to speak to* Ráma the *following words.)*

428. *"Even Indra and the other deities find it difficult to declare war with Rávana, and what art thou but a devotee? Dost thou then purpose to cope with him? Thy presumption is strange indeed: thou ignoramus, venture not to march against Rákshasas, but, abandoning the thought of regaining Sítá, return to thy home without delay."*

429. *Nikum. (to* Ráma.) I tell you also that your earnest desire to regain your beloved, who has been carried off by Rávana, from Lanká, on the strength of the Vánaras, is like the desire one may have to obtain a carbuncle from the head of a snake.* Do think upon your welfare.

430. Rávana, who has willingly offered his heads as an act of devotion to Bhavání's husband (Shiva,) and who has subjugated the deities, has the power to assume any shape he likes. And can you by suspending a bridge over the ocean, expect to subdue him; yea such a one who held the mountain *Kailásha* in his hand, and made low the Regent of death's haughtiness?

431. Until Kumbhakarna comes to battle, furious with rage and as noisy as the clouds at the universal dissolution, you may entertain the intention of regaining Sítá. But when he comes, you and the corps of the Vánaras shall not be able to stand still by his strong respirations, which are like a heavy gale at the time of universal destruction.

[*Exit* Nikumbha.

Enter Mandodarí.

432. *Mando. (aside.)* You alone, Rávana, the youngest brother of Kuvéra,† have performed a surprisingly courageous deed by raising up *Kailásha*; but since Ráma has defeated Válí, he is now the person to endanger the Rákshasas.

* A gem said to be produced in the head of the Cobra de capella, and to be noted for its alexipharmic virtues.

† The Indian Plutus, or god of wealth.

433. Since Hanúmána has overleaped a dangerous ocean, entered Lanká, which was never discovered even by demons, and, having had a view of the city, has driven the porters from the garden, and destroyed the same, and has killed Akshaya, consumed the city, seen Jánakí, and returned with ease and safety, what am I to think of Ráma himself?

434. *(Aloud.)* Ráma is the descendant of the sun, and the son of Dasharatha, the great king; and he is himself ruler of the world, and obeyed by all for his justice. It is his arms that protect the *three* worlds, and it is he, who will destroy you for having carried Sítá away. Why then will you not acknowledge him?

Enter Aravinda.*

435. *Ara.* My lord, we shall not at this crisis address you with panegyrics as bards do generally, but we shall advise your lordship in such manner as may tend to your prosperity. Please to consider, that you yourself were incapable of overstepping the circle which was made by Lakshmana on the ground with his bow, to secure Sítá; but as Ráma's Vánara has, though reluctantly, overleaped the ocean, certainly his master must be of greater prowess.

436. Is Ráma to be considered a common man when a menial servant of his, Pávana, has overleaped the ocean in the same manner as he would the print of a cow's feet, and having done so, has entered Lanká as he would his own habitation, and has seen and spoken to Sítá, nay spoiled the garden, and before you consumed Lanká?

437. *Mando.* A Vánara of great valour or one of Sugríva's has burnt Lanká and returned safely; but you who possess ten mouths, have observed taciturnity: what then can your warriors do? Now is Ráma accompanied by a strong body of the Vánaras, and on the eve of coming here by means of the bridge. Reflect, and give Síta up, for your beloved wife entreats you earnestly to do so.

[*Exeunt.*

* One of Rávana's ministers.

ACT VII.

SCENE, *the ocean and the hill Subéla on one side, and Lanká on another.*

Re-enter Mandodarí.

[Mandodarí *persists in her counsel to* Rávana, *on seeing that* Sítá *had not been given up by him.*]

438. *Man.* Mandodarí, finding Sítá still cherishing her love towards her husband, was led to look upon Rághava, engaged against the Rákshasa family, as a raging fire in a forest, threatening total destruction. Observing, therefore, that the contest would not end but in defeat on her own side, unless Sítá's attachment towards Ráma diminished, she was in great apprehensions about the result.

Enter Ráma.

439. *Ráma.* O chief of the Vánaras! He alone can venture to Lanká, who is the most courageous, and who has descended from a king and a learned man.

[To Sugríva.

440. *Sug.* There may be men of royal extraction and yet not warriors, and there may be soldiers and yet not men of noble descent.

[To Ráma.

441. *Man.* Ráma, who resides at the foot of the hill *Subéla,* who possesses a considerable force, and is well able to cross the formidable ocean and proceed in all directions, has commanded Angada, Indra's grandson, to go to Rávana.

442. The son of Tárá (Angada) having overleaped the newly-built palaces, shook their walls with his foot, which occasioned a great noise like that of the clouds. Rávana then inquired what all that was, and coming out muttered something.

Enter Angada *and the guard of* Rákshasas.

443. *Anga.* Tell me, ye Rákshasas, where Rávana is, who having stolen the gem of Rághava has decamped, who shall be like a grasshopper before the flaming points of Ráma's arrows, which illuminate the three worlds.

444. *Rák.* Do not enter the place that Rávana is in, but stay here without the camp, and in a few minutes retire: or thou, O brute, shalt faint from suffering under the weight of Rávana's powerful arms; when thou shalt be like a deer under the paws of a lion, who will be able to save thee?

[*To* Angada.

[Angada *appears as* Kétu* *and in pomp sits on* Rávana's *throne.*]

445. *Ráva.* Who art thou? *Anga.* I am the son of Válí, and the ambassador of Rághava. *Ráva.* Tell me, O Vánara! who Válí is, and who Rághava is? *Anga.* Ah! do you now forget him (Válí,) under whose strong arms you were once crushed, and actually fainted? Ráma is he who chopped off your sister's nose.

446. *Ráva. (again absent minded.)* Who art thou? *Anga.* I am the son of Válí. *Ráva.* Why art thou here? *Anga.* I have been sent by Shrí Ráma. *Ráva.* Hast thou heard any thing of Hanúmána? *Anga.* He is gone some where for fear of our king. *Ráva.* What is the cause of his fear? *Anga.* His not destroying Rávana and his strong army, his sons and his brothers.

[Rávana *on hearing this, was greatly surprised.*]

447. *Ráva.* Who art thou? whose ambassador? and where art thou come from? Perhaps thou takest me for a straw; but know thou that I have conquered the whole world. *Anga.* Hark, O great grandson of Pulusta,† I am the progeny of him, who has subdued thee, and am come from the hill *Subéla,* as an ambassador and minister from Ráma; O brute, give Sítá up, or your life is in jeopardy.

448. Ráma that has perforated a range of seven palm trees‡ with a single arrow, and broken the great bow, and,

* In Hindu mythology, an Asúra, and the ninth planet; in astronomy, the dragon's tail or descending node, and a comet.

† A sage and the son of Brahamá.

‡ It is said in the *Adhyatma-Rámáyana,* that these trees stood circularly, and a serpent lay at the root of them under ground.

he that has lately erected a bridge over the ocean, and slain my father, is my royal master; know then assuredly, that this Lanká is but the pollen of his lotus like feet, and I the same.

449. ***Ráva.*** Who is Ráma? ***Anga.*** It is he that defeated Bhrigu. ***Ráva.*** Who is Bhrigu? ***Anga.*** It is he that made a proclamation of victory; art not thou aware of his renown? and it is he that slew the king Haihaya and others. ***Ráva.*** Who was Haihaya? ***Anga.*** It is he that kept you in confinement.

450. ***Ráva.*** Who art thou? ***Anga.*** I am the descendant of a king of the Vánaras. ***Ráva.*** What can the lord of the Vánaras say, when I am in my palace, and when Indra and others serve me daily as servants? What can Ráma do by coming here in company of his Vánaras, by his crossing the bridge made on ***Ratnákara?**** He will be like a grasshopper on the fire of my anger.

451. ***Anga.*** We have heard of many Rávanas like you, one of them was beaten by Kártavíryárjuna, one was supported by some female dancers, who were engaged by the king of Daityas (Titans,) in prison, and one fled from my father. Art thou one of those Rávanas, or of a different race?

452. ***Ráva.*** I have the pride of having raised the mountain ***Kailásha*** with my own hands, and I am known in all quarters as having ten heads. Observe my grandeur; as for your Ráma, he is but a miserable devotee, and surrounded with enemies, and has but a Vánara for his envoy.

453. *Anga.* A certain Kártavíryárjuna had a thousand arms, which were cut off by Parashuráma, this man was very vain, but his vanity was even destroyed by Rághava, whose envoy I am, and I am the son of him (Válí) by the hair of whose arm-pit you were suspended: my name is Angada.

454. *Ráva.* My brother is Kumbhakarna, who has overcome my powerful foes: my son is Meghanáda, who has been successful in binding the thousand-eyed Indra; even my enemies are the deities, and I have conquered the three worlds. My name is Rávana, and I am a ruler.

---

* The ocean is figuratively termed a mine of gems.

455. *Anga.* Take care, Rávana, that you yourself give Sítá up to Ráma, for you have been disgraced by Kártavíryarjuna, and protect your own children, lest Ráma in anger let off his arrows, he having defeated Parashuráma, who used to hold an axe with which he could cut off the bush-like ranged arms of the ruler of *Haihaya* (Kártavíryárjuna.)

456. *Páva.* What can Ráma do? *Anga.* He can put his enemy to flight. *Ráva.* Who is that enemy? *Anga.* Válí. *Rava.* Who is he? *Anga.* Do not you know him? *Ráv.* Who is to know any thing of a Vánara? *Anga.* It is surprising indeed, and you must have lost your senses to forget him who having taken you a captive, made a toy of you for the diversion of his son.

457. *Ráva.* What are Rághava's remarkable actions? he with the assistance of the Vánaras has erected a bridge over the ocean by way of sport, does not he know me? *Anga.* Ráma has heard of you from the inhabitants of Lanká, and from the chieftain of the place. *Ráva.* Who, O Vánara, is the ruler of Lanká? *Anga.* It is Vibíshana, who is well known to be a king.

458. *Ráva.* O thou obstinate young Vánara! whose father even was not classed among famous warriors. What may have been your Rághava's achievements, so that even hutman power cannot effect them, and what can they have been to induce you to speak so highly of him to me?

459. *Anga.* He who goes by the remarkable name of Ráma, chopped off your sister's nose with his sword, which being stained was washed in the gore which flowed from Khara's and Dúshana's heads after they were cut off by him. O thou impudent Rávana, hast thou forgotten my father (Válí,) who having wrapped thee up* whirled thee, and in a moment performed his evening prayer on the shore of the *four* oceans.†

* With his tail.

† Some Hindu historians have it, that there are four oceans at the four ends of the earth.

460. *Ráva.* Shame on thee, thou brute Vánara, for yet serving him (Ráma,) who has slain thy father without a cause: I would have punished thee well for thy daring expressions, had not thy father been a friend and an object of my kindness.

461. *Anga.* If a friend be of moral principles he is liked by honest people, but if a friend be of immoral principles, he is hated. For example, your own brother Vibhíshana has left you, and he obeys Shrí Ráma, though the latter is bent upon the destruction of the Rákshasas.

462. *Ráva.* I have heard of Vibhíshana's having sheltered himself under a certain Ráma's protection; but as there are many Rámas, I should like to know whom you are alluding to.

463. *Anga.* I mean the Ráma who has slain the Rákshasa Táraká and others, and broken Shiva's bow, as well as defeated Bhárgava, and pierced a range of seven palm trees; who has moreover made a bridge over the ocean. Is not that Ráma yet known to you?

464. *Ráva.* What if he has broken an old bow of Shiva and destroyed the dying Válí; nay perforated a range of seven palm trees with his arrow? And as to his having erected a bridge of mountain stones across the ocean, that even is of little consequence; inasmuch as Rávana is conscious of the strength of his own arms, from having raised with his hands the chief mountain *Kailásha,* which was the residence of Rudra.

465. *Anga.* You are bragging of having raised but one mountain, which was done solely by the favor of Mahádéva, a favor obtained from your devotion to that great deity. Now remember Ráma's having himself assumed the shape of a boar, and raised the earth (at the universal deluge) with thousands of mountains upon it.

466. *Ráva.* And what is all that compared to Ráma's destruction of a golden deer, which feeds upon grass; or a Válí, who goes from one branch to another? How can he who

is but a beggar, be skilled in archery? As for me, I am skilled in war and I have subdued even the Regent of death.

467. *Anga. (boasting.)* Know, thou Rávana, that I am the envoy of Ráma, whose arrows having penetrated through Khara and Dúshana, are now thirsting after blood from thy throat.

468. *Ráva.* Beware, O thou who speakest unadvisedly, and know that even the king of death and the sun serve me daily, the latter with his gentle rays; and that eight Dikpáls for fear of me apply the dust of my feet to their heads; moreover, that the celestial girls and females of the infernal regions feel abashed upon viewing my beautiful scimitar. How then can those two immodest devotees, Ráma and Lakshmana, in company of the Vánaras, dare to vie with me?

469. O thou infernal beast! know that thy effrontery deserves to be visited with death, but for my piety which rescues thee. If it be said, that an envoy should not be destroyed by a crowned head, that saying is worthy of attention in regard to an envoy that speaks with propriety; but thou, for being destitute of such propriety, deservest to be maimed.

470. *Anga.* A pious man you are indeed for robbing others' wives, of which I have heard and which I have witnessed! And a wise man you must really be for liberating an envoy.

471. *Ráva.* When it said, that a bridge has been made across the ocean by one Ráma, the reply is that it has been done by the Vánaras. And Ráma's boasting of the enterprise is the same as that of ants that live within the hills of earth made by white ants; and when the burning of Lanká is spoken of, the reply is, that it was the natural effect of fire; what then is there so very remarkable that Ráma has done?

472. *Anga.* O Rávana, you boast only of having raised the mount *Kailásha.* But how unreasonable would it be to believe, that you can wage war with Ráma, unless he urge you to it. Not to speak of Ráma, you had not sufficient courage to step within the circle marked by Lakshmana with

his arrow; whereas one of Ráma's menials leaped over the ocean, and set fire to Lanká.

473. *Káva.* True, the seven subterraneous regions were not strong enough for Ráma, who has pierced them. True, Ráma has bent one of Shiva's worn out bows; but is it not universally known, that Rávana has held on the palm of his hand the mountain of Hara, and that he is therefore like a comet; as also, that he is known in the world to be the descendant of Brahmá.

474. There is no need of further discussion, for you have heard of my valour. Tell me, what young Rághava's intentions are.

475. *Anga.* Ráma is now wishing to wash the gore from Súrpa-nakha's nose, which has stained his scimitar, in the blood flowing from your head.

476. *Ráva.* O young Vánara, you are not aware and cannot judge of the prowess of Ráma, and Sugríva, and the other warriors, nor of the fame I have acquired by conquering the three worlds. Go and communicate these things to them, and let me know the result.

477. *Anga.* First, Shrí Ráma has requested me to tell you to give Sítá up, whom you have either ignorantly or from being the lord of Lanká, decoyed in our absence. Should you not comply with the request, Lakshmana will pierce your heads with his arrows, and spill the blood flowing therefrom in all directions; and lastly, he will send you to the confines of the Regent of death.

478. Secondly. Kumára* Lakshmana has requested me to open his mind to you, that is, you shall be allowed after giving Sítá up to Ráma to enjoy always your kingdom uninterruptedly, and you shall always be served by the deities. Otherwise, you shall feel the consequence of your disobedience by slaps and blows from the Vánaras' generals.

479. Thirdly. Sugríva has directed you, the lord of Lanká, to look upon him as a great and courageous hero;

* A title given to princes.

and to leave off all your vain boasting, for, great as Válí was, he has been slain by Rághava; therefore give Sítá up, and acknowledge Ráma, that the race of Rákshasas be preserved, as well as your fame as Indra's superior.

480. Fourthly. Other generals have said, O thou infernal and stupid Rákshasa or Rávana, thou art plunged into a sea of grief, because of thy enemies who are near thee, this is not all that you should know, you should know also that Ráma and Lakshamana have bows and arrows, which like the Regent of death, are now near your city-gate.

481. *Anga. (to* Rávana *supposing him to have been a friend of his father's, says before any question is put by him.)* O Rávana, Ráma who is known in the world as a king, has arrived here with an army of the Vánaras (by means of a bridge,) to cause your destruction. He has deputed me to come to you, hear therefore what I say unto you, give Sítá up and acknowledge Ráma, whereby you shall enjoy your kingdom for ever.

482. *Ráva.* Cease from making use of such expressions about the valour of your father, be not astonished at the prowess of Ráma. Should his breaking Shiva's bow be taken into consideration, which enterprise you value so much, I say that it has not been a great enterprise.

483. *Anga.* Well, but Ráma has broken the bow. *Ráva.* It was a worn out one. *Anga.* He has destroyed Táraká. *Ráva.* She herself was a decrepit. *Anga.* Again he has slain Khara and Dúshana. *Rava.* They were but children. *Anga.* Moreover he has pierced a row of seven palm trees. *Rava.* They were like straws. *Anga.* He has destroyed Válí. *Rava.* He was but a Vánara. *Anga.* He has also constructed a bridge over the ocean.

[Rávana *on hearing this, was silent.*

Enter Prahasta.

484. *Pra. (finding* Rávana *silent, interrupts* Angada.) O Brahmá, read* no more at this time, but keep silent. O stupid Vrihaspati,† speak civilly, for it is not the banquet of

* That is, the Védas.

† Jupiter, or the preceptor of the gods.

Indra. O Nárada,* discontinue playing upon the lute and refrain from eulogizing, for the lord of Lanká is perturbed in mind, from his being pierced with the arrow-like words of Sítá.

Enter Satraváha.†

485. *Satra. (gives a color to the uneasiness of* Rávana.) Even the sun conceals itself at one place, and appears at another.‡ Hari§ sleeps on an ocean and Hara (Shiva) resides on the Himálaya mountain, and the chief of gods, Brahmá, does not quit the lotus.||

486. *Anga.* O king of Rákshasas, give Maithilí up immediately. Why art thou displaying thy self-conceit? Observe the Kinnaras themselves up-lifting their arms and singing her virtues; and hear the acclamations of praise to Sugríva, which flow from the mouths of the Vánaras with joined hands; by which the whole city of Lanká is in confusion.

487. *Ráva.* Look at these arms of mine which have defeated those of Indra. I, Rávana, who have conquered the three worlds, now learn that a bridge has been constructed over the ocean, and I find Lanká besieged by the Vánaras, which is a matter of surprise. When one's life is prolonged, one sees and hears what had not been seen or heard before.

488. *Anga.* O thou poor and senseless Rávana, dost thou take Ráma for a common man; Rambhá¶ for a mean woman; the golden age for a common age; Kámdéva for an ordinary holder of a bow; the Ganges for a common river; Airávata for a contemptible elephant; Uchaishrava** for a common horse; and Hanúmána for a common Vánara, whilst his influence is known all over the world.

---

* The name of a Hindu sage, who by telling tales, caused frequent quarrels among the gods.

† One of the ministers of Rávana.

‡ It is said in Hindu works, that the sun moves round the earth, rises from the eastern ocean and sets in the western ocean.

§ Vishnu, the preserver of the world.

|| Brahmá, being fond of the lotus, (which is produced in the water,) always sits upon it.

¶ In Hindu mythology one of the celestial dancing girls.

** The name of Indrá's horse, which is said to have sprung from the churning of the ocean.

489. *Ráva.* (*hearing of the might of* Hanúmána.) It is he who consumed the city, and in a frolic destroyed Akshaya and the great garden, as well as slew several Rákshasas and filled the caves of the mountain *Subéla* with their bodies. And it is he who having crossed the ocean came hither and returned safely. Tell me, if there is any other equal to him in the army of the Vánaras.

490. *Anga.* He who coming to you consumed the city of Lanká, destroyed the garden, and slew Rákshasas, as well as Akshaya, and filled the caves with their dead bodies, is not among the heroes or champions; but he goes here and there daily as a common messenger.

491. *Rava.* I guess the wisdom of Ráma in electing you as his envoy. Inform me candidly, O Vánara, of the virtue you possess.

492. *Anga.* If I knew the policy of an envoy in negociating an alliance or combat with two powers, I would positively make you, O king, roll either on a smooth or rough ground.

493. *Ráva.* O Vánara, go and request the two devotees, Ráma and Lakshmana, who are residing on the hill *Subéla,* which is guarded by an army of the Vánaras, to retire thence in safety; and tell them that the hero Kumbhakarna, who is the pride of Lanká, and by whose exploits I have gained the mansion of Indra, is resting near the ocean.

494. *Man.* Afterwards, Rávana ordered furiously; "Beat and punish this sinful son of Válí." Upon which several of the Rákshasas took hold of Angadá's arms. But he being strong knocked the Rákshasas under his feet; and kicked them so vehemently, that they were seriously hurt, and then he razed the palace to the ground.

495. *Anga.* (*appearing before* Ráma.) My lord, Rávana is much elated and heedless of my good advice. But as your arms are like fire in power, by which your enemy, who is ready to cope with you, will fall like a grasshopper, exert your might and slay him.

[*Exeunt.*

ACT VIII.

SCENE, *as before.*

496. *Man.* Ráma, hearing from Angada the particulars of Rávana's power, lineage and fortune, was for a little while concerned, and observed that Rávana was to be praised for his apparent courage in not giving Sítá up, (although he had witnessed Ráma's astonishing prowess,) and in not laying selfishness aside.

Enter Rávana.

497. *Rava.* (*from an elevated place.*) A Vánara whose tail and face were burnt, and who is the progeny of the wind, and who looks like death itself, has consumed Lanká; and though Ráma is of an azure colour, and like Cupid in appearance with a bow and arrow in his hand, yet his beloved Sítá, a delicate woman, has been decoyed by me.

[Rávana *then looks at all his enemies one after another.*

Enter Mandodarí.

498. *Mando.* (*from her own apartment with her hands folded.*) O! delay not you, who have raised the hill *Chandrashékhara* with your hand, and who have a brother that is capable of devouring all the creatures that are on the earth, to give up Jánakí, in order to enjoy Lanká comfortably. Consider, that Ráma, whose beautiful wife you have decoyed and who has slain Válí, is your antagonist. [*To* Rávana.

[Mandodarí *going.*

499. *Ráva.* (*stretching his hand.*) Be not afraid, my dear Mandodarí, for I have never considered Ráma a great antagonist, and should he declare war, he shall not be able to oppose me; since Indra and other mighty and immortal beings cannot dare to do so. When I shall let my arrows, they will cut off the heads of those two devotees. My intrepidity you shall witness by and by in the field of battle, and then you will find my sayings correct.

[*Exit* Mandodarí.

Enter Virúp ákshya.*

(Pronouncing a Benediction upon Rávana.*)*

Virú. Be renowned, my lord, and preserve your throne, which is set with the inestimable jewels that decorated the crown of Indra.

500. O king! although complimentary words are pleasing to all, yet they are rendered oppressive or hurtful in calamitous times.

501. A man of importance is always surrounded by sycophants. But unpleasant words are always beneficial for the security of one's fortune.

502. In prosperity, dinner and charity parasites are not wanting; but in adversity they fly away, when their sincerity is put to the test.

503. Though it is advisable to be silent before a tyrant, yet he who is loyal, cannot avoid using the following expressions:

504. Parasites cause their master to be in the burrow of distress, and nothing is able to deliver him from it, but they remain silent at it.

505. Will you not restore to Ráma his wife Sítá, until you see him, the ocean dried by the discharge of his fiery arrows, the crown of Lanká transferred to a youth, the women of the city widowed, or your brother Vibhíshana who disgraced your family?

506. *Ravá. (after deliberation.)* Good will is like a secret incantation to the learned, like possession to lovers, and like a sceptre to us valiants.

Re-enter Mandodarí.

507. *Mando.* O Lanká! thou art now plunged into the mire, and who is to preserve thee? Vibhíshana is away, Kumbhakarna is asleep, and thy ruler being resentful is highly stigmatized.

508. *Man.* Afterwards the sinful Rávana, having prepared two heads like those of Ráma and Lakshmana coloured them blood-red, and made them look as if they had

* One of Rávana's ministers.

been just cut off, with eyes closed like dead men's, and placed them before Sítá. [*Seeing the heads,* Jánakí *cries out.*

509. *Man.* Alas! said she, and cried bitterly, and tears gushed from her lotus-like eyes like streams of water, the drops of which looked like pearls and like a necklace on her chaste breast; and being in anguish for the death of her husband, she wailed much.

Sítá. (looking at the head of Ráma.) O God! What am I to do now without Ráma, the hero!

510. Ah! thou art now no more; thou sweet speaker, whose face was like the lotus. Wilt thou see me no more with those beautiful eyes of thine? Art thou now the husband of some celestial nymphs? And wilt thou enjoy the society of such nymphs? Moreover, hast thou embraced the faith of the *Param-hamsa*?*

[*She thinks of taking up the head of* Ráma, *and keeping it in her bosom.*

511. *Man.* At this time, a voice† was heard by Sítá, which said: "O mother, this is not the head of your husband. Be assured, that none can slay your royal consort in a conflict; therefore, touch not this head."—O how fraudulent is Rávana!

Enter Saramá.‡

512. *Sara. (near* Sítá *in the garden of Ashoka.)* Jánakí, cease from bewailing, for Ráma is furious now, and will *this day* destroy Rávana and his sons. O amiable Sítá of delicate make! thy husband will soon kiss thy honied lips.

[Rávana *reflects awhile, and in disguise contrives the following device.*]

513. *Man.* He caused the whole city of Lanká to resound with the mock sound of long-trumpets, the rattling of conches, the roaring of elephants, and the neighing of horses, and with the continued shrieks of Rákshasas, as well as the chattering noise of the Vánaras; and he himself assumed the shape of Ráma

* A particular sect of Hindus, who believe in one God, without any regard to pleasure or pain. † From heaven. ‡ The wife of Vibhíshana.

and put upon his head the forged severed head of Rávana; in which shape he proceeded on.

[Rávana *in this assumed shape comes into the Ashoka garden, and appears before* Sítá.]

514. *Man.* Sítá, beholding a person like Ráma, rose instantly with joy and very modestly covering her chaste breast with] her wearing apparel, cried out:—"Blessed am I, my dear lord, that you have cut off the heads of Rávana, rejoice at it and embrace me, as our distresses are now at an end."

[*At this time, a voice from the atmosphere was heard to the following effect.*]

515. "When the head of Rávana shall be destroyed by the shafts of Raghu, Mandodarí will kiss that head, and thus you will know it to be Rávana's. This, O lady, that you see, is a magical production of the vile Rákshasa, who is in disguise; do not take it to be Ráma's indeed."

Ráva. (aside.) Be that as it may, I shall slay those two devotees Ráma and Lakshmana, and enjoy the company of Sítá, and then retire from this garden.

ACT IX.

SCENE *in and before Lanká.*

Enter Vibhíshana.

Vibhí. O hero Angada, order the army of the Vánaras to be careful to-night; for Rávana sends here the female Rákshasa Prabhanjaní, to harm Ráma and Lakshmana whilst asleep.

Enter Prabhanjaní.

516. *Prabhan. (aside.)* Alas! how can I, a worthless being, harm Ráma the great, who is sleeping well guarded by the army of the Vánaras, who having raised their several arms, keep brandishing arrows over him. Let me therefore return to the lord of Lanká, and report it to him.

[*Exit* Prabhanjaní.

Enter Prabhanjaní *(into* Lanká.*)*

O lord of Lanká, be thou ever renowned! Ráma is guarded by the arrows which were turning like *Sudarshana*;* hence I was unable to kill him at night. Now please to declare war on the morrow. *Ráva.* Just so, I shall do as you say.

[*Exeunt.*

SCENE, *preparations for war.*

Enter Rávana, Ráma, *and* Lakshmana.

517. *Man.* Sugríva, the king of the Vánaras, Angada the prince, and other powerful Vánaras, have promised the divine Ráma to invade Lanká, which is surrounded with oceans and well peopled, by overleaping all barriers, and defeat the Rákshasas.

518. Many of the Rákshasas began the fight with the discharge of stones, thrown from the tops of palaces in Lanká, upon the army of the Vánaras, by which they shook and brought down the palaces.

[Rávana *viewing the force of the* Vánaras, *sent for* Mahodara,† *to be informed of a propitious day.*]

Enter Mahodara.

519. *Maho.* My lord, do you not remember, that when a Hanúmána was seen here, it looked as if the earth were depressed; the mountains oscillated; the ocean felt afflicted; the women of the city shed tears, as copiously as showers of rain; and the atmosphere was made impenetrable to the sun's rays by the cloud of dust caused by the enemy's movements? Command you now to fix a lucky day?

(Rávana *inquires into the state of* Ráma.)

520. *Maho.* Ráma is he who has caused a bridge to be easily constructed over the ocean; before whom bards always sing his praise; who has made of the skin of your maternal uncle‡ a carpet to sit upon; who has engaged your own brother (Vibhíshana) as prime minister; who takes a glance at the

* The discus or weapon of Vishnu.

† One of Rávaná's ministers, and an astrologer.

‡ Márícha, who assumed the shape of a golden deer.

arrangement of arrows; who laughs at the vain fear of Lakshmana for you; who places his hands upon the shoulders of Sugríva; and who stretches his feet into the bosoms of Angada and Hanúmána.

Ráva. *(in anger.)* Why are you vainly giving a flourish to your accounts? To-day you shall witness the power of my arms.

SCENE, *the breaking out of war.*

Enter the armies of Rákshasas and Vánaras.

521. *Vibhí.* Unexpectedly, the whole army of the Vánaras invaded Lanká in a body, and looked like the waves of the ocean, their colour being dark-blue or the colour of a peacock's tail.—The lord of Lanká was troubled at his not enjoying the company of Vidéhí. Now is prince Ráma's force, consisting of Vánaras, engaged in the fight.

522. *Man.* Rávana at this juncture, extended his breast, and raised his heads high as the most elevated walls, and looked as fierce as *Ráhu** when visible in the clear sky. At this time, all the denizens of Lanká held conference with one another.

523. *Maho.* *(looking on.)* The Vánaras that stood in lines before the lord of Raghu, were of a carnation colour, and skilled in the art of fighting, they have discomfited almost all the Rákshasas as the sun dispels darkness at dawn.

Ráva. *(when the* Rákshasas *were destroyed.)* You should awake my younger brother Kumbhakarna.

[*To his Ministers.*

Min. Very well, my lord, we shall attend to your command.

524. *Ráva.* *(aside.)* Wo unto me for having so powerful an enemy as the Vánaras, and these two persons who are near me, are devotees, but have destroyed the race of Rákshasas!—Wo unto Rávana for being yet alive! Accursed be Indrajit! What benefit can I derive by awaking Kumbhakarna? And

---

* The ascending node or dragon's head, according to Hindu astronomy. In mythology, it is the name of an *Asúra* or demon, which became immortal by drinking the nectar produced by the churning of the ocean.

cursed be my arms, which have acted in so small a compass under heaven!

525. *Man.* The royal priests and ministers awoke Kumbhakarna, by pouring some hot oil into his ear-holes.

Enter Kumbhakarna.

Kumbha. (*arising from his long sleep.*) May every happiness attend you!

526. Though the royal mandates are every where carried into effect, yet it is advisable to attend to the advice of the wise.

[*To* Rávana.

527. *Ráva.* Brother, I grant your words, but it is difficult to have good counsels in adversity.

528. Hear me brother, these arms of mine are famous for subduing deities and demons, and for raising *Kailásha;* wherefore my hand-ornaments have been rubbed, and they are very powerful; so I shall be victorious. But I find the present no easy enterprise, and therefore I fear there will be no success. You may therefore go to sleep.

529. *Kumbha.* I shall slay Ráma who has broken Shiva's bow, and slain Válí, who has erected a bridge over the ocean and destroyed several Rákshasas, and I shall slay Vibhíshana, and then kiss your feet.

530. O ruler of Rákshasas, be not sorry because of your enemies; they are but straw; I shall wash my javelin in their blood by slaying them. What is Ráma, or Lakshmana, or Sugríva, or Angada, or Hanúmána, or the regent of Death, or Brahmá, when compared with you? I shall set out to cope with them in your presence.

Ráva. My dear brother, now prepare yourself with other powerful Rákshasas for a combat.

[Kumbhakarna *does accordingly.*

531. *Kumbha.* I am not Válí, Subáhu* or Trishira,* Khara, Dúshana, Táraká, the bridge of the ocean, or Hara's bow. Look, Ráma, I am the destroyer of the enemies, I

* The names of warriors.

resemble fiery arms, and am like the regent of Death, and like the chief weapon of heroes, and now stand before my enemies in the field.

532. *Man.* Kumbhakarna slew several of his enemy's men, and took hold of Sugríva as he would a bludgeon, to hurt him, and then retired to the capital (Lanká) before the race of the Vánaras.

533. *Ráva. (on hearing the news.)* The weapon with which he pierced Válí, is now revenged by confining the head of the Vánaras in the bosom of Kumbhakarna.

534. *Man.* Kumbhakarna, putting one hand in Sugríva's armpit, and another around his neck, took him to Lanká. Sugríva finding Kumbhakarna unguarded, immediately bit his ears and nose, and beat his breast with his elbows, and regaining his liberty, went back to his own cantonment.

535. Kumbhakarna now sighed and bathed the wounds upon his person with his tears, and then resolving on self destruction, took hold of a trident in great anger, and looked like the fire of dissolution with his eyes reddened. He then went out and stood in the field of battle.

536. Some of the Vánaras being terrified at the sight of Kumbhakarna hid themselves in the caves of mountains; some of them flew upwards; some whirling before him fell on the ground, whereby blood flowed from their mouths; and some of them died from the effect of his hard breathing.

Enter Sugríva.

537. *Man.* Kumbhakarna levelled Shiva's invincible trident (which resembled a comet causing dissolution, and shone like millions of lightnings and a blazing fire,) at Sugríva's breast; which when Raghu saw, he kept it off by discharging one of his arrows.

538. When the son of Válí saw that his uncle, the head of the Vánaras, (Sugríva,) was in danger, he let off his weapon *Gárutma* at Kumbhakarna, and his enemy straightway fell, but rising afterwards, he caught hold of Sugríva and Angada

at once, though the former had been liberated by him for a while.

539. At this time, Nala and Níla* witnessing the seizure of both by a Rákshasa, let off their weapons in anger over his head and shoulders, face, ear-holes, and belly. The Rakshasa being weakened by the wounds he received, the Vánaras embraced the opportunity of rising and freeing themselves.

540. The lord of Lanká eyed from a lofty place Kumbhakarna in a state of conflagration from the effect of fiery weapons; and instantly caused a shower of rain to fall upon him. Kumbhakarna now being relieved, seized his enemies like death to devour them.

541. Jámbuvána, who is like thunder and a huge mountain, pressed (boastingly) Kumbhakarna under his knees, and furiously held him fast by the throat, by which Nala and Níla were freed. At this, some flowers were showered from heaven, and gentle zephyrs blew over his person. One of the Rákshasas then with a stroke of his dart liberated Kumbhakarna from Jámbuvána.

542. Prince Rághava with Lakshmana noticing all these circumstances, particularly Rávana's powerful army, became somewhat concerned, and looked at Hanúmána, who then proceeded to the field and appeared there with his eyes as red as those of Narasingha† when Hiranya-kashipu‡ was killed by him.

543. Kumbhakarna having defeated Hanúmána in the conflict, apprehended him and took him to his brother Rávana as an offering.

[Rávana *taking* Hanúmána, *goes to the Ashoka garden.*]

544. *Ráva.* Ráma, being separated from you, has lost his life, and Lakshmana has shared the same fate with him; Sugríva, afraid of Indrajit's force, has escaped and is hiding in the cave of mount *Vindha,* and none acknowledges Vibhíshana

---

* The names of the chief Vánaras.

† The fourth incarnation of Vishnu in the form of a man with a lion's head.

‡ The name of a demor

to be a warrior. Hanúmána, who was capable of bursting through the gate of Lanká, has been apprehended.

[*To* Sítá *repeatedly.*

545. O charming Sítá, the deities are now put to shame, and your Ráma, the brother of Lakshmana, shall not be able to stand in the day of battle: the host of Vánaras shall feel the consequence hereafter. *Sítá.*—O thou vile and mean ten-headed creature, thou, instead of them, shalt be put to shame. Ráma with Lakshmana shall stand boldly in the field, and the Vánaras shall be highly honored.

546. *Man.* Hanúmána placing his foot on the breast of Rávana, tore his ears with his sharp nails, and bit off his nose with his teeth, which are like iron nails; and then the valiant Hanúmána escaped.

547. Kumbhakarna, again angry, appeared in the dreadful field, and discharged his several unequalled weapons. Upon which Ráma with ease cut Kumbhakarna's body into pieces.

548. *Hanú. (when the head of* Kumbhakarna *was chopped off.)* O chief of the tortoise tribe! and O chief of serpents! support the earth. O elephants that are stationed in all quarters, support the great mountains upon your tusks; for the monstrous head of Kumbhakarna has been severed by Ráma's arrows.

549. *Man.* When the head fell down from the neck, all the deities, even the sun, getting into their respective vehicles, appeared and graced the field of battle with their presence, to witness the achievement. They then desired the Vánaras and Rákshasas to discontinue the fight, and, taking up the headless body of Kumbhakarna in the sky, threw it into the capital of Lanká, in order to terrify Rávana by that means.

550. When the body fell down, the wives of Rávana consoled their husband, and prevented him from going again to war. And Nárada, with some musicians and others began to sing and play, and speak highly of Rávana to ease his mind for his affliction for the loss of so valiant a person.

Enter Mandodarí.

551. *Mando.* O king of Lanká, your younger brother has been slain in the battle by Ráma, who in company of some of the Vánaras has entered this place, by means of a bridge and is now at your gate, and are you yet unmindful of him? yea, at whose separation Sítá has been all along in a rage? And do you still harbour a desire to have her?

[Rávana *keeps silent on hearing this.*

[*Exit* Mandodarí.

552. *Ráva. (aside, sighing.)* Alas! the Vánaras have now invaded Lanká, where the Wind, the Moon, the Sun, Indra, and other gods serve in fear—O what a pity! I now appoint you, Méghnáda, to go to war, for by your frown only you can conquer the universe.

Enter Méghnáda.

(*The Vánaras run awuy.*)

553. *Mégh.* O petty Vánaras, why are ye fearful? Know that even Airávata (Indra's elephant) can be killed with my arrows, to discharge which against you would be disgraceful. O Lakshmana, be easy, for you are not the object of my anger. It is Ráma, who has with facility erected a bridge over the ocean.

554. *Man.* Méghnáda, getting into a magical car, soared up, and roaring in the sky like heavy clouds, discharged his *Nágpásha** at his enemies Ráma and Lakshmana, who immediately fell to the ground like the two mountains *Suméru* and *Mandara.*

Enter Saramá.

[*This female* Rákshasa, *by order of* Rávana *goes to* Sítá *in the* Ashoka *garden, and gives her the sad news of* Ráma *and* Lakshmana.]

---

* In Hindu mythology it is the name of a particular rope used as a weapon; this when thrown at an enemy, has the efficacy of transforming itself into a serpent, and retaining him in its folds.

Sítá. Ah Ráma! Oh young Lakshmana! Are ye thus suffering for me?

555. Alas! It is owing to my ill-luck, that the saying of Bhárgava, Chyavana, Kashyapa, Goutama, Vashishta, Lomasha, and Kushika, the sages, have not come to pass.

556. *Man.* He (Méghnáda) who had subdued Indra, the lord of the immortal beings, entrapped Ráma and Lakshmana; but Garura appearing to their rescue, effected their liberation; now they go to war, and Lakshmana has with his arrow levelled Méghnáda.

557. Rávana being informed by the people of the warfare, and the destruction of his son (Méghnáda,) grew incensed at it and said:—"This is like the tale of a batch of elephants entering into the nostrils of musquittos."

Re-enter Mandodarí.

558. *Mando. (hearing of the destruction of* Rávana's *son.)* Alas! do you yet shamelesssly mean to face Ráma, although you yourself have witnessed the disgrace of your sister, and the slaughter of your maternal uncle Márichí? And have you not heard of the piercing of the seven subterraneous regions, the intimacy of Sugríva, the embankment of the ocean, and the spoiling of your garden?

[*To* Rávana.

559. *Ráva.* Tell me, my dear, shall I now restore Maithilí to Ráma my enemy, or shall I die under his arrows in the battle, to ascend to heaven? Of these two, whatever course you think better, shall be adopted by me; for I see that the whole race of the Rákshasas except myself is defunct.

560. Though I know Sítá to be the daughter of Janaka, and Ráma to be the self-incarnate being Madhusúdana;* though I am aware of all this, and that I shall certainly be destroyed by Ráma, yet I cannot give Sítá up.

[*To* Mandodarí.

* The destroyer of the demon *Madhu*,—one of the names of Krishna.

[Rávana *calls on the regent of Death to be present.*]

Enter the Regent of Death.

561. *Ráva.* Hear me, O Death, thou hast once gained wealth, now thou shalt be delighted to carry a necklace of human heads on thy person. Go therefore to Rághava, and desire him to prepare himself speedily with the implements of war; for the lord of Lanká will use his sword to-day in battle.

562. *Hanú.* The spear which Rávana discharged in the field at Vibhíshana, Lakshmana, to save Vibhíshana, received in his own breast, in the way that one receives his beloved into his bosom.

[Lakshmana *falls on the ground motionless.*

563. *Ráma.* (*seeing* Lakshmana *senseless, laments.*) Get up, my dear brother Lakshmana, and hold your arrows, for the enemy are about to destroy our forces; why are you idling to-day, and why do you appear as unconcerned as if you had either regained my beloved Sítá or slain Rávana? Speak, brother, be no longer insensible, and obey me as a king. O mother Kékaí! be now happy at the destruction of thy son.

564. My father is gone to heaven, and unexpectedly my darling Jánakí is gone to a distant place. As to my ingenious and well accomplished brother, (Lakshmana) I am in anxious suspense about him whether he be living or dead: O God! thou hast made us suffer pains in addition to pains which will be made manifest to all!

565. *Sug.* (*condoles* Ráma.) Why do you, who are a man, grieve thus? By such grief nothing can be achieved:—none can bring Valí* from the subterraneous regions; none has been able to kill the regent of Death; none has the power to remove the opacity of the moon; and none can bear the burden of the earth except Ananta.†

566. *Ráma.* (*on being condoled.*) Nothing is so valuable in the three worlds as a dear brother. O Lakshmana! art thou

* The name of a certain king.

† The name of a deified serpent.

gone into the regions of Death, leaving me disconsolate in this transitory world !

567. Ah ! my brother, my noble-minded brother, that wast with me all along in the wilderness, art thou now gone for ever from me into heaven ! Shame on me, for not having accompanied thee !

Enter Suséna.

568. *Man.* Suséna, a Vánara, the son of Dhanwantari,* feels Lakshmana's pulse, and reports to Ráma that he is yet alive, and may be restored to health, if the plant *Vishalya-karaní*† be had during the *day* and *night.*

[*The consultation of* Nala *and others about procuring the medicine.*]

569. If Nala go, he may bring the medicine in *three* whole days and nights ; if Mainda and Dwivida proceed, they may return in *two ;* if Sugríva, or Níla be commissioned to go, they may bring it in *one* day ; but if Válí be desired to go, he may bring it in *twelve hours.*

570. *Ráma. (after the departure of* Hanúmána *to bring the medicine.)* O Night! prolong thy continuance ; O Darkness ! remain in thy natural state by pervading the sky ; and O Sun ! appear not with thy rays until the progeny of the wind returns to me.

Enter Suka *and* Sárana.

571. *Suk.* and *Sára. (when* Hanúmána *had gone to bring the plant.)* My lord, Hanúmána, having killed the female Rákshasa, has destroyed the crocodile, and annihilated the force of Rákshasa, as well as defeated a million of the choristers of heaven, and he has brought the mountain (which was lighted with its gem‡) to Ràma, and the medicinal shrub produced there, with which Lakshmana will be cured and enabled to enter, with you, into contest again.

[To Ráma.

* The physician of the Hindu gods, who sprang into existence at the churning of the ocean.

† The name of a plant celebrated in the writings of the Hindus for extracting arrows and removing inward pains. *(Menispermum dichotoma.)*

‡ A kind of stone emitting light supposed to be in the caves of mountains.

572. *Vána.* and *Ráksha.* Look, Ráma now resembles the beautiful tree *Tamála** which is covered with flowers, and Rávana has changed color from fear: he looks blue like the sky, when he appears in the field of battle.

573. *Báva.* Come forward, ye Vánaras, why are ye all running away? Hold now these arms, when ye engage yourselves in a contest. I shall *this day* kill Jámbuvána, Nala, Níla, and Hanúmána with my bow. I am seeking for Ráma.

574. *Ráma.* O chief of Lanká, give Sítá up, I entreat you. What a vain thought are you still harbouring in your mind! If you do not release Sítá, you shall not be able to suffer the dart of my noted arrow which has destroyed Khara and others; and you shall contract friendship with my bow-strings and embrace them (that is, be severed by means thereof.)

575. *Báva.* Fly now, O Vánara, and be saved.—*Hanú.* Shame on me that I see thee yet alive!

576. *Báva.* (*when Ráma attempted to hold his sharp weapon.*) I am already burning at this separation from Jánakí, which resembles a fiery weapon, and which cannot be bathed even in the water from her eyes, while her respirations are like the winds which inflame a fire. Now, O devotee, do whatever you please with me, the lord of the Rákshasas.

577. *Ráma.* O lord of the Rákshasas, hold your bow immediately, and also the arrow† with which Shiva once severed Tripura, and I shall extinguish the fire of your separation from Sítá by the stream of Mandodarí's tears.

578. *Báva.* You have defeated only Táraká among the females, and the old devotee Bhragu among the males, and you have destroyed Máricha, the timid deer, and the monkey Válí. Now tell me whom among the heroes have you destroyed? why are you making a boast of your arms? take now your arrow.

---

* The name of a tree (according to some xanthocymus pictorius, according to others Disspyros tomentosa.)

† This arrow was gained by Rávana from Shiva at the time of his devotions to him.

579. Your origin is from the sun, whereas I am the great-grandson of Brahmá, and my likeness is that of the cruel Ráhu. I am possessed of ten mouths; whereas you have only one like the single moon; I have twenty hands, which have broken the thunderbolt of Indra, but you have only two arms, which were overcome by me; why then do you vainly boast of your lineage and prowess?

[*To* Ráma.

580. *Ráma.* True, you have sprung from the lotus,* but I from the sun its supporter; fie unto your ten mouths, which are of no consequence. Tell me candidly, whether, or not my arms are superior to yours.

581. Although your arms are renowned for conquering the three worlds, why did you cut off your heads with those arms for the worship of Shiva? Had you not been the great-grandson of Brahmá, you would not have repossessed those heads.

(*The Conversation of the two arms of* Ráma.)

582. *The left-hand.* O right-hand, you are always of service at meal time, why are you not the same in time of war; why do you hide yourself behind the back? *The right-hand.* It is not so, I approach Ráma's ears to know if he is vulnerable or not.

Man. When one of Rávana's heads was severed, the people that were in the field of conflict praised Ráma thus:

583. "When the first of Rávana's heads fell on the ground, the eyes which were in that head glanced at the bow and arrow, and burst into laughter, muttering at the same time these words in anger, 'Up to this day, women live in Lanká at ease and with comfort.'

584. "When the rest of Ravana's heads were cut off, they did not say as they had at one time yelled out before Shiva, viz. "Slay me, slay me, slay me; but they merely laughed heartily."

585. *Ráma.* O Rávana, when I was cutting off thy tenth or last head, all the deities viewed the enterprise from heaven.

---

* Brahmá is the progeny of the lotus, according to Hindu mythology.

Now is my late father equalled to Indra in honor; and I pray you to be my enemy even in the next life.

[*He then kissed the last head.*

586. *Man.* As soon as each of Rávana's heads was taken off, a new one immediately sprang up in its place; and the Vánaras, upon witnessing so extraordinary a sight, were filled with surprise.—Ráma then, listening to the advice of Máthali* from the firmament, took the sharpened *Brahmástra,*† and plunged it into the breast of Rávana.

587. Ráma in company of Lakshmana got into the car from the field of battle. At this instant, the celestial girls complimented Ráma with garlands of the flower *Mandara.* And all the birds commenced singing the song of victory in praise of Ráma, who was then served by the fortunate Sítá.

588. *Behind the Stage.* O wives of deities, retire to your respective stations, and there enjoy the agreeable company of your husbands; and O elephant driver, keep the elephant Airávata in its stable in heaven; O deities, get into your respective cars, and let the trees of paradise be transplanted again into the garden of Indra; for now have the servants of the regent of Death deposited Rávana's severed heads in different places.

589. *Mando. (bewailing.)* Cursed be my fate, for though I am the wife of Rávana, the daughter of the demon Maya, and the mother of him who defeated Indra; I am now made a subject of the Vánaras!

590. Ah! Though the shores of the ocean lay very distant from each other, bridges have been constructed at different places, and though mountains stood where the lord of Lanká resided, they are all levelled to the ground. Where then is the shore of the ocean that lay so very distant, and where are now the Vánaras? both have met together.—None can search out the divine will!

---

* The name of Indra's charioteer.

† A weapon which is consecrated by a formula addressed to Brahmá: it infallibly causes destruction to those against whom it is discharged.

591. Alas! I mourn for the loss of Rávana, in whose hand a scimitar used always to be in a state of wakefulness, who broke the great rod of the regent of Death with it without any difficulty, and who was the chief of heroes; I lament for his destruction by the arrow of Ráma.

592. The heads of Rávana, that were once borne by Shiva upon his own head, are now trodden of vultures. Ah, every one is subject to the inevitable decrees of fate, and must endure whatever may be in his destiny!

593. *Ráksha.* Alas! We now witness the slaughter of Rávana in battle, the defeat of Pushpaka,* and the conquest of Lanká by Vánaras. Man may witness many deeds if his life be prolonged.

594. Though Rávana originated from the sun, though he had an elder brother Yaksha,† and a younger brother Kumbhakarna (who defeated even Indra,) though he had twenty strong arms, and though he had his arrows always at command, and a flying chariot, yea, though he had Lanká for his capital surrounded as it was with the ocean; yet nothing has proved effectual to him. Ah, who can escape the decrees of fate!

595. He (Rávana) who had his capital enclosed by the ocean, the water whereof was of use to his gardens, at whose command even the head jewel of Indra had been brought, whose dominions were three worlds, and who worshipped Hara by severing his own heads, has been reduced to so painful a condition as to be stripped of his grandeur.—What more need be said! *Exeunt.*

SCENE—*Lanká.*

Enter Vibhíshana *and* Mandodarí.

596. *Vibhí. (on seeing* Mandodarí *lying prostrate before* Ráma.) My lord, this is the daughter of Maya, a giant whose

---

* The name of a car. The author means here those who drove this chariot.

† According to Hindu mythology, a king of the creatures that are supposed to possess supernatural power for attending Kuvéra, the god of riches, and superintending his wealth and gardens

son has defeated Indra, and she is the wife of the ten-headed Rávana: she now salutes you with folded hands.

597. *Ráma.* Mandodarí is now to be your queen, and the city (Lanká) your dominion; support and govern both of them.

[*To* Vibhíshana.

[Ráma *then desires* Vibhíshana *to bring* Sítá *into the assembly.*]

Enter Sítá.

598. *Sítá. (in a fiery ordeal.)* I see here my royal husband Ráma, and Lakshmana his younger brother, and here I find the progeny of the wind, and a body of Vánaras. Now I solemnly declare, that should my mind ever have been fixed on Rávana, mayst thou, O fire ! reduce me to ashes.

599. And should I ever have entertained any other person save my husband Ráma, either by words, or in mind, or in person, I pray thee, O fire ! to moulder my chaste body into ashes, for thou art the test of all actions both virtuous and sinful.

[*So saying* Sítá *enters the fire.*

600. *Man. (when* Sítá *entered the fiery ordeal.)* The fire near the soles of her feet and the palms of her hands changed into red colors ;* near her waist and her hair, into wreaths of red water-lilies ; and near her neck and breast, into a gold colored necklace.

601. While the praiseworthy Sítá was in the midst of the fire, all the deties with their consorts, in order to prepare some flowery garlands, purchased the flowers of paradise at a high value from the gardeners of heaven.

602. Sítá came out purified from the fire, having on her head the wreath (given her while in the wilderness by Anusúa the sage,) with a modest look, and with her attention directed to her toes and nails, and her waist-band.—She wore at this time a transformed gold bracelet.

---

* It is customary with native women, to dye their hands with red substances commonly called áltá, or lac leaves impregnated with lac.

[Sítá *creditably passes the ordeal.*]

603. Ráma, who in his infancy broke Hara's bow, has defeated Jámadagnya, having forsaken his empire by direction of his royal father, having erected a bridge over the ocean, and having cut off one by one Rávana's heads, what more shall be said of his exploits? He doubted for a moment the chastity of Sítá, but she has been found guiltless.

(*When* Sítá *came out of the fire unhurt, all the deities and* Ráma's *deceased father* Dasharatha *sang out from heaven.*)

604. "O Ráma, son of the Raghu tribe, know, and own thy wife to be chaste and pure, for we Dikpáls are a testimony to her noble character. Moreover, she like a golden creeper has undergone a fair ordeal, and is an invaluable ornament to your family.

605. "You, Ráma, have conquered Lanká and walked over the ocean by means of a bridge across it; killed Rávana with merely the assistance of Vánaras in the field of battle, and destroyed the race of Rákshasas. The achievements of the great are ever successful, even without adventitious aid.

606. "Ráma, you are famous in having obeyed your father's command by retiring to the wilderness; and you are respected even by Bharata your younger brother, who was regardless of his mother and his kingdom from his attachment to you; and you are so very liberal as to have conferred royalty upon Sugríva and Vibhíshana; and, lastly, you have made known your valour by destroying the race of the Rákshasas.

607. "You are renowned in the three worlds, and are the constant object of meditation to Sítá, whom you grace with a place in your heart."

Enter some persons from Lanká.

608. *Per.* This Hanúmána of yours, my lord, has destroyed Lanká, made a bridge over the ocean, and brought some good medicine for Lakshmana. Considering such services of Hamúmána, some Rákshasas painted his likeness on the walls and bit the portrait in a rage.

609. *Man.* Ráma, having destroyed Rávana the hero, intends to return in company of Sítá to Ayodhyá.

610. *Ráma.* Look, my dear, with your deer-like eyes at the capital of Lanká, in which even the sun from fear always gently distributes its rays, and the moon appears in full every night, and which is now to be styled the new kingdom of Vibhíshana.

611. My dear lady, look on, here we have been both hurt with a serpentine weapon, and Lakshmana has received the strong stroke of the spear, Hanúmána has brought the mountain *Gandha-mádana*, and my younger brother has slain Méghnáda, and *some one* has killed Rávana, the lord of the Rákshasas.

[*To* Sítá.

612. *Man.* The son of Dasharatha with Vidéhí got into the car (*Pushpaka*), and whilst proceeding they observed the wonderful and extraordinary appearance of Lanká which was like blackberries; of Jánakí which was like a lotus; the field of war which was like the mire of earth; and the ocean which was like a drop of water.

613. When Raghunátha, in company of his consort Sítá, who had so conspicuously undergone a fiery ordeal, drove the *Pushpaka* car, all the Vánaras joined in an acclamation of praise to Ráma for his conquest and to Vibhíshana; and the lord of the Raghu tribe attended by his ministers arrived at Ayodhyá. Kékaí now gave charge of his empire and its fortunes to him, and he received the same under his sway.

[*Exeunt.*

THE END.

ERRATA.

Page 7,	*l.* 9.	*before the word* " Ye" " and."
—	*l.* 10.	*after the word* " globe," *add* " all the three."
9,	*l.* 36.	*for* " Jamadagnya" *read* " Jamadagni."
13,	*l.* 13.	— " Ráma's" —— " Shiva's.
17,	*l.* 27.	— " occurence" —— " occurrence."
21,	*l.* 15.	— " bnt" —— " but."
22,	*l.* 1.	*after* " 114" *add* " Manager."
30,	*l.* 4.	*before the word* " Whither" *insert a dash*
31,	*l.* 7.	*for* " Máríchí" *read* " Máricha."
36,	*l.* 34.	— " Rhámayana" —— " Rámáyana."
39,	*l.* 7.	— " have" —— " to have."
—	*l.* 12.	*at the end of Sloka* " 233" *add* [" To Sugríva."
—	*l.* 15.	*dele* [" To Sugìrva."
43,	*l.* 30.	*for* " occasionrd" *read* " occasioned."
45,	*l.* 16.	— " you" —— " your."
—	*l.* 26.	— " at" —— " if."
48,	*l.* 11.	— " it" —— " this."
49,	*l.* 20.	— " Askhaya" —— " Akshaya."
51,	*l.* 27.	*after* " 314" *add* " Manager."
53,	*l.* 18.	—— " Dadhimukha" — " Sugríva."
54,	*l.* 10.	—— " 331" — " Manager."
54,	*l.* 21.	*for* " taken" *read* " token."
56,	*l.* 34.	*after the word* " of " *add* " the master."
57,	*l.* 1.	—— " 349" —— " Ráma."
63,	*l.* 32.	*for* " Sugríva" *read* " Vibhìshana."
64,	*l.* 24.	— " on " —— " about."
76,	*l.* 25.	*after* " it" *add* " is."
78,	*l.* 9.	— " Lakshamana" — " Lakshmana."
84,	*l.* 20.	*add* [*Exeunt.*
91,	*l.* 16.	*for* " awuy" *read* " away."
92,	*l.* 19.	— " Máríchí" —— " Márícha."

श्रीमन्महानाटकः

अर्थात्

वीरश्रीयुत नृपति रामचन्द्रचरित

श्रीमद्धनुमता विरचितग्रन्थः

इदानीन्तु

मूलसंस्कृतादुद्धृत तदर्थैङ्गलण्डीय भाषया

शोभाबाजारस्थ

श्रीलश्रीयुत महाराज कालीकृष्ण बाहादुरेण

अनुवादितः ।

नगरवर कलिकातान्तर्गत

सारसंग्रहयंत्रे श्रीनवकृष्ण सरकारेण मुद्राङ्कितः ।

शकाब्दा १७६२ ।

प्रधानतम ब्रीटन आइरलण्ड महाराज्यद्वयाधिकारिणी कृपाप्रकाशिनी

परमाराधिनी विविधयशस्विनी प्रतापशालिनी महाराज्ञी

श्रीश्रीमती विक्टोरिया

साम्राज्यवर्द्धिनी विजयिनी लोकप्रतिपालिनी नानानीतिशास्त्रविनोदिनी

गुणिगणगुणग्राहिणी सम्मत्यनुसारतः संस्कृतप्रचलित

श्रीमन्महानाटकग्रन्थस्य

इंलण्डीय भाषयानुवादः

सेनकराजश्रीकालीकृष्णदेवकर्तृकः

तन्महाभिधानोद्देशतः

कृतोपायनः ।

भूमिका ॥

श्रीगोपीनाथ पादाम्बुज युगलमहं सर्वमङ्गल्यगेहं स्तुत्वानत्वाचयत्नात्पवनसुतकृत श्रीमहानाटकस्य । ग्रन्थस्यैवानुवादं गुणिगणसुखदं भाषयाभूपतीनां श्रीकालीकृष्णनामा नरपतितनयः सत्प्रहर्षोवितन्वे ॥ १ ॥

मधुसूदनमिश्रेण कृतं सन्दर्भशोभनं । रामचरितोदयस्यास्य नाटकानुक्रमेणवै ॥ २ ॥

नर्त्तकीनर्त्तकादीनां निर्गमागमबोधकं । प्रयुक्तं तत्र यद्वाक्यं तन्नसम्यक् समीरितं ॥ ३ ॥

ग्रन्थस्योपक्रमे तत्तद्विवृतेरनुरूपतः । चित्रप्रकटनं तेषु पाठकेषु न दृश्यते ॥ ४ ॥

नटादीनां क्रियातेषां चित्रप्रकटनादिकं । गद्यैर्विरचिते ग्रन्थे तत्सर्वं कथितं मया ॥ ५ ॥

विहाय प्रपद्यं नियतच्छन्दसां प्रयुक्तानु यत्नाद्विरचितं कादम्बं । कुसुमाद्भिरं नागरैरत्नैस्तत्प्रयाचेऽहमस्मिन्निदं भो गुणज्ञाः ॥ ६ ॥

दोषं हित्वा गुणिगणाः स्वगुणग्राहितां नयम् । यदि गृह्णाति तद्भावं तदा सार्थःश्रमोभवेत् ॥ ७ ॥

कालीपुरसदृशा कान्ता या परा नगरीपरा । श्रीकालीसदना देवोऽस्याः शोभावैषणिकेस्थितः ॥ ८ ॥

भूमिकायाः प्रथमश्लोके भाषयाभूपतीनामित्यत्र इंरेजीय भाषयेति बोद्धव्यम् ॥

महानाटक रङ्गस्थलीस्थ पात्रादीनामनुक्रमणिका ॥

पुरुषगणः ।

दशरथः — अयोध्याधिपतिः ।

श्रीरामः — दशरथस्य प्रथमात्मजः दशवदन निधनकारीच ।

लक्ष्मणः — दशरथस्य द्वितीयपुत्रः रामानुगतः ।

शत्रुघ्नः — दशरथस्य तृतीय तनयः ।

भरतः — दशरथस्य चतुर्थाङ्गजः ।

परशुरामः — ब्राह्मणैकः क्षत्रिकुलनाशकः ।

जनकः — मिथिलाधिपः ।

मारीचः — कल्पितस्वर्णमृगोराक्षसश्च ।

रावणः — दशवदनोलङ्काराजः सीतापहारकः ।

कुम्भकर्णः — रावणानुजः ।

वाली — कपीन्द्रः ।

सुग्रीवो — रामसखः किष्किन्धाधिपश्च ।

हनूमान् — लङ्कादाहकः ।

अङ्गदः — वालिपुत्रः श्रीरामदूतः ।

विभीषणः — रावणभ्राता ।

सूत्रधारः — नटस्थलीस्थः ।

स्त्रीगणः ।

सीता — रामभार्य्या ।

कौशल्या, कैकयी, सुमित्रा — दशरथदाराः ।

तारा — सुग्रीवपत्नी ।

मन्दोदरी — रावणपत्नी ।

सरमा — विभीषणजाया ।

एतद्भिन्न वैतालिक, मुनि, सारथि, सखीगण, एवं पथिक, नगरवासि, सेनाध्यक्ष, राक्षस, राक्षसी, सभासद, राजमंत्रि, द्वारि, यम, भिषक्, दूत प्रभृत्यादि ॥

श्रीमन्महानाटकः ॥

अर्थात्

रामलीलोदयः।

विश्वेशोवः सपायात्त्रिगुणसचिवतां योवलम्ब्यानुवारं विश्वध्रीचीन सृष्टि स्थितिविलयमजः स्वेच्छया निर्मिमीते। यस्येयत्तामतीत्य प्रभवति महिमा कोपिलोक व्यतीतस्त्वसौ यश्चक्षुराद्यैरपि निपुणतमो वीक्षणादि क्रियासु ॥ १ ॥

विघ्नेशोवःसपायाज्जलनिधिमखिलं पुष्करायेणपीत्वा यस्मिन्नुद्धृत्यतोयं विसृजति सकलं दृश्यते व्योम्निदेवैः। क्वाप्यम्भः क्वापिविष्णुः क्वच कमलभूः क्वाप्यनन्तः क्वचश्रीः क्वाप्यौर्व्वः क्वापिशैलाः क्वचनमणिगणाः क्वापिनक्रादिचक्रं ॥२॥

जयति रघुवंशतिलकः कौशल्यानन्दवर्द्धनोरामः दशवदननिधनकारी दाशरथिः पुण्डरीकाक्षः ॥ ३ ॥

नमामिदेवं सुरकल्पवृक्षं धनुर्धरं नीरद नीलगात्रं। जनाभिरामं कमलाननं तं यदास्पदं लक्षणमुज्झति श्रीः ॥ ४ ॥

रामं लक्ष्मण पूर्व्वजं रघुवरं सीतापतिं सुन्दरं काकुत्स्थं करुणामयं गुणनिधिं विप्रप्रियं धार्मिकं। राजेन्द्रं सत्यसन्धं दशरथतनयं श्यामलं शान्तमूर्त्तिं वन्दे लोकाभिरामं रघुकुलतिलकं राघवं रावणारिं ॥ ५ ॥

मनोभिरामं नयनाभिरामं वचोभिरामं श्रवणाभिरामं सदाभिरामं सतताभिरामं वन्देसदा दाशरथिञ्चरामं ॥ ६ ॥

श्रीरामचन्द्र भुविविस्तृतकीर्त्तिचन्द्र स्मेरामस्यचन्द्र रजनीचर पद्मचन्द्र आनन्दचन्द्र रघुवंशसमुद्रचन्द्र सीतामनःकुमुदचन्द्र नमोनमस्ते ॥ ७ ॥

कल्याणानां निदानं कलिमलमथनं जीवनं सज्जनानां पाथेयंयन्मुमुक्षोः सपदि परमपदप्राप्तये प्रस्थितस्य विश्रामस्थानमेकं कविवरवचसां पावनं पावनानां बीजं धर्मद्रुमस्य प्रभवतु भवतां भूतये रामनाम ॥ ८ ॥

एतौ द्वौ दशकण्ठकण्ठकदली कान्तारकान्तिच्छिदौ वैदेहीकुचकुम्भकुङ्कुम रजः सान्द्रारुणाङ्काङ्कितौ लोकत्राणविधान साधुसवन प्रारम्भयूपौभुजौ देयास्तामुरु विक्रमौ रघुपतेः श्रेयांसिवः ॥ ९ ॥

बालक्रीडितमिन्दुशेखर धनुर्भङ्गावधि प्रभुता तातेकानन सेवनावधि कृपा सुग्रीवसख्यावधि आज्ञावारिधिबन्धनावधि यशोलङ्केशनाशावधि श्रीरामस्य पुनातु लोकमहिमा जानक्युपेक्षावधि ॥ १० ॥

नान्द्यन्ते सूत्रधारः ।

सूत्र । वाल्मीकेर्वदनामलेन्दुगलितं हृद्यं परं पावनं श्रोतं वागमृतं पिबन्त्यनुदिनं येश्रोत्रपात्रैर्जनाः । विष्णोःसच्चरितं चराचरगुरो रामायणं सादरास्तेषां श्रीर्विमला भवत्यनुदिनं नश्यन्ति चारातयः ॥ ११ ॥

अपिच । वाल्मीकेर्हृदयदेशतः स्वयमहो वक्ताहनुमान्कपिः श्रीरामस्य रघूद्वहस्यचरितं सौभ्यावयं नर्त्तकाः । गोष्ठीतावदियं समस्तसुमनः संघेनसंवेष्टिता तद्धीराः कुरुत प्रमोदमधुना वक्ताक्षिरामायणं ॥ १२ ॥

अथ प्रथमोऽङ्कः ।

अयोध्याराजसदन कल्पनं ।

राम लक्ष्मण भरत शत्रुघ्न सहित दशरथागमनं ।

सूत्र । राजासीत्समहारथोदशरथस्सत्वांशुवंशाग्रणीस्तस्या सन् कमनीय केलिनिलयाश्चित्रो महिष्यःशुभाः वीरांस्तां श्चतुरः सुताम् सषुविरे रामं तथा लक्ष्मणं शत्रुघ्नं भरतश्च कैटभरिपोरंशावताराइमी ॥ १३ ॥

शत्रुघ्नोराजपुत्र स्तदनु समभवच्छत्रुनिघ्नैकवीरः सोयं स्नेहानु वृत्या भरतमनुगतः कैकयी सूनुमेव सौमित्री राममेवानुगम दथसदा धर्मकर्म प्रवीरः श्रीमद्दाशरथाः स्वयं मुररिपोरंशावताराइमी ॥ १४ ॥

विश्वामित्रागमनं ।

सूत्र । तेषां रामः कुशिकतनय प्रार्थितो यज्ञसिद्धै तातस्याज्ञां शिरसि विदधल्लक्ष्मणेनानुयातः । पोरस्त्रीभिर्नयन कमलैः सादरं वीक्ष्यमाणः श्यादाणी निधनकुतुकी यज्ञभूमिं प्रतस्थे ॥ १५ ॥ निष्क्रान्ताः ।

तपोवन कल्पनं ।

ततःलक्ष्मणसहितःश्रीरामचन्द्रे तपोवनंप्रविशति वैतालिकवाक्यं ।

वैता । विद्यां विशिष्टां विजयां जयाञ्च सम्प्राप्य सम्यङ्मुनगाधिपुत्रात् ।
रक्षांसिहन्तुं क्रतुबन्धुबन्धुः समागतःसम्प्रति रामचन्द्रः ॥ १६ ॥

पुनर्वैता । मारीचं निजघान राक्षसचमूनाथं स्वयंराघवः सर्वेऽन्ये-

किल लब्धाशस्य विश्विखैर्याताः कृतान्तालयं । तेषं प्रापुरथोमहर्षि सहिताः सर्व्वैपुराब्राह्मणास्ताभ्यां संयुयुजुः शुभाशिषमतिस्फीताः समाप्ताःक्रियाः ॥ १७॥

सूत्र। इतेरक्षः कुलेतत्र रामेण विधिवत्कृता । निर्वृत्ते कौशिकः प्रायात्ताभ्यां जनकपत्तनं ॥ १८ ॥ निष्क्रान्ताः।

मिथिलाराजभवन कल्पनं।

अथ मिथिलां प्रविशति रामे वैतालिकैः पठितं।

वैता । योदत्तः कुशिकात्मजायमुनये तातेन यज्ञोत्सव प्रत्यूह प्रशमाय वर्मविपिने हत्वार्चितां ताड़कां । लब्धाखाशि मुनेरवेक्ष्यचमखं तस्यानुगः कौतुकात् सोयं सम्प्रति राघवो निमिपतेः प्राप्तःपुरीं सानुजः ॥ १९ ॥

जनक । असुरसुर भुजङ्ग वानराणामथ नरकिन्नर सिद्धचारणानां । नमयति यदि कोपि चापमेतं मम दुहितुः सपरिग्रहं करोतु ॥ २० ॥

तत्श्रुत्वा रावणदूतः सौष्कलः सकोपः ।

सौष्कल । सार्द्धं हरेण हरवल्लभया गिरीशं हेरम्बषण्मुख बृष प्रमथावकीर्णं । कैलासमुद्धृतवतो दशकन्धरस्य कोयस्तवधनुषि दुर्मददोः परिद्धा ॥२१॥

तयोरुक्ति प्रत्युक्ती।

माहेश्वरंधनुः कुर्य्यादधिज्यखेदरान्यहं । गुरोः शम्भोर्धनुर्मोचे चूर्णतां नयति क्षणात् ॥ २२ ॥ इत्युक्ता दूतेगते ।

शतानन्दागमनं ।

सूत्र । सभायां नृपयुक्तायां जनकस्य पुरोहितः । शतानन्दोवचःप्राह शृण्वतां सर्व्वभूभृतां ॥ २३ ॥

शता । शृणुत जनकशुल्कं क्षत्रियाःसर्व्वएते दशवदनभुजानां कुण्ठिता यत्रशक्तिः । नमयति धनुरैशं यःशरारोपणेन । त्रिभुवन जयलक्ष्मी मैथिली तस्यदाराः ॥ २४ ॥

नृपतिभिरव गृहीतेधनुषि जनकवाक्यं ॥

जनक । आद्वीपान्तरतोऽप्यमी नृपतयःसर्व्वे समभ्यागताः कन्येयं कलधौत कोमलछविः कीर्त्तिस्तुनातःपरा । नाकृष्टं नच टङ्कितं ननमितं नोत्थापितंस्थानतः केनापीदमहो महद्धनुरतो निर्व्वीरमुर्व्वीतलं ॥ २५ ॥

ससखीगणसीतागमनं ।

सखी । रामोदूर्व्वादलश्यामो जानकीकानकीलता । अनयोर्योग्यउद्वाहो धनुरैशःपणोमहान् ॥ २६ ॥

कमठपृष्ठकठोरमिदंधनु र्मधुरमूर्त्तिरसौरघुनन्दनः । कथमधिज्यमनेन विधीयतामहहतात पणस्तवदारुणः ॥ २७ ॥

श्रीरामेलज्जांकुर्व्वति सीताया उत्साहंवर्द्धयन्लक्ष्मणः ।

लक्ष्मण । देवश्रीरघुनाथ किं बहुतया दासोऽस्मिते लक्ष्मणोमेर्व्वादीनपि भूधरान्नगणये ज्जीर्णः पिनाकःकियान् ॥ २८ ॥

तन्मामादिश वीरयस्य भवतोवाक्यादहं कौतुकी । प्रोद्धर्तुं प्रचलायितुं नमयितुं भङ्क्तुं सदैवंक्षमः ॥ २९ ॥

सूत्र । गृहीते हरकोदण्डे रामे परिणयोन्मुखे । पस्पन्दे नयनंवामं जानकी जामदग्न्ययोः ॥ ३० ॥

गृहीतेधनुषि रामेणलक्ष्मणः ।

पृथ्विस्थिराभव भुजङ्गमधारयैनां त्वंकूर्मराजतदिदं द्वितयं दधीथाः । दिक्कुञ्जराः कुरुत तत्रितये दिधीर्षामार्य्यः करोति हरकार्मुकमाततज्यं ॥३१॥

पृथ्वी यातिरसातलं फणिपतिर्मग्नं फणामण्डलं विभ्रत् क्षुभ्यति कूर्मराज सहितो दिक्कुञ्जराःकातराः । आतन्वन्तिच हं द्वितं दिविभटैः सार्द्धंधराधारिणः कम्पन्ते रघुपुङ्गवे पुरजितः सज्यंधनुः कुर्व्वति ॥ ३२ ॥

तत्र नृपतीनां चेष्टा ।

सूत्र । रामेणदशरासनं तुलयति क्षित्वाक्षितं पार्थिवैः सिञ्जासिञ्जनतत्परे च हसितंदत्वामियस्तालिकां । आरोप्यप्रचलाङ्गुली किसलयैर्मानं गुणास्फालने सर्व्वाकर्णनभग्न पर्व्वनिपुणाः सिंहासने मूर्च्छितं ॥ ३३ ॥

उत्क्षिप्तं सहकौशिकस्य पुलकैः सार्द्धंमुखैर्नामितं भूपानां जनकस्य संशय धिया साकंसमास्फालितं । वैदेहीमनसा समंचसहसाकृष्टं ततो भार्गवप्रौढाहं कृतिकन्दनेन महता तद्भग्नमैशंधनुः ॥ ३४ ॥

सन्धानत्वविधेः श्रुतीर्मुखरयन्नष्टौदिशः क्रोडयन्मूर्त्तीरष्टमहेश्वरस्य दलयन्नष्टौकुलक्ष्माभृतः । अत्युच्चैर्बधिराणि पन्नगकुलान्यष्टौच सम्पादयन्नुन्मीलत्ययमार्य्य दोर्बल दलत्कोदण्ड कोलाहलः ॥ ३५ ॥

लोकाग्सप्तविनादयन् हरिहयागुद्‍ाभयन्सप्तच ध्यामात्सप्तविवा-

रयमुनिवरास्सप्तार्णवान् क्षोभयन् । उन्मूलानि रसातलानि जनयन्स-
प्तापि संभूतवान् श्रीमद्राघवबाहुदण्डविदलत्कोदण्डचण्डध्वनिः ॥ ३६ ॥

शुभ्राज्ञीमधनुः कठोरनिनदस्तत्राकरो विस्मयं नश्यद्दाजिरवेर्विमार्गगम-
नं शम्भोः शिरःकम्पनं । दिग्दन्तिस्खलनं कुलाद्रिचलनं सप्तार्णवान्दोलनं दे-
देहीमदनं मदान्धदमनं त्रैलोक्यसम्मोहनं ॥ ३७ ॥

कोदण्डभङ्गाम्मुखरीकृताशं वरं वरेण्यं जनकात्मजायाः । अनन्यसामान्य
धनुर्विलासं नमामितं लोकविसर्पिकीर्त्तिं ॥ ३८ ॥

अथ शतानन्देनानीते दशरथे मिथिलां वैतालिकैः पठितं ।

वैता । जनकनृपतिवाक्यं पुत्रसम्बन्धकृत्यं सरभसमुपगृह्य श्रीशतानन्द
वक्त्रात् । अपरमपितमूजद्दन्दमादायहृष्टः श्रुतरघुपतिशौर्य्यः कोशलेन्द्रोय-
मेति ॥ ३९ ॥

सूत्र । आतिथ्यमानमहितं मिथिलाधिनाथः कृत्वातिथिं दशरथंपरमा-
तिथेयः । खीयेसुतेप्यथ कुशध्वजकन्यके च प्रत्याददौ विधिवदेव तदात्मजेभ्यः ॥ ४० ॥

निःशालमर्दल रसालगभीर भेरीढक्कारतालवर काहलनादजालैः ।
पूर्णांबभूवधरणी गगनान्तरालं पाणिग्रहे रघुपतेर्जनकात्मजायाः ॥ ४१ ॥

रघुजनकमहीन्द्रयोस्तदानीमभवदपत्य विवाहमङ्गलश्रीः । त्रिभुवन
जनतानमन्द यत्र प्रमदमवाप मनोरथव्यतीतं ॥ ४२ ॥

सीतां श्रीरघुनन्दनोथ भरतःकौशध्वजींमाण्डवीं सौमित्रिः शतपत्रपाणु
वदनां सीतानुजामूर्मिलां । शत्रुघ्नःश्रुतकीर्त्तिमुत्तमगुणां कौशध्वजीमूढ्वां
स्तामादाय कृतोत्सवो दशरथः खीयांपुरीं प्रस्थितः ॥ ४३ ॥ निष्क्रान्ताः ।

॥ इतिप्रथमोऽङ्कः ॥

द्वितीयोऽङ्कः ॥

चित्रपथ कल्पनं ।

अथ पथिपरशुरामेण संसर्गः ।

सूत्र । यद्भग्नं जनकात्मजाकृते राघवःपशुपतेर्महद्धनुः । तद्ध्वनिश्रवण रोषितस्त्वरन्नाजगाम जमदग्नि जोमुनिः ॥ ४४ ॥

लक्ष्मणः श्रीरामम्प्रति परशुरामं स्मारयति ।

कुर्व्वन् कोपादुदग्र द्रविकिरण सटापाटलैर्द्दष्टिपातैरद्यापि क्षत्रकण्ठच्युत रुधिरसरित्सिक्तधारंकुठारं ।तीव्रै र्निश्वासपातैःपुनरपि भुवनोत्पातमा सूचय-नन्नाक्रान्तर्लौल्मौर्व्वी कलापं त्रिभुवनविजयी जामदग्न्योयमेति ॥ ४५ ॥

अपिच । चूडाचुम्बितकङ्कपत्रमभितस्तूणीद्वयं पृष्ठतो भस्मस्निग्ध पवित्र लाञ्छनमुरो धत्तेत्वचंरौरवीं । मौञ्जामेखलया नियन्त्रित मधोवासश्चमाञ्जि-ष्ठिकं पाणौकार्मुक मक्षसूत्रवलयं दण्डंपरंपैप्पलं ॥ ४६ ॥

सोयंसप्तसमुद्रमुद्रितमही येनार्ज्जुनादुद्धृता छित्वा भैरवसङ्करेतिकठिनं कण्ठं कुठाराग्रतः । रेवानीरनिरोधहेतुगहनं बाह्वोःसहस्रंजवात् खण्डं खण्डमखण्डयत् पितृवधामर्षेण वर्षीयसा ॥ ४७ ॥

यत्राक्रामति सङ्कराङ्कभुवं दुर्व्वार धारास्खलत्कुप्यत् क्षत्रकिशोर कण्ठरुधिरैर्नीरेणुकाभूरभूत् । तादृग्वीरवर स्वयम्वर परस्त्रीककन्याकर क्रीडापुष्करदामरेणुभिरभूद्दूरेव रेणूत्कटा ॥ ४८ ॥ क्रोधं नाटयित्वा ।

जाम । कोनेदं कालदण्डान्तरमिच्छता भग्नमजगवं धनुरिति सापशङ्कं वारत्रयं ॥ ४९ ॥

पार्व्वत्यानिजभर्त्तुरायुधमिति प्रेम्णायदभ्यर्च्चितं निर्म्मोकेनमहवासुकेर्निगुम्फितं यत्सादरं नन्दिना। भव्यंयत्त्रिपुरेन्धनं धनुरिदं तन्मन्मथोन्माथिनः सत्येवंभुवि रामनाममनिमयि द्वैधीकृतं दृश्यते ॥ ५० ॥

इत्युक्त्वा सतर्कंसासूयम्।

सहस्रबाहुस्त्वमहंद्विबाहुस्त्वं चक्रवर्त्ती मुनिनन्दनोहं। त्वं सैन्ययुक्तोऽसहमेक वीरस्तथापिनो पश्यतसर्कमर्कः ॥ ५१ ॥ इति सूर्य्यंदृष्टवान्।

उत्कृत्योत्कृत्यगर्भानपि शकलयतुं क्षत्रसन्तान रोषादुद्दामानेक विंशत्यवधि विशसतः सर्व्वतोराजवंश्यान्। पैत्रंतद्रक्तपूर्णह्रदमवनि महानन्दमन्दायमान क्रोधाग्नेः कुर्व्वतो मेनखलुविदितः सर्व्वभूतैः प्रभावः ॥ ५२ ॥

कुप्यत्क्षत्रशिरोरकण्ठविगलद्रक्तौघधारासरिन्निवृंताभिषवस्य कृत्तशिरसःकेशान्कृशान् कुर्व्वतः। तावद्रक्तजलाञ्जलिः पितृगणैर्यस्य ग्रहीतःसन्तोषेणजुगुप्सया करुणया हासेनशोकेन वा ॥ ५३ ॥

अपिच। आस्वर्थंकार्तवीर्य्यार्ज्जुनभुजविपिन छेदलीलाखभिज्ञः केयूरग्रन्थिरत्नोत्करकषण रणत्कारघोरःकुठारः। तेजोभिः क्षत्रगोत्रप्रलयसमुदित द्वादशार्कानुकारः किंनप्राप्तः श्रुतिं ते पुरमथन धनुर्भङ्गपर्य्युत्सुकस्य ॥ ५४ ॥

स्वकुठारं प्रदर्शयति।

अभ्यग्निं जमदग्निराश्रमपरैर्यैः श्रूयते श्रोत्रियैः श्रूयेचाहमहं दुभिर्नृपतिभिस्त्रोभयेसाक्षिणः। इक्ष्वाकोरथवाभृगोर्भगवतो भाविस्वधाविप्लवः स्वाध्यायेमशपेशपे परशुनापत्यापशूनांशपे ॥ ५५ ॥

श्रीरामःसानुनयं।

वाह्वोर्बलंनविदितं नचकार्मुकस्य त्रैयम्बकस्य सुतरामयमेवदोषः। तच्चापलं परशुराममममक्षमस्व डिम्भस्य दोर्विलासितानिमुदेगुरूणां ॥ ५६ ॥

रामकथनमनाकर्ण्यैव परशुरामः ।

परशु । क्वासदाशरथी रामो मद्यशखक्कवारितः । पुरारेःकार्मुकं येन भग्नं तिष्ठतिभार्गवे ॥ ५७ ॥

एवमाकर्ण्य श्रीरामःसविनयं ।

राम । सृष्टंत्रायिनवासृष्टंकार्मुकं पुरवैरिणः । भगवन्नात्मनिर्वेद मभज्यत करोमिकिं ॥ ५८ ॥

हारःकण्ठेप्रभवतुतरामत्रकिंवाकुठारःस्त्रीणां मैत्रायधिवसतुनः कान्तंवाजनं वा । संपश्यामोनिरूपममुखं प्रेतभर्तुर्मुखं वा यद्वातद्वाभवतु नवयं ब्राह्मणेषु प्रवीराः ॥ ५९ ॥

अपिच । निहन्तं हन्तगोविप्राञ्शूराराघवा वयं । अयंकण्ठे कुठारस्ते कुरुराम यथोचितं ॥ ६० ॥

अथ युद्धोद्यते परशुरामे दासरथिःमुने चमस्व ।

भोब्रह्मन्भवतासमं नघटतेसंग्राम वार्त्तापिनः सर्व्वेहीनबलावयं बलवतां यूयंस्थितामूर्द्धनि । यस्मादेकगुणं शरासनमिदं राजन्य कानाम्बलं युष्माकं द्विज जन्मनां नवगुणं यज्ञोपवीतंबलं ॥ ६१ ॥

अथ परशुरामंप्रति लक्ष्मणः ।

पुरोजन्मानाद्य प्रभृति ममरामः स्वयमहो नपुत्रः पौत्रो वा रघुकुलभुवाक्षत्तितिभजां । अधीरंधीरं वाकलयतुजनो मामयमयं मयावद्धो दुष्टद्विजदमनदीक्षा परिकरः ॥ ६२॥

लक्ष्मणं सान्त्वयन् श्रीरामः ।

श्रीराम । जातः सोहंदिनकरकुले क्षत्रिय श्रोत्रियेभ्यो विश्वामित्रादपि

भगवतो हस्तदिव्यास्त्रपातः । च्युतिस्त्वन्वं भ्रेकजयतुजनोदुर्यशो वायशोवा विप्रेशस्त्व
पदनयगुरवः साहसिक्याद्विभेमि ॥ ६३ ॥

तथापिरामंप्रति परशुरामः ।

तथापमीशभुजपीडनपीतसारं प्रागप्यभज्यत भवांस्तुनिमित्तमात्रं ।
राजन्यकप्रधनसाधनमस्मदीयमाकर्षकार्मुकमिदं गरुडध्वजस्य ॥ ६४ ॥

सूत्र । रामस्तदादायधनुःसहेलं बाणञ्चसंधुक्ष्य तदाचकर्ष । भातिस्कला-
त्मकरध्वजोयं गतिंप्रचिच्छेदच भार्गवस्य ॥ ६५ ॥

तथापमाकर्षति ताडकारावाकार गुणापिविश्राजनेभा । सासूयमेघित्त
विदेहकन्यावान्यां किमन्यांपरिणेष्यतीति । ६६ ॥

भार्गवस्तानुनयं ।

यःकार्त्तवीर्यस्य भुजागसहस्रं चिच्छेदवीरोयुधिजामदग्न्यः । ससायके
रामकराधिरूढेष्वमग्नएव प्रबभीबभूव ॥ ६७ ॥

यावद्धूर्जटिधर्म्मपुत्रपरशु द्युम्नाखिलक्षत्रियश्रेणीप्रोक्षितपिच्छिलावरुम-
तीकोस्याम्नधास्यत्पदं । त्रैलोक्याभयदानदक्षिणभुजावष्टम्भदिव्योदयो देवोयं
दिनरत्नमुखे कतिपको न प्राभविष्यद्यदि । ६८ ।

जामदग्न्य परंपतितोरामः ।

उत्पत्तिर्जमदग्नितः सभगवान् देवः पिनाकीगुरुर्वीर्यं यत्तु नतद्गिरां पथि-
ननुव्यक्तं हितत्कर्म्मभिः । त्यागः सप्तसमुद्रमुद्रितमही निर्व्याजदानावधिः सत्यं
ब्रह्मतपोनिधेर्भगवतः किं किं नलोकोत्तरं ॥ ६९ ॥

सूत्र । ज्ञात्वाप्रभावं रघुनन्दनस्य तदङ्गमालिङ्ग्य ततोतिगाढं । विन्यस्यत-
स्मिन्जमदग्निसूनुस्तेजो महत्तत्र वधान्निवृत्तः ॥ ७० ॥

ययौरामं परित्यज्य भार्गवः स्वीयमाश्रमं । राजापि सहरामाद्यैः पुत्रैरगात
कोशलां ॥ ७१ ॥

तद्वागतिं परशुराममुनेः सशोकानाटम न्यूसर्वसुजनान् पितृमातृवर्गान् ।
सम्मान्यमान्यतमविप्र गुरुस्वजातीन्मित्रासमं निजपुरीं प्रजगाम रामः ॥ ७२ ॥

अत्रान्तरे जनकजा रघुनन्दनेन दृष्ट्वाचिरान्मदनबाणनिपीडिताङ्गी ।
गत्वास्तशैलशिखरं खररश्मिमाली हर्षात्पपातसलिले चरमस्य सिन्धोः ॥ ७३ ॥

कल्पितशयनागारम्प्रति सीतामन्दगमनं ।

अस्तंयाते सपदिनलिनी बान्धवे सिन्धुपुञ्जे प्राचीभागेसरसमुदिते पङ्कजा-
रङ्ककल्पे । रामःकामंगुरुजन गिरामन्दिरे सङ्गतोभूत् वामोरुस्तं जनकतन-
या मन्दयन्ती जगाम ॥ ७४ ॥

सूत्र । ननन्दस्वजनैराजा गृहेरामैः सम्पूजितः । कौशल्या च सुमित्रा च
कैकेयीच सुमध्यमा ॥ ७५ ॥

वधूप्रतिग्रहेयुक्ता याश्चान्याराजयोषितः । ततःसीतां महाभागामूर्मिला
चयशस्विनीं ॥ ७६ ॥

कुशध्वजसुतेचोभे जगृहुर्नृपयोषितः । मङ्गलालापनैर्होमैः शोभिताः
क्षौमवाससः ॥ ७७ ॥

देवतायतनान्याशु सर्वास्ताः प्रत्यपूजयन् । अभिवाद्याभि वाद्यांश्च सर्वा
राजसुतास्तदा ॥ ७८ ॥

शुश्रूषमाणाःपितरं वर्त्तयन्तिनरर्षभाः । कस्यचित्त्वथकालस्य राजादश-
रथःसुतं ॥ ७९ ॥

भरतंकैकयीपुत्र मब्रवीद्रघुनन्दनः । अयं केकयराजस्य पुत्रोवसति
पुत्रक ॥ ८० ॥

त्वां नेतुमागतोवीरोयुधाजिन्मातुलस्तव । श्रुत्वा दशरथस्यैतद्भरतः
कैकयीसुतः ॥ ८१ ॥

गमनायाभिचक्राम शत्रुघ्न सहितस्तदा । आपृच्छ्यपितरं शूरोरामञ्चा
क्लिष्टकारिणं ॥ ८२ ॥

मातॄंश्चापिनरश्रेष्ठः शत्रुघ्न सहितोययौ । युधाजित्प्राप्यभरतं सशत्रुघ्नं
प्रहर्षितः ॥ ८३ ॥

स्वपुरंप्राविशद्वीरः पितातस्य तुतोषह । गतेच भरतेरामो लक्ष्मणश्च
महाबलः ॥ ८४ ॥

पितरंदेवसङ्काशं पूजयामासतुस्तदा । पितुराज्ञांपुरस्कृत्य पौरकार्याणि
सर्वशः ॥ ८५ ॥

चकार रामः सर्वाणि प्रियाणि च हितानि च । मातृभ्यो मातृकार्याणि कृत्वा परमयंत्रितः ॥ ८६ ॥

गुरूणां गुरुकार्याणि काले कालेऽन्ववैक्षत । एवन्दशरथः प्रीतो ब्राह्मणा नैगमास्तथा ॥ ८७ ॥

रामस्य शीलवृत्तेन सर्वे विषयवासिनः । तेषामति यशा लोके रामः सत्य पराक्रमः ॥ ८८ ॥

स्वयम्भूरिव भूतानां बभूव गुणवत्तरः । रामश्च सीतया सार्धं विजहार बहून् ऋतून् ॥ ८९ ॥

इति सर्वे निष्क्रान्ताः ॥

इति द्वितीयोऽङ्कः ।

अथाऽयं वृत्तान्तः । सद्भिः सह पुनर्विवेचनायामस्मिन्नङ्के पञ्चसप्ततितम श्लोकादारभ्यैकोननवतितमश्लोक पर्यन्तं यद्यपि पञ्चदशश्लोकाः आदिरस घटिताः सुश्राव्यास्तथापि महावीराग्रेसरकेसरि श्रीरामचन्द्रपत्न्याः श्रीजान-क्याः अन्तःपुरक्रीडावर्णनं पाठकवर्गाणां सङ्कोचावहमतस्तान्परित्यज्य तत्रस्थ गार्हस्थ्यसुवृत्तान्तघटित श्लोकान् श्रीमद्वाल्मीकि रामायणादुद्धृत्यास्मिन्नङ्के सूत्रधारोक्ति रूपेणनिवेशनाच्च पद्यानां परिपूर्तिः कृतेतिविदाङ्कुर्वन्तुविद्वांसः ॥

तृतीयोऽङ्कः ॥

पुनरयोध्या ।

प्रथमं सूत्रधारः ततः ससभाजनदशरथ सुमन्त्रागमनं ।

भुक्त्वाभोगान्सुरम्यान् कतिपयदिवसं राघवोधर्म्मपत्न्यासार्द्धं वर्द्धिष्णुकामः श्रवणमुनिपितुः प्रापशापप्रकालं । यत्नेकस्मादिवसाम्मलिन किरणातां शाम-होत्पात केतोरुल्कादण्डः प्रचण्डःप्रपततिनभसः कम्पतेभूतधात्री ॥ ६० ॥

दिङ्नागोधूसरोभूदहनिवक्रतराःस्फारताराःस्फुरन्तिस्वर्भानोर्भानवीयं ग्रहणमसमयेरोधिरी ग्रक्रवृष्टिः । मध्याह्ने ध्वांत्तघोषः श्वगणशतमति स्फीत फेरप्रचारो वारंवारंगभीरप्रलयइवमहाकोलचीत्कारघोषः ॥ ६१ ॥

अत्रान्तरे दशरथस्य चेष्टा ।

सूत्र । रामेनयचवंदृष्ट्वा लोकधर्मासदहयत् । यौवराज्याभिषेकाय नि-श्चिकाय दिदेशच ॥ ६२॥

अथ रामाभिषेकप्रसङ्गे सुमन्त्रोवहिर्निःसृत्य नागराम्प्रत्याह ।

सुमन्त्र । स्वीयांजरामुपगतामवलोक्यराजा रामस्यराज्यकहनस्यममा-कलय्य । राज्याभिषेक परमोत्सवमस्य कर्त्तुं ध्यादिशत्नागपुरजनाः कुरुतप्रमो-दं ॥ ६३ ॥

सूत्र । रामाभिषेके मदविह्वलायाः कक्षाच्युतोहेमघटस्तरुण्याः । सोपा-नमार्गेण करोतिशब्दं ठठं ठठं ठं ठठठं ठठं ठः ॥ ६४॥

कैकयीप्रविशति ।

अथ कैकयीस्वगतं पतितमनर्थान्तरं राजानमुपसृत्यप्रकाशं जयति जयति महाराजोदशरथः ।

सूत्र । व्याकोशेन्दीवराभं वरनयनयुगं बिभ्रतीस्वर्णकान्ति गत्वाराजानमुच्चैर्दशरथमवदत् कैकयीसाधुमध्ये । राजन्रामाभिषेको विरमतुजडधीर्निष्कलङ्के कुलेऽस्मिन् भूपुत्री यस्यपत्नीसहिभवतिकथं भूपतीरामचन्द्रः ॥ ९५ ॥

राजाचाह ।

कैकयिहहास्यतांउपविश्य कैकयीएवमेवं कथयतिराजानं किंतत्त्वमङ्गलेयंवधूः यतोऽस्याआगमनानुपदमेव महोत्पाताः दृश्यन्ते तदेनांदूरते। निःसारय महास्वप्राकस्वीकृतं वरद्वयं प्रदीयतांतदेवसीतालक्ष्मण सहितस्य रामस्य वनप्रयाणं भरतस्यचक्रवर्त्तित्वे अभिषेकः ॥

ततोदशरथः ।

हारामभद्रप्राणाधिकभूपुत्री तवपत्नी तथापितस्यभुवःपरिग्रहश्च अनुचितं इदमिति मत्वाकैकयीत्वां निवारयामास ॥

ततःसुमन्त्रःस्वगतं राज्ञएषो अभिप्रायस्तत्स्वयमेव गत्वारामचन्द्रायनिवेदयामीति निष्क्रान्तः । जयतिजयतिश्रीरामचन्द्रः भृत्यस्ते सुमन्त्रोऽस्मि निवेदयाम्यात्मानमिदमन्यच्च ॥

श्रुत्वैवकैकयसुतानगरीजनानां माङ्गल्यमुन्मदकुलाकुलवारघोषं । तुभ्यं श्रियंन्यसति शक्रसखेनरेन्द्रे प्राक्स्वीकृतंवरयुगं समयाचतैनं ॥ ९६ ॥

तदेव वरयुग्मं ।

रामोयातुवनंचतुर्दशसमामूर्ध्नि जटांधारयन् वन्यांवृत्तिमुपागतो विरचितांसीतासखःसानुजः । राज्यंसानुचरं समुन्नतमिदं संन्यस्यतांमत्सुते श्रुत्वैवं सतुनिष्ठुरं वचइदंभूमिंगतोविह्वलः ॥ ९७ ॥

कैकयींप्राप्य श्रीरामः ।

वैखानसैःपरिवृतेषु वनेषु वासस्तातावज्ञया जननिलक्ष्मतवानुरोधः । प्राणाधिकस्य भरतस्यचराज्यलाभो रामेण देविकिमतःपरमर्जितव्यं ॥ ९८ ॥

पुष्पश्चरणाःप्रणाममित्यन्तःपुरान्निष्क्रान्तः ।

राम । श्रीरामोलक्ष्मणंप्रति वत्सलक्ष्मणप्रजावतीमादायाग्रेभव अहंतातं नत्वा यावदागच्छामि ॥

सूत्र । तातंदशरथंनत्वा मातरौजननीं ततः । मैथिल्यासहितोरामोलक्ष्मणोनवनंययौ ॥ ९९ ॥

गुर्वाज्ञापरिपालनात्प्रतिवनं संप्रस्थितंराघवं दृष्ट्वासौत्वरिता विदेहतनया संखंजनंपृच्छती । नत्वाकोशलकन्यकांघ्रियुगलं पश्चात्सुमित्रांपुनः पृष्ट्वासौशुक सारिकापिककुलं रामानुगाप्रस्थिता ॥ १०० ॥

अथ सुमित्रागमनं ।

लक्ष्मणंप्रति सुमित्रावचनं ।

रामंदशरथंविद्धिमांविद्धि जनकात्मजां । अयोध्यामटवींविद्धिगच्छपुत्रयथा सुखं ॥ १०१ ॥

रामंप्रति सुमित्रावचनं ।

बालाविदेहतनयाजनितौ भवन्तौ दिग्दक्षिणाच रजनीचरचक्रदुष्टा ।
तद्वत्सवत्स यतयेदमुदाहरामो मारामम्मच्चनयदक्षिणदक्षिणाभ्यां ॥ १०२ ॥

अथावसरे पौराः प्राहुः ।

सूत्र । अभिनवगुणग्रामेरामेविमुञ्चतिपत्तनं सकलकरुणापारावारे निमज्जतिसज्जने । अयमवसरवैरंगुर्वींगुर्वीपरं नतुकेकयीकुलिशघटितं प्रायंप्रायोमनोवतयेोचितां ॥ १०३ ॥ ततःसर्वे निष्क्रान्ताः ।

अथ वनगमनं ।

सीतागमनं ।

अथ वनप्रस्थाने पथि सीतावचसारामखेदः ।

सद्यःपुरीपरिसरेषु शिरीषमृद्वी सीताजवात्त्रिचतुराणि पदानिगत्वा
गन्तव्यमस्तिकियदित्यसकृद्ब्रुवन्तीरामाश्रुणः कृतवतीप्रथमावतारं ॥ १०४ ॥

सद्यैवकर्णाभरणप्रसूनै रिद्यैवबालातपतापितासि । दिनान्तरम्यानिवना-
न्य मूनित्वंकेन वैदेहिविलङ्घयेथाः ॥ १०५ ॥

लक्ष्मणा वनं दर्शयति ।

मुनिगणाः प्रविशन्ति ।

नायंभिक्षुर्ध्वरयुवतिमान् मातिविक्षुर्धनुष्मान्राज्ञः पुच्छेनछिन्नछिन्नजटाजू-

द्भारं दधानः । नायंत्याधीनवगुणधरः पश्यकस्मादकस्मात्पुरण्येरण्ये नवनवघन-श्यामलः कोयमेति ॥ १०६ ॥ इति परस्परमवलोकयन्तस्तस्थुः ।

धरणींप्रति श्रीरामः ।

अयमदलतनिम्नाम्लिग्धपादारविन्दाकठिनतरधरण्यां यात्यकस्मात्स्खल-न्ती । अवनितवसुतेयं पादविन्यासदेशेत्यजनिजकठिनत्वंजानकीयात्यरण्ये॥१०७॥

पथिकवधूनामागमनं ।

पथिपथिकवधूभिःसादरं पृच्छमाना कुवलयदलनीलःकोयमार्य्येतवेति । स्मितविकसितगण्डं व्रीडविभ्रान्तनेत्रं मुखमवनमयन्ती स्पष्टमाचष्टसीता ॥१०८॥

मत्तवरणपातंगम्यतां भूःसदर्भाविरचय सिचयान्तं मूर्द्धि घर्म्मःकठोरः । तदितिजनकपुत्रीलोचनैरश्रुपूर्णैः पथिपथिकवधूभिः शिक्षितावीक्षिताच ॥ १०९ ॥

इति पथिकवधूनां प्रस्थानं ।

सूत्र । प्रथमपथिकमस्मिन् काननेरामभद्रं तदनुचरणचारिण्येवमेकाकि-नीसा । त्वरितममगयन्तीपर्य्यटन्ती दिगन्तान् क्षणरुचिमचिरेन्दुं रोहिणी बन्निनाय ॥ ११० ॥ निष्क्रान्ताः ।

पुनरयोध्याकल्पनं ।

सुमन्त्रदशरथयोरागमनं ।

अथ श्रीराममनुव्रज्यागतः सुमंत्रो दशरथंप्रति ।

सुमन्त्रः । भवद्भिराराज्यमपास्यतूर्णंवनं जगामैवरघुप्रवीरः । निषङ्गपृष्ठं शरचापहस्तं तंलक्ष्मणोगा दनुसीतयाच ॥ १११ ॥

तदाकर्ण्य दशरथः ।

आहूतस्याभिषेकाय प्रस्थितस्यवनायच । नमयालक्षि तत्तस्यस्वल्पोप्यस्वारविभ्रमः ॥ ११२ ॥ इत्युक्त्वा ।

दशरथः स्वगतमाक्षिपति ।

हृदयंनोपयातोसि दिक्षुसर्वासुवीक्षसे । वत्सरामगतोसीति सन्तापादनुमीयते ॥ ११३ ॥

सूत । श्रुत्वासुमन्त्रवचनेनवनप्रयाणं शापस्यतस्यच विचिन्त्यविपाकवेलां । हाराघवेति सकृदुच्चरिते नृपेण निश्वस्यदीर्घतर मुच्छ्वसितंनभूयः ॥ ११४ ॥

अथ पौरजनागमनं सदुक्तीच ।

पौरजनाः । जातःसूर्य्यकुलेपितादशरथः क्षोणीभुजामग्रणीःसीतासत्यपरायणाप्रणयिनीयस्यानुजोलक्ष्मणः । दोर्द्दण्डेनसमोनचास्तिभुवने प्रत्यक्षविष्णुः स्वयंरामोयेन विडम्बितोपिविधिना चान्येजनेकाकथा ॥ ११५ ॥

जामातापुरुषोत्तमो भगवतीलक्ष्मीःस्वयंकन्यका दूतीयस्यवभूववोधिषणः मुनिर्यज्वा वशिष्ठःस्वयं । योदाताजनकः प्रदानसमये चैकादशस्याग्रहाः किंब्रूमो भवितव्यतांहतविधे रामोपियातोवनं ॥ ११६ ॥

प्रविश्यकैकयीभरतः ।

अथ मन्त्रिभिरानीतो भरतोमातरमुक्तिप्रत्युक्तितयापृच्छति ।

मातस्तातःक्वयातः सुरपतिभवनं हाकुतःपुत्र शोकात्कोसौपुत्रश्चतुर्णांत्वम-

परजनतया यस्य जातः किमस्य । प्राप्तोसौ काननान्तं किमिति नृपगिरा किंतदा-सौबभाषे महाम्बहुः फलंते किमिहतवधराधीशता हाहतोस्मि ॥ ११७ ॥

रामंप्रति तत्प्रयाणं ।

रामोमूर्द्धि निधायकाननमगान्मालामिवाज्ञां गुरोस्तद्भक्त्यापिच लक्ष्मणेन सकलंमात्रासहैवोज्झितं । श्रीश्रीराममयात्वया सहवनेस्थेयं यतस्तेनुजः सौमित्रिःसम्प्रिपुर्नृपोपि भवतस्त्वापादितः खःपथं ॥ ११८ ॥ इत्युक्त्वा ।

पुनःस्वगतंकैकयींभरतः ।

भरत । मैवानिर्णसमतिरात्मकुलोचितेषु वंशेषु सत्स्वपिखलामिश्रितायनीव । माकन्दशालिनिवने विषवल्लिकेवहाहन्त केकयसुताकथमाविरासीत् ॥ ११९ ॥

आगम्यमौलिमतिवाञ्छितराजवेशमानन्दयन्तमखिलानवलोकनेन । हाहन्तकेकयसुता नयनाभिरामं रामंकथंच मुनिवेशधरं चकार ॥ १२० ॥

इति सर्वे निष्क्रान्ताः ।

अथ पुनर्वनरचनं चित्रकूटाश्रम कल्पनञ्च ।

ततो भरतंवनेसमायातंप्रति श्रीरामः ।

राम । परस्त्रीमातेवक्वचिदपिनलोभः परधनेनमर्य्यादाभङ्गः क्षमापि नीचेष्वभिरुचिः । रिपौशौर्य्यं धैर्य्यंविपदि विनयःसम्पदि सतामिदंवर्त्मभ्रात भरतनियतोयास्यसिसदा ॥ १२१ ॥

वाञ्छासज्जनसङ्गमेपरगुणे प्रीतिर्गुरौनम्रता विद्यायांव्यसनंस्वयोषितिरतिर्लोकापवादाद्भयं । भक्तिःशूलिनि शक्तिरात्मदमने संसर्गमुक्तिःखलेष्वेते येषु वसन्तिनिर्मल गुणास्तेभ्योनरेभ्यो नमः ॥ १२२ ॥

अन्योपदेशेन भरतं शिक्षयति ।

सामान्योयंधर्म्मसेतुर्नराणां कालेकालेपालनीयोभवद्भिः । सर्वानेतान्भाविनः पार्थिवेन्द्रान्भूयोभूयो याचतेरामभद्रः ॥ १२३ ॥

भरतः स्वगतं ।

भरत । हाहन्तमातरहहज्वलितानलोमांकामंदहत्यघनिघ्नेलक्ष्मणायबाणाः । मथ्यन्तुताम् विपद्भुतेभरतःसलीलं श्रीरामचन्द्र पदयोःपुनविप्रयोगं ॥ १२४ ॥

श्रीराम । मांवाधतेभवितया विपिनेषुवासो राज्येदर्शवितजंनकबान्धव वत्सलस्य । रामानुजस्यभरतस्य यथाप्रियायाः पादारविन्दयुगलेच्छति सत्यवाच्याः ॥ १२५ ॥

ततः सीतांप्रणामति भरतः ।

सूत्र । मूर्द्धं बद्धजटेन वल्कलभृतादेहेन पादानतिं कुर्व्वाणे भरतेतथा प्ररुदितं तारस्वरैःसीतया । येनोद्विग्न विहङ्गसंकुलतरु निःसंमदः श्वापदः शैलेन्द्रोपिकिलेषभूरितिरभूत्साश्रःपयःप्रस्रवैः ॥ १२६ ॥

ततः श्रीरामपादानतोभरतः ।

आर्य्योराज्यमलंकरोतु विपिनेवासोमयास्त्वीकृतस्तातज्ञा परिपालनंवत कालंगृह्णातुमत्तोभवान् । इत्युक्तोभ्युपगम्य चाहृतमनाराज्येयदाराघवः संप्राप्तो-भरतस्तदानिजपुरी मादायतत्पादुके ॥ १२७ ॥

राज्येतेऽभिषिक्त्वाथ नन्दिग्रामगतःस्वयं । राघवागमनापेक्षी भरतोपालयन्महीं ॥ १२८ ॥ निष्क्रान्ताः ।

अथ सगोदावरी पञ्चवटीवन कल्पनं ।

तत्र सीतासहित रामलक्ष्मणयोरागमनं ।

सूत्र । दृष्ट्वाश्रमानथ चिरायविहाय चित्रकूटस्थलीमिह विराधवधं वि-
धाय । कुम्भोद्भवेनमुनिना सहमन्त्रयित्वा रामोनिवासमकरोदथपञ्चवट्यां॥१२९॥

तंपयोदमिववीक्ष्यसभ्रमं कम्पमान कमनीयकलापाः । ताण्डवानिविदधुस्त-
त्रषण्डे दण्डकाननशिखण्डियुवानः ॥ १३० ॥

राघवेनलघुनारघुनाथ प्रेरितेनविपिनादुपनीतं । स्वर्णवर्णमकरोदधिकर्णं
कर्णिकारकुसुमंकरभोरुः ॥ १३१ ॥

तत्र गमनसमये रामचन्द्रंप्रति सीता ।

सीता । पदकमलरजोभिर्मुक्त पाषाणदेहामलभत यदहल्यां गौतमो-
धर्म्मपत्नीं । त्वयि विचरतिशीर्णग्राव विंध्याद्रिपादे कतिकतिभवितारस्तापसा-
दारवन्तः ॥ १३२ ॥

अथ लक्ष्मणोनदीं दृष्ट्वानाविकमाह्वयति नाविकः प्रविश्य रामचन्द्रंप्रति ।

नाविक । मानुषीकरणरेणुरस्तिते पादयोरितिकथा प्रथीयसी । क्षालया-
मि तवपादपङ्कजे नाथदारुदृषदोः किमन्तरं ॥ १३३ ॥

उपलतनुरहल्या गौतमस्येहशापादियमपि मुनिपत्नी शापिताकापिवा-
स्यात् । चरणमलिनसङ्गानुग्रहन्ते लभन्तीभवतुचिरमियंनः श्रीमती प्रात-
पात्री ॥ १३४ ॥

अथ पर्णशालाकल्पनं तेषां तत्रनिवासश्च ।

सूत्र । दृष्ट्वातिदैन्यं जनकात्मजाया स्तत्रैवरामः सहलक्ष्मणेन । गोदावरी
तीरसमाश्रितेषु देशेषुचक्रे निजपर्णशालां ॥ १३५ ॥

ततः शूर्पणखा प्रविशति ।

स्त्रीमायया हरति शूर्पणखेति बुद्धा सौमित्रिणा सपदि लक्ष्मणि नासिका सा । सारावणस्य भगिनी कुपिताथ गत्वा प्रत्यानिनाय खरदूषणसैन्यमुग्रं ॥ १३६ ॥

चतुर्दशसहस्रकं परमचण्डरक्षोगणं निहत्य युधि सत्वरं सकलमेकवाणेन सः । खरं त्रिशिरसान्वितं तदनु दूषणं दुर्द्धरं जघान घनघोषवाः स्फुरितकार्मुको राघवः ॥ १३७ ॥

सीतारूपं सुधाहृद्यं श्रुत्वा शूर्पणखामुखात् । राममोहाय मारीचं प्रेषयामास रावणः ॥ १३८ ॥ निष्क्रान्ताः ।

ततः कियद्दूरेऽपसृत्य मारीचः प्रविश्य ।

मारीचः स्वगतं ।

मारीच । प्रतापान्तदक्षप्रकाण्डदोर्दण्डः सकलभुवनाभोगवंशाखण्डलो रामचन्द्रः । अयमपि महेन्द्रावस्कन्धस्थानं लङ्केश्वरस्तदवश्यं शमनभवनातिथिना भवितव्यं जीवितेनाद्य ॥ १३९ ॥

राघवादपि मर्त्तव्यं मर्त्तव्यं रावणादपि । उभाभ्यामपि मर्त्तव्यं वरं रामान्न रावणात् ॥ १४० ॥ इत्युक्त्वा मारीचो निष्क्रान्तः ।

ततः पञ्चवाटिकां हेममृगरूपी मारीच आगमनं ।

सूत्र । सुललितफलमूलैस्तत्र कालं क्षियन्तं दशरथकुलदीपे सीतया लक्ष्मणेन गमयति दशकण्ठोत्कण्ठया प्रेरितं प्राक् कनकमयकुरङ्गं जानकी संददर्श ॥ १४१ ॥

ततः सीता श्रीरामंप्रति।

प्रियतम मृगमद्भुताङ्गमेनं मृगपतिविक्रम देहि मे प्रसीद। इति जनकसुतावचोनुरोधात् कनकमृगं सशरोऽन्वियायरामः ॥ १४२ ॥

ततोगच्छन् श्रीरामोलक्ष्मणंप्रति।

श्रीराम। वत्सलक्ष्मण त्वमस्याः प्रजावत्याः सहायोभव। यावदहं कनककुरङ्गं निहत्यसमागच्छामीति निष्क्रान्तः ॥ १४३ ॥

रामान्वेषणं।

सूत्र। आलोकयन् विशिखमेककरेणमन्दं कोदण्डकाण्डमपरेण दधार सव्यं। संनह्यपुष्पलतया पटलंजटानां रामोमृगं मृगयते वनवीथिकासु ॥१४४॥

मृगचरितं।

हस्तप्राप्यमुपैति लोढिचतृणं नस्पृश्यतां गाहते गुल्मान् प्राप्य निवर्त्तते किसलयानाघ्रायचाघ्रायच। भूयः पश्यति गच्छति प्रतिदिशं कण्डूयतेश्रान्तमुदूरंधावति तिष्ठति प्रचरति प्रान्तेषु मायामृगः ॥ १४५ ॥

तत्र सीतालक्ष्मणंप्रति।

चिरयति मृगान्वेषीनाथः कथं रघुनन्दनो वनपरिसरास्तेते क्रूरश्वापदभैरवाः। मुहुरपिभवानुत्तोमत्व्यायसः परिमार्गणो व्रजतितदहोचेतः किं किं न लक्ष्मणशङ्कते ॥ १४६ ॥

चिरात्हस्ते रामेकरुणकटुभिर्मैथिलसुता वचोभिः कोदण्डाटनिजनित-रेखान्तरगतां । निधायैनां रामःस्फुरितपदपद्माङ्कितभुवं तदध्वानं पश्यन् कथमपि स सौमित्रिरगमत् ॥ १४७ ॥

सूत्र । सीतोदूरं कनकहरिणच्छद्मना रामभद्रः पश्चादेनं द्रुतमनुसरत्येव वत्सःकनिष्ठः । बिभ्यद्भिभ्यत्प्रविशति ततः पर्णशालां सभिक्षुर्धिग्धिक्कष्टंप्रथयति निजामाकृतिंरावणोयं ॥ १४८ ॥

रामान्मुक्तैकबाणप्रतिहतहृदयः काञ्चनाङ्गः कुरङ्गः सद्योमारीचनामाऽजनि रजनिचरः सान्द्ररक्तान्तवक्त्रः । भिक्षुःकोपिक्षणार्द्धान्मणिखचित चलत्कुण्डल श्रेणिशोभावीचीलेखत्कपोलस्फुरित दशशिराः कुम्भकर्णाग्रजोभूत् ॥ १४९ ॥

अपिच । बाणेन दिव्येन रघुप्रवीरो मृगस्यवक्षःस्थल बद्धलक्ष्यः । विव्याध यावत्तरसा तपस्वी दशाननस्तावदिहाजगाम ॥ १५० ॥

भिक्षुः । भिक्षांप्रयच्छ ननु सूर्य्यकुलावतंसे कन्ये विदेहनृपतेः प्रथितासिसाध्वि । एतद्गृहाण हरिपादरजोविमिश्रं निर्माल्यदामसकलेप्सित सिद्धिहेतु॥१५१॥

इति तुलसीं दर्शयति ।

सीता । दृग्भङ्गिमङ्गिमशतैरसतीरहस्यमन्वेषयन् कपटभिक्षुकलक्षितोसि । आसं प्रभुः सुभगनाहमिति क्षमस्वभैक्षायमाकुरु मृणालयमञ्जलिस्ते ॥१५२॥

सूत्र । सव्याहरद्दर्म्मिणि देहिभिक्षामलंघयल्लक्ष्मणदत्त रेखां । क-याहृतां पाणितले क्षिपन्तीं समाहूयन्तीं रघुराज पुत्रौ ॥ १५३ ॥

मार्गंमार्गंमृगयति मृगाराति रामेविरामेशोकंशोकं गतवति गते लक्ष्मणे लक्ष्मणेन । सीता सीतातपसतनया राज्यलक्ष्मामलक्ष्मान्नीतानीता सुरसुरवधूरा-वणेरावणेन ॥ १५४ ॥

रावणेनहृतासीता कृष्णापक्षेऽष्टसिताष्टमी । अर्द्धरात्रौदिनस्यार्द्धेअर्द्धचन्द्रा-
र्द्धभास्करे ॥ १५५ ॥

सीता दशमुखनीता भीतावदतिस्म काननथोता । रघुनन्दन रघुनन्दन
रघुनन्दन रामचन्द्रेति ॥ १५६ ॥

हाराम हारमण हा जगदेक वीर हानाथ हा रघुपते किमुपेक्षसेमां ।
इत्थंविदेहतनया बहुधालपन्तीमादाय राक्षसपतिर्नभसा जगाम ॥ १५७ ॥

रावणस्य रथसङ्गतासती नूपुरं परिससर्ज सत्वरा । उत्तरीयमपि कङ्कणं
क्वचिद्धारहारमपिचक्ष्मस्थले ॥ १५८ ॥

अथ तत्रवनस्य जटायुवृत्तान्तः ।

सूत्र । इतोबाणंरामः क्षिपति हरिणे मुक्तकरुणः सचापः सौमित्रिः स्वजन-
मनुयातिद्रुतमितः । इतः सीताभिक्षामुपनयति भिक्षोः करतले नयं श्यामि
प्रेक्षन् युगपदहमालोकयमिदं ॥ १५९ ॥

रावणरथस्थां सीतांदृष्ट्वाजटायुः स्वगतं ।

मारीचमृगयाव्यग्रे रामभद्रे च लक्ष्मणे । कथमेषा कुरङ्गाक्षी रावणस्य
रथोपरि ॥ १६० ॥ एवमालोचयन् ।

अम्बरादवतरन्तं जटायुं दृष्ट्वारावणःस्वगतं ।

मैनाकःकिमयंरुणद्धि गगनेमन्मार्गमव्याहतं शक्तिस्तस्यकुतःस वज्रपतना-
द्भीतोमहेन्द्रादपि । तार्क्ष्यःसोपिसमं निजेन विभुनाजानाति मांरावणं व्यज्ञातः
सजटायुरेष जरसाग्लोवधंवाञ्छति ॥ १६१ ॥

रावणंप्रति जटायुः ।

जटा । जन्मब्रह्मकुलेहरार्चनविधौ छित्वाशिरःकर्त्तनं भक्तिर्वञ्चिशिवा बाहु-दण्डदलनव्यापारशक्तिः परा । हेलोत्तोलितकेलिकन्दुकनिभः कैलासउत्पाटितस्तत्किंरावण लज्जसेनहरसे चौर्य्येण पत्नींरघोः ॥ १६२ ॥

अपिच । जन्म ब्रह्मकुले तपस्त्वनुपमं वीर्य्यञ्च लोकोत्तरं किञ्चैश्वर्य्यमहो त्रिलोक जयिनः स्वर्गाङ्गनास्वामिनः । इत्यस्मादपि वाञ्छितं किमधिकं सीता समाकृष्यते तस्मात्त्वं सहबान्धवैः पशुमते यातासि निःशेषतां ॥ १६३ ॥

अविदुषस्तवदोषमहं सहे विसृजवीरवधूं पतिदेवतां । शरणमस्मिजटायुरहं सखा दशरथस्य रथस्तवतिष्ठतु । १६४ ॥

तथापि तमवधीर्य्यगतेरावणे ।

जटा । रेरे भोः परदारचौर किमिदं धीरं त्वया गम्यते तिष्ठाधिष्ठितगन्धमादनतटप्रान्तोजटायु स्वयं । मुञ्चैनांपतिदेवतां नखलु चेन्मत्तुण्डचण्डांकुश क्रीडाकर्षणनिर्गतासृगुरसः पास्यन्तिगृध्रास्तव ॥ १६५ ॥

सीतामाश्वासयन् रावणंप्रतिक्रोधं नाटयति ।

माभैर्वोःपुत्रिसीतेव्रजतिममपुरो नैषदूरंदुरात्मा रेरेरक्षः क्वदारान् रघुकुलतिलकस्यापहृत्य प्रयासि । चञ्चाक्षेप प्रहारैस्त्रुटितधमनिभिर्दिक्षु विक्षिप्य मांसैरासाशापालोपहारं दशभिरपिभृशं त्वच्छिरोभिः करोमि ॥ १६६ ॥

आः पापिन् पश्यतोमे रघुतिलकवधूं चोरयित्वाप्रयातुं सीतांशीतांशुलेखामिव गिरिशशिरःशायिनीमुद्यतोसि । रभिच्छित्वाशिरांसि प्रखरनखमुखैर्दीप्तचूडामणीनि त्वा मद्याहं गरुत्मानुरगमिव सुधाहारिणं संहरामि ॥ १६७ ॥

अथ जटायुरावणयोर्युद्धं ।

सूत्र । अक्षं विक्षिपति ध्वजं विभजते मूर्द्धानि नद्धं युगं चक्रं चूर्णयति क्षिणोति तुरगान् रक्षःपतेः पक्षिराट । वक्षं गर्ज्जति तर्ज्जयत्यभिभवत्याक्षिपते ताडयत्याकर्षत्यपकर्षति प्रचलयत्यवत्युदवत्यपि ॥ १६८ ॥

क्रुद्धस्ततो धृतचपेट शिलातलेन रक्षः पिपेष गगने ऽङ्कुतपक्षिराजं । ईषत्स्थितासुरपतद्भुवि राम राम रामेति मन्त्रमनिशं निगदन्जटायुः ॥ १६९ ॥

अथ हतरथभङ्गं पक्षिराजं निहत्य क्षितिगतमवलोक्य श्वासमात्रावशेषं । जनकनृपतिपुत्रीं क्षिप्रमादाय लङ्कां सरभसमुपदध्रे ऽशोककेलीवनान्ते ॥ १७० ॥

अथ पतितजटायुखेदः ।

गमैत्रीनिर्व्यूढा दशरथनृपेकार्य्यविषया न वैदेही त्राता नच रणहतो राक्षसपतिः । न रामस्यास्येन्दुर्नयनविषयोभूदहतिनो जटायोर्जन्मेदं वितथमभवद्भाग्यरहितं ॥ १७१ ॥

अथ पथिरामलक्ष्मणयोरुक्ति प्रत्युक्ती ।

एकाकिनी मुटजसीम्नि विहाय सीतां किंवत्स मत्सविध माकुल मागतोसि । अनागते चिरयति त्वयिवीर देव्या नैवस्थितः कटुकदुक्ति कदर्थितोहं ॥ १७२ ॥

सूत्र । बाणेनैकेनाद्भुतं तं निहत्य मारीचाख्यं यातुधानं जवेन । सीताशून्यां पर्णशालां विलोक्य किं किं वृत्तं नतदा राघवस्य ॥ १७३ ॥

रामः । मायाकुरङ्गं विनिहत्य बाणै र्भ्रात्रा सहागत्य च पर्णशालां । कोऽयं तत्र समीक्ष्य तूर्यां द्रष्टुं चतुर्थं न शशाक रामः ॥ १७४ ॥ इतिसर्वे निष्क्रान्ताः ।

इति तृतीयोऽङ्कः ।

अथ चतुर्थोऽङ्कः॥

रामःप्रविशति।

अथ रामविलापः।

बह्निरपिमपदानां पंक्तिरन्तर्मकाचित् किमिदमिहनसीता पर्णशाला क्रिमन्या। अहमपि किलनाहं सर्व्वथा राघवश्चेत्कथमपिनहिसोढा हन्त सीता वियोगं॥ १७५॥

हापर्णशालाङ्कणवासयष्टे हाभूतलाविष्कृत चन्द्रलेखे। मज्जीवना नामव-लम्बशाखे वैदेहि वैदेहि कुतोऽगतासि॥ १७६॥

सूत्र। सभूरजोरञ्जित सर्व्वकायो बभौ विभुर्मन्यु विदीर्णचेताः। योषि-द्वियोगानलदह्यमानः स्वकान्त मालिङ्गयतीवभूमिः॥ १७७॥

अत्रावसरे मुनिजनागमनं।

मुनि। एकदैवतुरामेण सम्प्रमर्थं चतुष्टयं। राज्यनाशो वनेवासोहृता-सीता मृतःपिता॥ १७८॥

असम्भवं हेममृगस्यजन्म तथापिरामो लुलुभे मृगाय। प्रायःसमासन्न-विपत्तिकाले धियोऽपिपुंसां मलिनीभवन्ति॥ १७९॥

कर्म्मणाबाध्यतेबुद्धि र्नबुध्याकर्म्म नबाध्यते। सुबुद्धिरपियद्रामो हैमंहरि-णमन्वगात्॥ १८०॥

राज्यान्निर्गयता वनंगमयता वैरिक्रियामापरे क्लैरंकारयता मतिं हृत-

यया मायामृगच्छना । दारान्हारयता वनेभ्रमयता नानावनालीतलं रामस्यापि कृतं शठेनविधिना दुःखातिदुःखंमहत् ॥ १८१ ॥

उत्थायरामः ।

राम । हावल्लभे जनकवंशज वैजयन्ति हामद्विलोचन चकोर नवेन्दुलेखे । इत्थंस्फुटं बहुविलप्य विलप्य रामस्तामेव पर्णवसतिं परितश्चचार ॥ १८२ ॥

पुनःपर्णशालां विलोक्यरामः ।

आलिङ्गिताञ्च सरसीरुहकोरकाभ्यांपीतोधरोञ्च मधुरो विधुमण्डलोस्य । रङ्गावतार मकरन्द विमर्द्दितानि पुष्पाण्यमूनि दयिते क्वगतासि सुभ्रू ॥१८३॥

अथ गोदावरीतीरे सीतान्वेषणे रामचरितं ।

राम । हेगोदावरि रम्यवारि सुभगे दृष्टात्वया जानकी साहर्तुं कमलानि किं गतवती याता विनोदायवा । इत्येवं प्रतिपादपं प्रतिदिशं प्रत्याश्रमं प्रत्यगं प्रत्येणं प्रतिवर्हिणं तत इतस्तांयाचते मैथिलीं ॥ १८४ ॥

भो भो वृक्षाः पर्व्वतस्था बहुकुसुमयुता वायुना घूर्णमाना रामोहं व्याकुलात्मा दशरथ तनयः पृच्छते शोकदग्धः । बिम्बोष्ठी चारुनेत्रा गजपतिगमना दीर्घकेशीसुमध्या हासीता केननीता ममहृदयगता केनवाकुत्रदृष्टा ॥ १८५ ॥

सारेवातटिनी तदेवविपिनं सैवाग्निकुञ्जस्थली सोयं भूमिधरः सएवमलयः प्रोद्भूत मन्दानिलः । तान्येतानि सरांसि सन्ति विमलान्युत्तुङ्ग वक्षोरुह द्वन्द्वापीडनभार मन्दगमना नालोक्यतेजानकी ॥ १८६ ॥

सूत । गाहं गाहं गह्वरे काननेतां दर्शंदर्शं दर्शवल्लीं मतल्लीं । स्मारं स्मारं भूषणं तत्त्वकान्तां रामःकान्तामन्विचारी मरोत्सीत् ॥ १८७ ॥

अथ सीताया मलब्धायां रामः।

मध्यं केसरिभिः स्मितञ्च कुसुमैर्नेत्रं कुरङ्गीगणैः कान्तिश्चम्पककुड्मलैः कलरुतं हाहाहृतं कोकिलैः। वल्लीभिर्ललितंगतं करिवरैरित्थं विभज्याङ्गसा कान्तारैः सकलैर्विलास पटुभिर्नीतासि किं मैथिलि॥ १८८॥

सीताया नूपुरंप्राप्य रामः।

चक्षुर्मेप्रीणयत्येतत्सीताया इव नूपुरं। अवधारय सौमित्रे भूषणान्तर-मन्यतः॥ १८९॥

लक्ष्मणः। नाहं जानामि केयूरे नाहं जानामि कङ्कणे। नूपुरावेव जा-नामिनित्यं पादाभिवन्दनात्॥ १९०॥

ततः कियद्दूरंगत्वापतित सीतोत्तरीय प्राप्तोरामः।

द्यूते पणप्रणयकेलिषु कण्ठपाशः क्रीडापरिश्रमहरं व्यजनंरतान्ते। श-य्यानिशीथ कलहे हरिणेक्षणायाःप्राप्तंमया विधिवशादिदमुत्तरीयं॥ १९१॥

ततश्चन्द्रं दृष्ट्वा।

रामलक्ष्मणयोरुक्ति प्रत्युक्ती।

सौमित्रे ननुसेव्यतां तरुतलं चण्डांशुरुज्जृम्भते चण्डांशोर्निशिकाकथा रघु-पते चन्द्रोय मुन्मीलति। वत्सैतद्विदितं कथंनुभवता धत्तेकुरङ्गं यतः क्वासि प्रे-यसि हाकुरङ्गनयने चन्द्रानने जानकि॥ १९२॥

ततश्चन्द्रंप्रतिरामः।

शीतरश्मिरसि चन्द्रमांकथं तापयस्यनलगर्भमयूखैः। त्वां शरेण शतधा विभजेयं जानकी मुखसमोयदि नस्यात्॥ १९३॥

अथ स्मृति विभ्रमे राम लक्ष्मणयोरुक्ति प्रत्युक्ती।

यथा। केयूरं रघुनाथ नाथ किमिदं भृत्योस्मि तेलक्ष्मणः कोहं वत्सवदास्व देवभगवानार्य्यो भवान्राघवः। किंकुर्म्मो विजनेवने ततइतो देवीसमन्वेष्यते कादेवी जनकाधिराज तनया हाहाप्रिये जानकि॥ १९४॥

अथ रामानुस्मरणं।

हारोनारोपितः कण्ठे मया विश्लेषभीरुणा। इदानीं मावयोर्मध्ये सरित्सागर भूधराः॥ १९५॥

सोढस्तात वियोगः सोढोराज्य वियोगोपि। सोढो वनेचवासः सोढुं नभवामि जानकी विरहं॥ १९६॥

इयंगेहे लक्ष्मीरियममृत वर्त्तिर्नयनयो रसावस्याः स्पर्शोवपुषि बहुलचन्दनरसः। इमौबाहुःकण्ठे सरसमसृणो मौक्तिक सरः किमस्यान प्रेयोयदि परमसह्यास्तु विरहः॥ १९७॥

वासिवात यतःकान्तां तांस्पृष्ट्वा मामपिस्पृश। त्वत्तो मां त्वया नाम्यः शक्यमेतेन जीवितु॥ १९८॥

तद्वियोग समुत्थेन तच्चिन्ता विपुलार्चिषा। रामन्दिवंशरीरं मे दह्यते मदनाग्निना॥ १९९॥

वायुर्दक्षिणतो वनानि पुरतो भृङ्गध्वनिर्वामतः पश्चाद्दुःसह चक्रवाकरु-दितं चोर्द्धं सुधादीधितिः । इत्थं दुःसह पञ्चताप सहिते मध्येमया ध्यायताने-ध्यन्ते कतिवा प्रजागर भवैरत्यन्त दीर्घाःक्षपाः ॥ २०० ॥

चन्द्रश्चण्ड करायते मृदुगति र्वातोपि वज्रायते माल्यासूचि कुलायते म-लयजालेपः स्फुलिङ्गायते । आलोकस्तिमिरायते विधिवशात्प्राणोपि भारायते हाहन्त प्रमदा वियोग समयःसंहार कालायते ॥ २०१ ॥

रेरेनिर्द्दय दुर्निवारमदन प्रोत्फुल्लपङ्केरुहान् बाणान् संवृणु संवृणु त्यज धनुः किं पौरुषं सांप्रति । कान्तायास्तु वियोग जातकृतभुग्ज्वालाप्रदग्धं वपुः शूराणां मृतमारणे नहिपरोधर्म्मः प्रयुक्तोबुधैः ॥ २०२ ॥

आपृच्छाम्यममीश्वरामनसि मेमग्नासमं पश्यते निर्द्दग्धं विरहाग्निना वपु-रिदं तैरेव सार्द्धं मम । तत्कान्दर्प निरायुधोसि भवताजेतुं नपश्यःपरो दुःखी स्यामह मेकएवसकलो लोकः सुखी जीवतु ॥ २०३ ॥

एवं दैवादस्तं गते मार्त्तण्ड मण्डले प्रचण्डमार्त्तण्ड मिवोदयन्त मच-ण्डरश्मिमन्तश्चन्द्रमण्डलमवलोक्य लक्ष्मणंप्रतिरामः ।

राम । सौमित्रेदाववह्नि स्तरुशिखरगतो वार्य्यतां निर्झरोदैः कावार्त्तादाव वह्नेरयमुदयगिरे रुज्जिहीतेहिमांशुः । धत्तेधूमं पुरस्तात्किमिति कथमयं नैषधूमोधरण्याश्छायेयं सङ्कता भूदयिधरणिसुते कुत्रसीतेस्थितासि ॥ २०४ ॥

यत्रयत्र न जगामराघव स्तत्रतत्र बुबुधेस मैथिलीं । अधदाश्रममगान्न भिक्षुक स्तत्तदर्थ परिपूर्णा मीक्षते ॥ २०५ ॥

सूत्र । विचिन्वता तेनविदेह पुत्रीं दृष्टोजटायुः श्वसितावशेषः । सीता हृताते दशकन्धरेणे त्यावेद्य सद्यः सतनुं मुमोच ॥ २०६ ॥

श्रीरामः । आत्वादशरथस्येनं मित्रं प्राणु निषूदनं । हाहातात किमिदं नाम रामः पक्षीन्द्रमब्रवीत् ॥ २०७ ॥

पारलौकिकं कृत्वा कृताञ्जलिः ।

राम । तातत्वं निजतेजसैव गमितः स्वर्गं व्रजस्त्वि ते ब्रूमस्ते किमिमां वधू हृतिकथां तातान्तिके माऽऽख्याः । रामोहं यदितद्दिनैः कतिपयैर्व्रीडानमत्काननः सार्धंबन्धुजनैः सुरेन्द्र विजयी वक्ताखयं रावणः ॥ २०८ ॥

राज्यनाशो वनेवासो हृतासीता मृतःपिता । एकैकमपि यद्दुःखं समुद्र-मपिशोषयेत् ॥ २०९ ॥

एकस्य दुःखस्य नयावदन्तं गच्छाम्यहं पारमिवार्णवस्य । तावद्द्वितीयं समु-पस्थितं मे छिद्रेष्वनर्था बहुलीभवन्ति ॥ २१० ॥

युक्तमेवहि कैकय्या भरतस्याभिषेचनं । भार्य्यामपिन योरक्षेत्सकथं पा-लयेन्महीं ॥ २११ ॥

भर्ग्नंकृतंहि तातेन येनाहं वनवासितः। एषापि हीनमेबुद्धिः कामृगः काञ्चि-रण्मयः ॥ २१२ ॥

सगरात्सागरःकीर्त्तिं गंङ्गाकीर्त्तिं भंगीरथात् । अस्माक मीदृशीकीर्त्तिं रेकाभार्य्या न रक्षिता ॥ २१३ ॥

लब्धव्यमर्थं लभते मनुष्यो देवोपितं वारयितुं नशक्तः । अतो न शोचा-मि न विस्मयोमे ललाटलेखा न पुनःप्रयाति ॥ २१४ ॥

विलपतिच ।

यापाणिग्रहलाञ्छितासुतरणी तन्वीसुवंशोद्भवागौरी स्पर्शसुखावहा

गुणवती नित्यं मनोहारिणी । साकेनापि हृतातया विरहिणो गन्तुंमयुक्तावयं हे भिक्षो तवकामिनी नहिनहि प्राणप्रियायष्टिका ॥ २१५ ॥

अर्द्धेचेतसि जानकी परिपतत्यर्द्धेन लङ्केश्वर क्षणार्द्धं मदनामलः कवल त्यर्द्धं च रोषानलः । इत्थं दुर्विधि सङ्गम व्यतिकरस्तुल्यद्वयोरंग्रयो रेकांवेद्मि तुषाग्निदग्ध मपरंदग्धं करीषाग्निना ॥ २१६ ॥

नमेदुःखं प्रियादूरे नमेदुःखं हृतेतिसा । एतदेवहि शोचामि वापो यद-भिवर्त्तते ॥ २१७ ॥

श्रीरामोलक्ष्मणंप्रति ।

कोवेद हेमहरिण ग्रहणाय वत्स दूरंगते मयिहृता जनकात्मजेति । व्रीडैव पीडयतिमां श्वसतोपि कुत्र त्यक्ष्यहि श्रुतिचरो वनितापहारः ॥ २१८ ॥

व्यसनं किमितोप्यास्ते ज्ञातव्याभ्युदयोमम । यद्वयं मरणंराज्यं मापुनर्व्यंसनान्नुतत् ॥ २१९ ॥

ततो भुजङ्गमवलोक्य द्रुतगमनंनाटयतिश्रीरामः ।

सूत्र । ततोरामस्तिरस्कृत्य पुरस्कृत्यच लक्ष्मणं । धन्योधन्य यदग्रस्य म-रणार्णवगाहत ॥ २२० ॥

तत्रच कबन्धंदृष्ट्वा ।

लक्ष्मणः । आयोजनप्रहत दीर्घभुजोनमार्ग माक्रम्यकण्ठकुहरे कुरुतेकु-कोयं । सौमित्रियोसि गदितः सकबन्ध कण्ठंचिच्छेद गर्भकदली मिवरामभद्रः ॥ ॥ २२१ ॥

सूत्र । पूतोरामशरेण दिव्य मगमद्दिवं कबन्धस्ततस्तद्वाक्याच्छ्रमणाश्रमे

हनुमता संयोज्य सीतापतिः। सीतोद्धार विधौसमं निजबलैः स्वीकृत्य साहाय्यकं संप्राप्तः प्रतिपन्न वालिनिधनः सख्यं कपीन्द्राधिपात्॥ २२२॥

ऋष्यमूकगिरौ रामो निःसहायः परिभ्रमन्। सख्यं समानदुःखेन सुग्रीवेण सहाकरोत्॥ २२३॥

पादाङ्गुष्ठेन दूरं धरणिधर गुरुं दुन्दुभेरस्थिकूटं क्षिप्त्वासक्षिप्रकारी विषम विनिहितान् वज्रवत्सप्ततालान्। बाणेनैकेन शब्दप्रतिहत सकलश्रोत्रमर्भान् विभेद्य प्रत्याशां वालिवधे प्लवगबलपतेः प्रेषयामासरामः॥ २२४॥

तालवेध समये रामो बाणंप्रति।

भावीनिघ्नं कुक्षि काननदन पादयोर्मे यद्यस्त्यवं द्विजतिरश्चू तरोविहीनः। मान्यङ्गाना सुमनः शरसप्ततालान् भित्वा तदाप्रविश भूतलमप्यगाधं॥२२५॥

एकेनैवशरेणगर्भकदली काण्डेष्विवानुक्रमात् विद्धेषु प्रथमेन दाशरथिना तालेषु सप्तस्वपि। शैलाःसप्तगजास्तु सप्तमुनयः सप्तापिसप्तार्णवास्तेषुःसमरसातलान्युभयतः संख्यानसाम्यादिव॥ २२६॥ निष्क्रान्ताः।

एकांशे रणस्थल कल्पनं।

ततोवाली प्रविशति।

सूत्र। श्रुत्वाहतान् समरमूर्ध्नि सुसप्ततालान् रामेणदीन हृदयेनविनायराधं। कोपानल ज्वलित हृत्कमलोथ वालीरङ्गावतारमगमद्गिरि गह्वरात्सः॥ २२७॥

अथ पर्वतगुहाकृतिः ।

ततस्तारा प्रविशति ।

सूत्र । ततस्तारा सहर्षमात्मगतं अद्यावश्यं श्रीरामचन्द्रचरण प्रसादा-
न्निजवल्लभस्य चिरविरहियोवक्षः पीठेलुठिष्यामि ॥ २२८ ॥

वीरसुग्रीवस्येत्याशिषः पठति ।

सूत्र। तारासंत्यक्तहारा गिरिशिखरवरव्यस्तधम्मिल्लधारा शोकाब्धि प्राप्त
पारार्पितमदनशरा वीरसुग्रीवदाराः । नानानाराच धारानिजरमणरता ता-
पिनो पापिनोस्य प्राणान् मालावतीर्णाहरतु कलिकलाशालिनो वालिनो-
द्य ॥ २२९ ॥

श्रीराम मुद्दिश्यलक्ष्मणः ।

लक्ष्मणः । पृथिव्यां चतुरन्तायां नास्तिवालि समोवली । वचसानेन लोका-
नां शङ्कितव्योमहेन्द्रजः ॥ २३० ॥

श्रीरामः सहासः । माभैषीर्मयि सान्निध्ये राघवेधिज्यधन्वनि । सतां
देहं परित्यज्य निर्गच्छत्यसतोभयं ॥ २३१ ॥

वाली । गृहाणबाणं रघुराजपुत्र सुत्रामसूनं समरेवतीर्णं । जानीहिमां
दुन्दुभि घातवज्रं नेष्यामिवां कालगृहाति चित्वं ॥ २३२ ॥

इत्युभौयुद्धायावतरतः ।

लक्ष्मणः सुग्रीवंप्रति ।

आर्य्यबाणेन भिन्नोयं वालीलुठति भूतले । तदिमच्छस्यशिरसि पुष्पवृष्टिः
सुरैःकृता ॥ २३३ ॥

वाली। सुग्रीवोपिसमः कर्त्तुं यत्कार्य्यं तवराघव। तदहं महमःकस्माद-पराधं विनाहतः॥ २३४॥

रामः सकरुणं।

शुद्धिर्भविष्यति पुरन्दरनन्दनस्य मामेवचेदहह पातकिनं प्रणाय। सख्य र्थ्यनं निरपराधिनमाहनिष्यं आवः पुनर्ज्जनकजा विरहक्षतोमे॥ २३५॥

वाली। सोहं श्रीमतो रघुवंशावतं सस्यभवतः प्रसादान्महावीरोचितां गतिंगच्छामि। अयं वत्सोऽङ्गद स्तवदासः परिपालनीय एवेति स्वर्गारोहणं नाटयति॥ २३६॥

सूत्र। सद्योनिर्भिद्यबाणैः समरभुवितदा वालिनं रामचन्द्र किष्किन्धा राज्य-मादा विदमयस ददौ तत्र सुग्रीवहस्ते। वर्षाकालं घनालीघमरवदलितोद्दाम दिक्चक्रगर्भं द्योमुल्वासं वितेने शिखरवरतटे माल्यवत्पर्व्वतस्य॥ २३७॥ निष्क्रान्ताः सर्वे।

इति चतुर्थोऽङ्कः।

अथ पञ्चमोऽङ्कः॥

माल्यवत्पर्वत कल्पनं।

तत्र रामलक्ष्मणौप्रविशतः।

सूत्र। रामाद्बलीयाश्चपरोस्ति कश्चिद्दारापहाराश्चपरोपमानः। तथापि रामः शरदं समीक्ष्य प्रतीक्षते सम्प्रति कालमेतं॥ २३८॥

तत्र माल्यवति वर्षासु विरही रामः।

यत्तन्नेत्रसमानकान्ति सलिलेमग्नं तदिन्दीवरं मेघैरन्तरितः प्रियेतवमुख-

च्छायानुकारीश्रियः । येपित्वदूमनानु कारिगतयस्तेराजहंसागतास्तत्सादृश्य विनोदमात्र मपिमे दैवंनदृष्टाम्यति ॥ २३९ ॥

लक्ष्मणः । मन्दं मरुद्वहति गर्ज्जति वारिवाहो विद्युल्लता स्फुरति कूजति नीलकण्ठः । एतावतिव्यतिकरे रघुनन्दनस्य मूर्च्छैव केवलमभूदवलम्बनाय ॥२४०॥

सीतायाः पूर्वावस्थां सूचयन् ।

रामः । पूर्वंपुरारिधनुषोनिनदेमहत्यं रामंमुनिं रणमुखे परितोविलोक्य । शङ्काग्रग्राह परितप्त मुखारविन्दां तामेव मैथिलसुतां सततंस्मरामि ॥ २४१ ॥

स्निग्धश्यामलकान्ति लिप्तवियतो वेल्लद्बलाकाघना वाताःशीकरिणःपयोद सुहृदा मानन्दकेकाःकलाः । कामंसन्तुदृढं कठोरहृदयो रामोस्मि सर्व्वं सहे वैदेहीति कथं भविष्यति ह हा हा देवि धीराभव ॥ २४२ ॥

नीलेन्दीवरशङ्कया नयनयोर्बन्धूकबुद्ध्याधरेपाणौ पद्मधियामधूककुसुम-भ्रान्त्या तथागण्डयोः । लीयन्ते कबरीषु बान्धवजन व्यामोह जातस्पृहा दुर्वा-रामधुपाः कियन्ति तरुणि स्थानानि रक्षिष्यसि ॥ २४३ ॥

रामोलक्ष्मणंप्रति ।

कार्य्येषु मन्त्री करणेषु दासी धर्म्मेषु पत्नी क्षमयाच धात्री । स्नेहेषु माता शयनेषु वेश्या रङ्गेसखीलक्ष्मण सा प्रियामे ॥ २४४ ॥

जीवातुः कुसुमायुधस्य भवने सीमन्तिनीनां शिरोरत्नं मत्कुलदेवताप्रति निधिर्नेत्रोत्सवःकामिनां । माद्यद्दन्ति नितान्त मन्दगमना सामेप्रिया जानकी सौमित्रे शतपत्रपत्रनुवदना कुत्राधुनासीदति ॥ २४५ ॥

रामः स्वात्मानंस्वगतमधिक्षिप्य ।

ईदृग्भानुकुले न कोपि भविता यस्याङ्गना कामुकैराक्रान्तेति परस्परं निगदतांश्रुत्वा मुनीनां मुखात् । सौमित्रे कुलयांशुलस्य चरितंश्रीरामचन्द्रस्य मे प्राक्प्राणसमर्पितेन गुरुणा दुःखं परं धीयते ॥ २४६ ॥

अतीतायां प्रावृष्यनागते सुग्रीवे रामचरितं ।

सूत्र । ततोरामो महातेजा लक्ष्मणं समुपाह्वयत् । सुग्रीवं प्रेषयामास स्कन्दावारं चकारसः ॥२४७ ॥

किष्किन्धाराज्यकल्पनं ।

सुग्रीवःप्रविशति ।

ततःकिष्किन्धागत्वालक्ष्मणः ।

श्रीमद्रामोवनस्थः कपिवर नगरं लक्ष्मणः प्रेषितोऽस्मि किष्किन्धा द्वारमागां रघुपतिवचनाल्लक्ष्मणस्त्वं जगाद । श्रुत्वा रामेति वाक्यं हसति कपिवरो रामनामा किमेतत्कस्मात्किम्वा प्रमेयंसचकितमनसा विस्मितोसौप्रमत्तः॥२४८॥

लक्ष्मणःसुग्रीवंप्रमत्तंबुद्ध्वाभीययन्पुनर्बोधयति ।

बाल्येकौशिकताडका हतवधो यज्ञस्यरक्षाकरः सीतार्थे हरचापभङ्गकरोच्छिन्धोजितःभूतिनः । मारीचः खलुलीलयापि निहतो वालीहतः साम्प्रतं सोयं संप्रति राघवः कपिपते पञ्चाननोगर्ज्जति ॥ २४९ ॥

स्वस्ति श्रीरामपादाः कुशलिनः समाह्वयन्ति मां किं ।
इतिसुग्रीवोक्तिमाकर्ण्य पुनर्लक्ष्मणः ।

लक्ष्मणः । नमेसंकुचितोबाणो येनवाली हतोमया । समये तिष्ठसुग्रीव मा बालिपथमन्वगाः ॥ २५० ॥ इति श्रीरामोक्तिंलक्ष्मणमुखतःश्रुत्वा ।

श्रीरामान्तिकं समागत्यसुग्रीवः ।

यासौप्रकृतिरस्माकं वानराणांनरेश्वर । तामहंत्यक्तुमिच्छामि नसामां त्यक्तुमिच्छति ॥ २५१ ॥

पुनस्तानुनयं ।

दग्धंदग्धं त्यजति नपुनः काञ्चनं कान्तिवर्णं छिन्नंछिन्नं त्यजति नपुनः स्वादुतामिक्षुदण्डं । घृष्टं घृष्टं त्यजति न पुनश्चन्दनं चारुगन्धं प्राणान्तेपि प्रकृति विकृति र्जायते नोत्तमानां ॥ २५२ ॥

श्रीरामःप्रीत्यासुग्रीवं दृष्ट्वा ।

तातेनदत्तं भरतायराज्यं सीता हृता संप्रति रावणेन । विचिन्त्य रामोमनसाकुलेन विहायचापं वदितुं प्रवृत्तः ॥ २५३ ॥

अत्रावसरे पुनःसधीरंसुग्रीवः ।

एते सप्त पयोधयो दशदिशः सप्तैव गोत्राचलाः पृथ्व्यादीनि चतुर्दशैक-भुवनान्येकं नभोमण्डलं । एतावत्परिमाणमल्प विषये ब्रह्माण्डभाण्डोदरे क्वासौ यास्यति जानकी रघुपते किं कार्म्मुकं त्यज्यते ॥२५४ ॥

श्रीरामः । व्यसने महति प्राप्ते स्थिरैःस्थातुं न युज्यते । लङ्कां निःशङ्कमा-लोक्य का इहागन्तुमर्हति ॥ २५५ ॥

ततः प्रविशति जाम्बवान् ।

जाम्ब । आञ्जनेयः समानेयो योसौ कपिकुलोद्भवः । लङ्काप्रस्थापनेयोग्यः प्रोक्तो जाम्बवता सता ॥ २५६ ॥

श्रीरामं प्रणम्य स्वपराक्रमंप्रकटीकरोति हनुमान् ।

किं प्राकारविशालतोरणवतीं लङ्कामिहैवानये किम्वा सैन्यमयूक्तनभस्तलं तत्रैवसम्पातये । हेलोत्तोलित पर्वताग्रशिखरैर्बध्नामिवातोयधिं देवादेशय किंकरोमिसकलं दोर्दण्डसाध्यं मम ॥ २५७ ॥

सोत्कर्षं वदन्तं श्रीरामः समादिदेश ।

एतैर्महत्वमुत्कृष्टं मारुते तव तेजसः । वृथा परिश्रमः कार्य्यः सीता जीवति वानवा ॥ २५८ ॥

पुनः सोत्कर्षं ब्रुवन्तं हनुमन्तं पश्यन् श्रीरामः ।

कूर्म्मो । मूलवदालवालवदपां नाथो लतावद्दिशो मेघाः पल्लववत्प्रसूनफलवन्नक्षत्रसूर्य्येन्दवः । राजन् व्योम महीरुहो ममतले श्रुत्वेतिगां मारुतेः सीतान्वेषणमादिदेश सहसा रामः सहर्षः स्वयं ॥ २५९ ॥

सीतान्वेषणे तद्वृत्तमनभिजानतो हनुमतः परिदेवनं ।

कुत्रायोध्या क्व रामो दशरथवचनाद्दण्डकारण्यमागात्क्वासौ मारीचनामा कनकमयमृगः कुत्रसीतापहारः । सुग्रीवो राममित्रं जनकतनयान्वेषणे प्रेषितोऽहं योऽर्थोऽसम्भावनीयस्तमपि घटयति क्रूरकर्मा विधाता ॥ २६० ॥

सूत्र। आरम्भो विदधे महेन्द्र शिखरादम्भोनिधेर्लङ्घने वीरः श्रीरघुनाथ पाद रजसामुर्द्धिः स्मरन्मारुतिः। मूर्ध्ना जाम्बवतोभिवन्द्य चरणौ संस्तभ्य सेनापतीनाश्वास्यानुमुखान्मुहुः प्रियतमान्पश्यन् समादिश्य च ॥ २६१ ॥

अथ सम्पातेरागमनं ।

सूत्र। सम्पातेरवदच्छतयोजनशतात्पारे समुद्रं पुरी लङ्का तत्र विदेहराज तनयेत्याकर्ण्य वायोः सुतः। अभिसंक्षिप्य शरीरदुस्तरतरं दृष्ट्वा तथावर्द्धते यातं तेन तदीय केसर सटाटोपैर्नभोमण्डलं ॥ २६२ ॥

अथ सविलासदम्भस्तम्भिताब्धि प्रकाण्डं जलचर खरखेलत्स्फारवाचाखिलाब्धं । जलनिधिमभिवीरोलङ्घितुं वायुपुत्रः खगपतिरिव पक्षोड्डीनमङ्गीचकार ॥२६३॥

कपीनां कटके घोरो जातः कलकलध्वनिः। आञ्जनेयः किमेकाकी गच्छेज्जानकी सन्निधिं ॥ २६४ ॥

सुरसागमनं ।

सूत्र। प्रविश्य सुरसामुखान्तरमतोपि निष्क्रम्य च क्रमादुदितमम्बुधेः कुक्षिन शैलजं मानयन्। निहत्य पथि रोधिकां नभसि सिंहिकां राक्षसीं विलंघ्य जलधिं ययौ पवनजः स लङ्कापुरीं ॥ २६५ ॥

लङ्कापुरीकम्प नं ।

सूत्र। गत्वा लङ्कां निशायां पवनसुतवरोऽन्विष्य सीतां विनीतां गेहे गेहे प्रयत्नात्स्थल जल विटपे प्राचिरे वृक्षमध्ये यत्रास्ते कुम्भकर्णः सुरजितभवने कन्दरे गह्वरे वाऽदृष्ट्वा वैदेहपुत्रीं चिरमनुसरणाच्चिन्तितोऽसौ हनूमान् ॥ २६६ ॥

मातृभ्रातृकलत्र मंत्रि सचिव प्रख्यातजानां गृहं पौरव्यस्य मया निरूपित-

मपि श्रीसौधमेकैकशः । नानारत्न रहस्यवीथि चरिता सीता न दृष्टा क्वचित्
मग्ने सागरमङ्गने निपतिता चन्द्रेऽपि शङ्काकुला ॥ २६७ ॥

संक्षिप्यायतनुं निरीक्ष्य सकलां लङ्कां शरच्चन्द्रिका निर्धौताखिलसौध
मण्डलमहो दोलप्रसन्नान्तरां । दृष्ट्वा शोकवनेसराक्षसवधू संवेष्टितां जानकी-
मारूढो निभृतं स्थितः पवनजः कंकोलभूमीरुहं ॥ २६८ ॥

अत्रावसरे रावण प्रेषिता दूती सीतांप्रति ।

आज्ञाभङ्गविशङ्कामथि प्रणयिनी शक्तिस्त्रिलोकीजये भक्तिर्भूतपतौ पि-
माकिर्मिपदं लङ्केति दिव्यापुरी । सम्भूतिर्द्रुहिणान्वयेच तदहो नेदृग्वरो लभ्यते
स्याच्चेदेष न रावणः क्वनुपुनः सर्वत्र सर्वे गुणाः ॥ २६९ ॥

ततः स्वयमागत्यरावणः ।

मुग्धेमैथिलिचन्द्रसुन्दरमुखिप्राणप्रदानौषधि प्राणानुग्रहमृगाक्षि मन्मथ-
नदिप्राणेश्वरि त्राहिमां । रामस्तुमवति तेमुखं सुललितं वक्त्रैकमानेनातस्तुम्बिष्या-
मिदशानने वंऊविधं मुग्धाग्रहं मानिनि ॥ २७० ॥

अयिजनकतनूजे तापसेनत्वमेवं ननुकिमपिकुमंत्र जानिकाभिरुच्चितासि ।
ममदमरकिरीटोद्घृष्ट पादारविन्देप्रणमतिमयितस्मिन्मर्त्यकीटेऽनुरागः ॥ २७१ ॥

सीतेत्वंपरिमुञ्च मानमधुना राजादारोगृह्यतां पश्यत्वंकनकोज्वलां सुन्-
दरीं लङ्केश्वरंवीक्ष्य । एकोनाथ शतैकमहिषी त्यक्त्वाचमन्दोदरीं सेवार्थं वि-
नियुज्यतेचसकलं सुराधिपैर्भायतां ॥ २७२ ॥

सीतेयत्र शिरांसि यानिशिरसा धत्तेमहेशः स्वयं तानि त्वत्पदसंस्थितानि
सुभगे कस्मात्त्वजायते । श्रुत्वैतत्परदार लम्पटवचः सीताहृतंरावणं निर्माल्या
नि शिरांसि मूढत्वमधिकम् सीतावचःपातुवः ॥ २७३ ॥

सीता । कतरोऽसि त्वमुचित चिरमेव यस्य निर्वापितो युधि स येन सहस्रबाहुः । तस्यापि रे पुरभिदो शिवकार्मुकं वेद भञ्जयितस्य विजयी ममजीवनाथः ॥ २७४ ॥

सूत्र । अथतत्तदग्रमौलिजानकी पादपद्मे करधृत पदयुग्मे नाम्यमालोक्य ऊचे । सुरपतिरपिपादे न्यपतद्वीति योगाज्ञभवति तव तुष्टिब्रूहि किम्वाकरोमि ॥ २७५ ॥

पु० सूत्र । इत्थं विग्राम्यमधुरं नृपमाहवाक्यं नम्रानना सपदि कोपवतीच सीता । श्रीरामबाणहत रावणमस्तकेषु गृध्राःपदं दधति चेन्ममतुष्टियोगः ॥२७६॥

सीता । यदन्तरं वायसवैनतेययोर्यदन्तरं सिंह शृगालयोर्वने । खद्योत मार्तण्डकयोर्यदन्तरं तदन्तरं ते रघुनन्दनस्य ॥ २७७ ॥

रावणः । सीते त्वं ननु कम्पिता मम भये नाद्येन वाक्येन तद्रामं द्रक्ष्यसि च कृष्य मधिरा दाकारपूर्वं वद । मानेनैव तनुत्रयं ननुगता सत्यं वचोव्याधिना शु चारावणसीतयोरिति कपो हास्यं हनूमान्यधो ॥ २७८ ॥

त्रिजटाप्रविशति ।

सीतयाप्रतिषिद्धे रावणेचलिते त्रिजटासीतयोरुक्तं

सीता । पृच्छामि त्रिजटे सुखेन भवतीं कस्मादयं रावणोनीतिज्ञो नृपशेखरो हरति मामन्याङ्गनांकाननात् ॥ २७९ ॥

त्रिजटा । सीतेमन्मथ पुष्पसायकहते कामाम नीतेः कथा यावत्कामशरान्न हतो न पुरुषस्तावद्विवेकायते ॥ २८० ॥

अपिच । वज्रं जीर्य्यति वज्रिणोऽपिचहरेश्चक्रायसंचक्रं तथा दण्डः खण्डशतं यमस्य दलितः पाशोभवत्पाशिनः । लङ्केशोरसितत्र मन्मथशरो मग्नोनिमग्नस्ततः कः श्लाघ्यो सखि तस्य पुष्पमभत्पुष्पायुधस्यायुधं ॥ २८१ ॥

अथ सीतादर्शने हनूमान् ।

कान्तं पद्मपलाशाक्षि पीतकौशेयवासिनि । द्रुमस्य शाखामालम्ब्य तिष्ठसि त्वमनिन्दिते ॥ २८२ ॥

किमर्थं तव नेत्राभ्यां वारि स्रवति शोकजं । पुण्डरीकपलाशाभ्यां विप्रकीर्णमिवोदकं ॥ २८३ ॥

ततः सीतोक्तिः ।

दुहिताजनकस्याहं विदेहस्य महात्मनः । सीतेति नामतश्चाहं भार्य्या रामस्य धीमतः ॥ २८४ ॥

कीदृक्प्रभावोराम इति हनूमता पृष्टे ।

सीता । रक्षितारघुवंशस्य जनकस्य च रक्षिता । रक्षिताजीव लोकस्य धर्म्मस्य च परन्तपः ॥ २८५ ॥

धनुर्वेदे च वेदे च वेदाङ्गेषु च निष्ठितः । विपुलांसो महाबाहुः कम्बुग्रीवो महामनाः ॥ २८६ ॥

अथ हनूमान्मुद्रां दर्शयति ।

सुवर्णस्य सुवर्णस्य सुवर्णस्य वरानने । प्रेषितं रामभद्रेण सुवर्णस्याङ्गुरीयकं ॥ २८७ ॥

अथ सीता हनूमतो वक्ति प्रत्युक्तौ ।

मातर्जानकि कोभवान् वनमृगः केनात्र संप्रेषित स्त्वद्दैत्येन रघूत्तमेन कि-

मिदं हस्तोल्लिखितं मुद्रिका । दत्ता तेन तदैव तां निजकरे चालिंग्य चादाय प्रेम्णा मूर्च्छितसर्व्वसन्धिगु रभूद्गात्रेषु रोमोद्गमः ॥ २८८ ॥

अथ सीता मोहः ।

सूत्र । मुद्राङ्गुरीयकमणौ प्रतिबिम्बमासीद्रामस्य सादरमतीव विलोकयन्ती । मद्रूप एव किमभून्मम चिन्तयेति मीमांसया जनकराजसुता मुमोह ॥ २८९ ॥

पुनश्चेतना मासाद्य हनूमन्तमाह सीता ।

श्रीरामस्य तनुरीदृशी सगुतांगतेति ।

अथ हनुमान् ।

अनुदिनमनुशोचं त्वामनालोच्य सीतां प्रतिदिनमतिदीनं वीक्ष्य रामं विरामं । गिरिरपि विनयोसौ यत्तदा मद्विधाभूत्क्षितिरपि नविदीर्णा साक्षिसर्वं सहैव ॥ २९० ॥

समुद्रतरणे तव कीदृग्व्यवसाय इति प्रश्ने हनूमान् ।

तव प्रसादात् पवनप्रसादात्तवैव भर्तुश्चरण प्रसादात् । त्रिभिः प्रसादैरनुकूलितोहं व्यलङ्घयं गोष्पदवत्समुद्रं ॥ २९१ ॥

पुनर्हनूमन्तं सीतास्वावस्थांप्राह ।

सीता । चन्द्रोयञ्च दिनेश दीधितिसम स्त्रोतं स्फुलिङ्गायते कर्पूरः कुलिशोपमं प्रभिकाः संचारमातन्वते । वायुर्बाडववह्निवन्मलयजं दावाग्निवत्साम्प्रतं सन्देशं नयन रामचन्द्रविधिमितो यास्यान्द्रुतं मारय ॥ २९२ ॥

ससन्देश आम्रफलरूपः।

सीता। श्रीमद्राम पदारविन्द युगले दातव्य मेकं फलं सैन्येभ्योयुगलंफले कपिवरायात्यन्तरम्यंफलं। एकञ्चापिफलं ततश्चदगुजे देयं शुभाशीःशतं पश्चात्वे-न्य निराकुलप्रकृतिना भोक्तव्य मेकंफलं॥ २९३॥

ततो हनूमान्।

किन्दूरमिन्दुमुखि राम शिलीमुखानां किंदुर्गमं कुलभिदां हरियूथपा-नां। देवं प्रसन्नमिव देवि तवाद्यसत्यं रक्षांसिकानि कुपितस्य च लक्ष्मणस्य॥२९४॥

लङ्काकारान्तरालाशोद्यान रचनं।

सूत। सीतासम्भावनान्ते पवनसुतवरोऽरण्यमिभेंक्तु कामोध्याजे ना-पिद्विजोऽभूद्गगन विगलितश्चक्षुषी रक्तवर्णौ। श्वेतोमुखोऽपि भूत्वा गत वन निकटोभाषते मन्दमन्दं भ्रातर्युष्मत्प्रसादात्पतदमृत फलं किञ्चिदभ्यर्थयामि ॥ २९५॥ ततस्तैर्निराकृतोवनंभंक्तुमारब्धवान्।

रावणंप्रत्युद्यानपालाः।

यत्रारण्येवहति सततंमारुतो मन्दमन्दं सूर्य्योयत्र वसतितपितुं तोयदस्तो-यदाने। भग्नाभग्नं कुटति सहसाप्राचिरं विश्वकर्म्मा तत्तेरण्यद्यकमधु-ना वानरे णैवभग्नं॥ २९६॥ इति दूताःसर्वे निष्क्रान्ताः।

अथ भग्नदूतागमनं।

दूतः। देवाकर्णय कर्कशेन कपिना केनापि केलीवने खेलदालधिपालि-ताविटपिनःसाटोपमुत्पाटिताः। तत्रान्ये वनपालकाः सरभसं सर्वेपि निर्वापि-तास्तद्वार्ता कथनाय केवल महं देवेन संरक्षितः॥ २९७॥

इति श्रुत्वा प्रहितेन रक्षः सैन्येन समं युद्धं कुर्व्वति हनूमति तद्वृत्तान्त मासाद्य रावण चेष्टा।

सूत्र। हन्तीतिज्वलित क्रुधाकपिरिति व्रीडानमत्कन्धरो द्वेषोल्लासित याहिनी पतिरितिश्लाघा चलत्कुण्डलः। रामस्यायमितीर्षया कलुषितो लङ्का मुपेत्योद्भटे विक्रामत्यनिलात्मजे दशमुखः कां कां दशां नोगतः॥ २९८॥

अत्रान्तरे सीता हनुमतो रहस्यं त्रिजटयाकथिते रावणः।

त्रिजटा। मुद्रामर्कट कोन राम निकटा दागत्य दत्ता करे सीतायाइति सम्भ्रमा त्त्रिजटया प्रोक्तोऽथ लङ्केश्वरः। किं किं किं किमिति ब्रुवन्निरनिशं सिंहासना दुत्थितैरक्षो मुख्यसुत समेवहिकपिं धर्त्तुं नियुक्तो कृतः॥ २९९॥

अथ रावणाज्ञया चलत्यक्षयकुमारे पारिपार्श्वक वाक्यं।

प्रविशत्यक्षयकुमारः।

पारिपार्श्वकः। प्राकार तोरणमयीं पुरमध्यसंध्यां लङ्कामयं विशति कोऽपि कपि प्रवीरः। तत्सं मुखं प्रचलितः स्वयमक्षनामा नन्वेष राक्षसपतेः कुपितः कुमारः॥ ३००॥ ततोहनुमतासमरेऽक्षयकुमारोव्यापादितः।

अथाक्षेपतिते रावणाज्ञया गच्छति शक्रजितिपारिपार्श्वक वाक्यं।

हत्वाकथञ्चि दधिराज कुमारमक्षं रेवाबरापसद कुत्रपलायितोसि। त्वां हन्तु मिच्छति दशानन शासनेन दर्पोद्धतो धृत धनुर्ननु मेघनादः॥ ३१०॥

हनूमन्तंप्रति शक्रजित्।

शक्रजित्। रामस्यागमनं निवेद्य सुचिरादाश्वास्य सीतांततस्त्वीमक्षम-

यितदा रघुपतेः प्रत्यायनायाददे । भङ्क्त्वाशोकवनं निहत्य सहसा चाक्षादिकान् राक्षसान्दग्ध्वा रावण मात्मबन्धविषये सौम्ये भवन्मारुतिः ॥ १०२ ॥

अथ हनूमन्तं रावणः ।

रेरे दूत किमेवमेव चरितं वारां निधिं दुस्तरं लङ्घित्वा जलजन्तुभिः परिवृतं भीमं तरङ्गोत्करैः आयातोसि विनाशयं कथमिह प्रस्थापितः केनवा ब्रूहि त्वं नहि वध्य एव न भयः किं नामधेयो भवान् ॥ १०३ ॥

ततो हनूमान् ।

श्रीरामेण सलक्ष्मणेन जयिना श्रीचित्रकूटे स्थितः सीतान्वेषण कार्य्य साधनविधौ प्रस्थापितोयत्नतः । लब्ध्वा चैव वरं चिरात् सुरभिदः सर्वत्रगामी त्वहं विद्धि त्वं पवनात्मजो दशमुख श्रीमान् हनूमानहं ॥ १०४ ॥

अपि च । हत्वा वालि महाबलः कपिचमू मास्थाय सुग्रीवकं राजानं कृतिनं सदाविजयिनं सख्युः सदानन्दनं । कृत्वा चैव विशेष दैवमिव च ख्यातः स्य चिन्ताश्रितः श्रीरामो जनकात्मजा हरणतः कालोप मोराजते ॥ १०५ ॥

रावण हनूमतोरुक्ति प्रत्युक्ती ।

रेरे वानर कोभवानहमरे त्वत्सूनुहन्ताहवे दूतोहं खरखण्डनस्य जगतां कोदण्डदीक्षा गुरोः यद्दोर्दण्ड कठोरताडनविधौ कोसौभि कूटाचलःकोमेरुः क्व च रावणोद्य गणना कोटिषु कीटायते ॥ १०६ ॥

रावणंप्रति हनूमान् ।

एकोहं पवनात्मजो दशमुख त्वद्वापि कोटीश्वर त्वां जित्वा समरे प्रभोः

प्रणयिनीं सीतामानेतुं क्षमः। किन्तु प्रौढितया पुराभगवता रामेण सुग्रीवतो दत्वा दक्षिण पाणिना वसुमतीं त्वां हन्तुमुक्तं वचः ॥ १०७ ॥

अपिच। रेरे रावण राक्षसाधम पशोमुर्खोऽसि मूढाधम गर्वं वर्बर मुञ्च मुञ्च झटिति प्रीत्याहितं ब्रूमहे। मुर्द्धां सेवय रामचन्द्र चरणौ दत्वा पुरोजानकीं तस्माद्राज्य मकण्टकं कुरुचिरं पुत्रैश्च पौत्रैर्युवा ॥ १०८ ॥

आत्मानं परिरक्षितुं यदिभवान् पुत्रञ्च पौत्रादिकं भ्रातृवर्गं कुटुम्बकंपरिजनं चान्यत्तथा सैनिकं। राज्यञ्चापि महोदितं दशशिरः कांक्षस्यदः स्वेच्छया श्रीरामाय महात्मने विजयिने तद्दीयतां मैथिली ॥ १०९ ॥

यावद्दाशरथेर्नपश्यसिमुखं यावन्नवारां निधिर्बद्धो यावदियञ्च वानरचमूभ्रान्ता न लङ्कापुरी। यावत्सोदर बन्धुपुत्र सुहृदां मृत्युं न चालोकसे तावद्रावण लोकनाथ दयिता सीतास्वयं दीयतां ॥ ११० ॥

अथवा किं बहुना।

तावल्लङ्केश्वरो राजा यावन्नायति राघवः। आयाते राघवेवीरे लङ्कालङ्केश्वरः कुतः ॥ १११ ॥

आगत्य च विभीषणः।

अत्रावसरे क्रुद्धे रावणे विभीषण वाक्यं।

वैरूप्यमङ्गेषु कशानिपातो मौण्ड्यं तथालक्ष्मण सन्निवेशः। एतान् वधार्हेष्वहितत्ववादी प्राक्तेषु दूतस्य वधोनदृष्टः ॥ ११२ ॥

अपिच। कपीनां किललाङ्गूल मिष्टमेषां विभूषणं। तदस्य दीप्यतामाशु तेनदग्धेन गच्छतु ॥ ११३ ॥

छेत्तुं तं जनितोद्यमः क्षितिभुजां वध्योन दूतो भवेदित्याकर्ण्य विभीषणास्य वचनं क्रुद्धस्तथा रावणः । बद्धावालधिवल्लरीं बहुविधैर्वासोभि राज्यस्तुते दत्वावह्निं मदीयपत्रनुमतः कर्तुं विरूपंवपुः ॥ ३१४ ॥

रावण हनुमतो वह्नि प्रयुक्ती ।

अग्निःप्रज्वलितःसमादिशभृशं वर्षन्तुधाराधरावातो वाति नवास्यन्ति धूम ममी देवास्तवाज्ञावशाः । इत्थंसुप्य थकोत्तरे हनुमतो लङ्कापतेर्मानसं दग्धं याद्दश माक्रमेणाच तथा दग्धापि लङ्कापुरी ॥ ३१५ ॥

अत्रावसरे जनानां वितर्क्काः ।

अब्धिः किं बडवानलेनतरणोर्बिम्बेन किम्वावियन्मेघः किं चपलाञ्चलेन शशिभृत्त्विंभाल नेत्रेणवा । कालः किं प्रलयवह्निनेन्द्र धनुषाधाराधरः किं महाम्भेरुः किं ध्रुवमण्डलेन सकपिः पुच्छेन सराजते ॥ ३१६ ॥

अथ हनूमान् ।

रामाग्रे नच लक्ष्मणस्य पुरतः कृत्वा शरैराहवं सीता निस्त्रप वेपमान हृदया चौर्य्येण नीतात्वया । प्रत्यक्षं तवदुर्मते वरगृहैः पूर्णाजनैरावृता सर्वस्फाटिकरत्न मौक्तिक मयीलङ्कामया दह्यते ॥ ३१७ ॥

सूत्र । उल्कामुखानां भयविह्वलानां जलंजलं व्याहरतां मुखेभ्यः । निर्गात्यवह्निर्द्विगुण प्रभावो ददाहलङ्कामनिवारितार्चिः ॥ ३१८ ॥

रावणः । शीघ्रं रक्षत वाजिवारणगृहं शय्यागृहं स्त्रीगृहं रत्नागार धनालयं बलवता वातेन दीप्तोनलः । धूमव्याकुल नेत्रवक्त्रयुवती वक्षस्थले ताडनात् क्रन्दद्बालक वृद्धभीत वनिता हाहारवः श्रूयते ॥ ३१९ ॥

सूत्र । श्रीलङ्कामवलोक्य घोरदहनैः संदह्यमानां भृशं प्रोवाचेति वचांसि

सर्व्ववदनैस्तोयार्थिं लङ्केश्वरः । अर्घ्येनीरधि रम्बुधिर्जलनिधिः पाथोनिधिः स-
म्भ्रमादम्भोधि र्जलधिः पयोधिरुदधिर्वारां निधिर्वारिधिः ॥ १२० ॥

रावणः । निकुम्भकुम्भोदर कुम्भकर्णा कुम्भैरलं केवल नामधेयैः । मन्दोद-
री मन्दिर पावकोऽयं पानीय मानीय नकैर्विनीतः ॥ १२१ ॥

ततोऽशोकवनें वायुपुत्रः सीतान्ति केऽब्रवीत् । लङ्कादग्धामया देविविदायो
दीयतामिति ॥ १२२ ॥

सीता धूमशिखाग्रस्तोः कालव्याल वधूरिव । उदस्यच शिरोरत्नं विशार्द्रं
स्वामिनेददौ ॥ १२३ ॥

सीता । मनःशिलायास्तिलकं तथामेगण्डस्थलें पार्श्वतलेच घृष्टं । स्मरेति
विज्ञानमथोतृतीयकं जीवाम्यहं राघव मासमेकं ॥ १२४ ॥

सूत्र । दग्धालङ्कामशङ्कं जनकनृपसुतां तां समाभाष्यभूयो वायोः सूनु-
स्तरस्वीपुनरपिमिलितोजाम्ब वन्मुख्ययूथैः । तेभ्यःसर्व्वं निवेद्य प्रमुदितहृदयेस्तैः
समंसंनिवृत्तः सुग्रीव प्रेमपात्रं मधुवनमथ संरक्ष्य भोगंसचक्रे ॥ १२५ ॥

तैःपिबद्भिरभितो मधूचयं वारितो विनिहतो महाबलैः । रक्तकोदधि-
मुखोऽवधीरितः सप्लवङ्गपति सन्निधिं ययौ ॥ १२६ ॥

इति सर्वे निष्क्रान्ताः ।

इति पञ्चमोऽङ्कः ।

अथ षष्ठोऽङ्कः॥

विंध्याचल रचना।

ततोवनपालैसहप्रविशति दधिमुखः। जयतिजयति देवः। इतिसुग्रीवं प्रणम्य।

दधिमुखः। विंध्यं भूमिधरं तदन्तरवनं तद्गोप्तु मिच्छाद्यपि तत्राधिष्ठित देवतापरिकरन्तत्प्रीति दत्तं फलं। वैदेही मभितो विचिन्त्यहरयः सुग्रीवसंप्रेषणा दारोहन्तिविशन्ति यान्ति दधति ध्यायन्ति खादन्तिच॥ १२७॥

हनूमदागमन मजानन् सुग्रीवं प्रति रामः।

मासमेकं गतोलङ्कां हनूमान्ननिवर्त्तते। चिरंदूतेषु कल्याणं यदि बद्धो न तिष्ठति॥ १२८॥

अपिच। हे सुग्रीव हनूमतः कथमहो वार्त्तापि नासाद्यते दुर्गम्योजलधिः पुरीचविषमा तस्मादिदं कल्प्यते। दुष्टैर्धर्म्मपराङ्मुखै र्दशमुखैः सार्द्धं किमालापतो यातो वानरविवासवायुतनयः कालानुकम्पक्रियः॥ १२९॥

अथ दधिमुखात् हनूमदागमनं श्रुत्वा श्रीरामंप्रति सुग्रीवः।

यथा। अस्यस्मार्क मधुवनमिदष्माभुजा मेकभोग्यं भंक्त्वा भुंक्ते पवनतनय खेदसौ लब्धकार्य्यः। सत्यंप्रत्या गतइव तयोरित्य माख्याय भाजोत्तआयातः स्मित किलकिलोन्वीस पुर्मा हनूमान्॥ १३०॥

प्रविशति हनूमन्तं।

सूत्र। ततोमरचुम्बितचारुशेखरः प्रसन्नताराधिप मण्डलाग्रणीः। वियुक्तरामातुर दृष्टिवीक्षितो वसन्तकालो हनुमानिवागतः॥ १३१॥

अथ राम हनुमतो रुक्तिप्रत्युक्ती ।

हं हो मारुतनन्दनादिशइतो दृष्टात्वयाजानकी दृष्टा जीवतिजीवति प्रियतमा मांशोचते शोचते । मद्विच्छेद कृशा कृशा वदतिकिं हाराम हाराघवेत्येवं तत्पृच्छितं किमस्ति सुतरा मथ्येष चूडामणिः ॥ ३३२ ॥

इति प्रथमाभिज्ञानं चूडामणि मर्पयति ।

ततश्चूडामणिमासाद्य श्रीरामचेष्टा ।

सूत्र । कण्ठेसंतनुते चिरमुरः पीठे निवेश्य प्रियास्पर्शोल्लासभरं समाकलयतिप्रेम्णाचिरंपृच्छति । स्वामिन्याः कुशलं तवेति पुरतः पश्यं श्रुणासंप्लुतं निष्पन्देक्षण वीक्षणंप्रकुरुते चूडामणिं राघवः ॥ ३३३ ॥

ततःपुनर्हनूमान् । मनःशिलाया स्तिलकं स्मरगण्डस्थलेमम । संघृष्टजामकीपक्षः स्पर्शात्काणीकृतःखगः ॥ ३३४ ॥

इत्यभिज्ञानद्वयं दर्शयति ।

तत आलिङ्गितु मुपक्रान्तं श्रीरामंप्रतिहनूमान् ।

पीतोनाम्बुनिधि र्नरावणपुरी निःशेष चूर्णीकृतानानीतानिशिरांसि राक्षसपते र्नानायि सीतामया । आश्लेषार्पण पारितोषिकमहंनार्हामि वार्त्ताहरः संजल्पत्य निलात्मजे च लपति व्रीडानतोराघवः ॥ ३३५ ॥

रामः । अहो नविच्छितं किम्बा भवता राक्षसाहताः । दग्धा लङ्कापुरी सर्वा सीतावार्ता समाहृता । हनू । त्वत्प्रतापानलेनैव नाथ श्रीरघुनन्दन । दग्धापुरैव लङ्केयं पश्चादग्निर्मयार्पितः ॥ ३३६ ॥

रामः । अहोकिं नविहितं भवता । यदयं लङ्घितः समुद्र इत्युक्ते ।

हनूमान् । देवत्वत्प्रबलप्रताप तपनै रम्भोनिधिः शोषितस्तेनेत्थं स्थलवर्त्म नैव गतवान् लङ्कामलङ्कामहं । रक्षोनायक नागरीनयनजैर्नीरैर्यथा पूरितस्तेनायं जलधिस्तदाममक्षतास्फालेन किंवाफलं ॥ ३३७ ॥

अथोपविश्य राम हनुमतोक्ति प्रत्युक्ती ।

क्वास्तेसीता वसति विपिने देव लङ्काभगुप्ते कीदृक्पन्था जलधि पिहित-स्तीर्यते दैवयोगात् । इत्याख्याते पवनतनये व्रीडविभ्रान्त नेत्रो हर्षव्रीडाबभय चकितो विह्वलो रामचन्द्रः ॥ ३३८ ॥

ततःप्राप्तचेतनेन रामेण कीदृशीसीतेति प्रत्ययार्थं पुनःपृष्टोहनूमान् ।

हनू । इन्दुर्लिप्तइवाञ्जनेन दलितादृष्टिर्मृगीणांतथा पाण्डये नवमेघविद्रु-मदलं श्यामेव हेमप्रभा । पारुष्यं कलरव कोकिल वधूकण्ठेष्विवप्रस्तुतंसीता-याः पुरतोऽथहन्त शिखिनां बर्हाःसगर्हाइव ॥ ३३९ ॥

इदानीं कीदृगवस्थेति श्रीरामेण पुनः पृष्टो हनूमान् ।

हनू । कार्श्यं चेत्प्रतिपत्कला हिमनिधेः स्थूलाऽथचेत्याखुना नीलाचैव मृणालिका नयनयोर्बाष्पः कियान् वारिधिः । सन्तापो यदि शीतलो ऊतवहस्त-स्याःकियद्वर्ण्यते रामत्वत्स्मृतिमात्रमेवहृदयं लावण्य शेषं वपुः ॥ ३४० ॥

अपिच । स्वभावादेवतन्वङ्गी त्वद्वियोगा द्विशेषतः । प्रतिपत्पाठशीलस्य विद्येव तनुतांगता ॥ ३४१ ॥

अथ कथं समुद्र उत्तीर्ण इति प्रश्ने।

हनू। शाखामृगस्य शाखायाः शाखां गन्तुं पराक्रमः। यन्मया लङ्घितो ऽम्भोधिः प्रभावोऽयं तवप्रभो ॥ २४२ ॥

अपिच। राम नाम तव जातु जपन्तः पामरा अपि तरन्ति भवाब्धिं। अङ्गुलीयं भवदङ्गुलिमुक्तः किं विचित्र मतरत्पयिरब्धिं ॥ २४३ ॥

रामः। चतुरस्रपुरीलङ्का सप्तप्राकार वेष्टिता। रथीनाञ्च चतुर्लक्षै र्‌था- नाञ्च त्रिकोटिभिः ॥ २४४ ॥

त्रिकोटि शाखासंयुक्ता नवकोटि सुराक्षया। कथं पुरी त्वया दग्धा विद्य- माने दशानने ॥ २४५ ॥

त्रिदशैरपि दुर्द्धर्षा लङ्कानाम महापुरी। कथं वीर त्वया दग्धा विद्यमाने दशानने ॥ २४६ ॥

हनू। निश्वासेनैव सीताया राजन् कोपानलेन ते। दग्धा पुरीव लङ्केशं निमित्तमभवं त्वहं ॥ २४७ ॥

रावणं जयेभवतः कीदृग्व्यवसाय इति प्रश्ने।

हनू। रक्षस्तद्दुर्जकन्दरं बज्रभुजं बद्धाननं दीप्तिम द्रंष्ट्रारौद्रमहं विलोक्य सहसाद्ध्रे मनोर्हिंसितुं। देव त्वत्कृपया विजृम्भितधिया किं किं भवेद्दुष्करं भर्त्तुःकर्म्म भटस्य नोचितमिति त्यक्तोमया रावणः ॥ २४८ ॥

रामः। एकैकस्योपकारस्य प्राणान्दास्याम्यहं कपे। अन्यैकैवोपकारेण शेषेण ऋणिनोवयं ॥ २४९ ॥

हनूमान् । मद्विधा बहवो भृत्या यत्र तिष्ठन्ति राघव । त्वद्विधो गुणसम्पन्नः स्वामी नैव च लभ्यते ॥ १५० ॥

इति सर्वे निष्क्रान्ताः ।

ततः ससमुद्र लङ्कारचनं ।

अथ श्रीरामचन्द्रस्य लङ्काप्रयाणं ।

सूत्र । अथ विजयदशम्यामाश्विने शुक्लपक्षे दशमुख निधनाय प्रस्थितो रामचन्द्रः । द्विविदगयसहायैर्यूथनाथैस्तथान्यैः कपिभिरपरिमाणैर्व्याप्तदिक् चक्रवालः ॥ १५१ ॥

उत्फालैः स्थगयन्नभः किलकिला शब्दैर्दिशो नादयन् भञ्जन्पर्वत कानमानि धरणी मुद्धूनयन् सर्वतः । प्रस्थाने रघुनन्दनस्य स तदा सुग्रीव संपालितो लङ्कासंमुख मुच्चचाल सहसा हृष्टः कपीनांचयः ॥ १५२ ॥

क्षोणीमज्जति भूधरो विचलति क्षोभं प्रयात्यम्बुधिः कूर्माःकुप्यति संकुचत्यहिपति र्देवाधिप स्त्रस्यति । हेलानिर्जित वैरिवारलक्षिता रामेप्रयाणोत्सवे गन्तुं खेनविभीषणोपिसभयः स्थानान्तरं वाञ्छति ॥ १५३ ॥

ततः समुद्र तीरावस्थितो रामः स्वगतं ।

पारेसिन्धुपुरी पुरी परिसरे प्राचीर मभ्रंलिहं सिंहदेशिबलं रिपुर्जयबला स्तेकुम्भकर्णादयः । भ्रान्तीकः सरिपु स्तनन्धयइव भ्रातासखा वानरो मत्वैवं रघुपाकेप्ररियुवा कोदण्ड मुदीक्षते ॥ १५४ ॥

ततो हनूमान् । देवाज्ञापय किंकरोमि सहसा लङ्कामिहैवानये जम्बुद्वीप मतोनये किमथवा वारांनिधिं शोषये । हेलोत्तोलित विंध्यमन्दरगिरि स्वर्णभकूटाचल क्षेपक्षोभितबद्धमार्गसलिलं बध्नामि वारांनिधिं ॥ १५५ ॥

अथ समुद्रोपरतीरे लङ्कावृत्तान्तः ।

सूत । लङ्काख्यानतिवृद्धतापसभटा नानीय प्रश्नः कृतो लङ्केशेन विलोक्य वीरनगरीं लङ्कांसशङ्कामिव । ध्यानज्ञानपरायणा मुनिगणा देवं किमत्र श्रुतं येषां यद्धृदये स्फुरत्यपि वच स्तेनैव तत्कथ्यतां ॥ ३५६ ॥

रावणस्यमाता निकषया व्यसनाद्रावणो निवार्यतामित्युक्ता विभीषणः । लङ्कानाथपदं प्रणिपत्याह । राजन् सेयं राक्षस कालरात्रिः सीतापरित्यजतां । यस्यवानरमात्रेण पूरीयं व्याकुलीकृता । कस्तेन सहयुध्येत बुद्धिमान् राक्षसेश्वर ॥ ३५७ ॥

अपिच । त्यजप्रकोपं कुलकीर्त्तिनाशनं भजस्व रामं कुलकीर्त्ति वर्द्धनं । अलं विवादेन समोविधीयतां प्रदीयतां दाशरथाय मैथिली ॥ ३५८ ॥

लङ्कादग्धा वनंभग्नं लङ्घितश्चमहोदधिः । यत्कृतं रामदूतेन स रामः किं करिष्यति ॥ ३५९ ॥

नरावणोवा नमहोदरोवा नकुम्भकर्णोपि नचातिकायः । नचेन्द्रजिद्दाशरथिं प्रसोढुं शक्तास्तुतं शक्र सत प्रभावं ॥ ३६० ॥

सुवर्णपुंखाः सुभृशं सुतीक्ष्णावज्रोपमा वायु समानवेगाः । यावन्नगृह्णन्ति शिरांसिबाणाः प्रदीयतां दाशरथायमैथिली ॥ ३६१ ॥

तत आगतः कुम्भकर्णतनूजो रावणंप्रेक्ष्यवदति ।

तस्यैतेनोद्धृत्यस्फाटिकशिखरी सोपिविदधे समन्तादामूलं त्रुटितवसुधाबन्ध विधुरः । अमुं येनाद्यापि त्रिपुरहर नृत्यव्यतिकरः पुरस्तादन्येषामपि शिखरिणां मुल्लसयति ॥ ३६२ ॥

रावणः । शूराः सन्ति पथेषु नः कतिकतिप्राज्ञाः पदं चक्रिरे तेषामेव विलंघ्य चास्त पदवीं जागर्त्ति लङ्काभटः । यद्दोर्मण्डल चण्डपीडन वशान्निष्यन्दिरक्ताच्छटा शङ्कामङ्कुरयन्ति शङ्करगिरेरद्यापि धातुद्रवाः ॥ ३६३ ॥

इन्द्रं माल्यकरं सहस्रकिरणं द्वारि प्रतीहारकं चन्द्रं छत्रधरं समीरवरुणौ सम्मार्ज्जयन्तौ गृहान् । पाचकत्वे परिनिष्ठितं कृतवहं किं मद्गृहे नेक्षसे रक्षोभक्ष्य मनुष्यमात्र वपुषं तं राघवं स्तौषि किं ॥ ३६४ ॥

विभीषणः । रामोऽसौ भुवनेषु विक्रमगुणैः प्राप्तः प्रसिद्धिं गिरा मस्म राज्य विपर्य्ययाद्यदि पुनर्द्देवो नजानाति तं । बन्दीवैष यशांसि गायति मरुद्यस्यैकबाणाहतिश्रेणीभूत विशालतालविवरोद्गीर्णैः स्वरैः सप्तभिः ॥ ३६५ ॥

अजनि रजनिमध्ये मण्डलं चण्डरश्मेर्धनु रुदयमदभ्रं बिभ्रती यास्यकान्ति । अहह विधिरिदानीं दृश्यते रामएव प्रदिश जनकपुत्रीं मित्रता सेतुरामः ॥ ३६६ ॥

यस्यैकः कपिशावकः समतरल्लंघ्य मम्भोनिधिं दुर्भेद्यामपि देव दैत्य निवहैर्लङ्कापुरीं प्राविशत् । छित्वातान् वनरक्षिणो जनकजां दृष्ट्वा च भंक्त्वा वनं हत्वाक्षं प्रदहन् पुरीमथगतो रामः कथं मानवः ॥ ३६७ ॥

गतायुषं त्वां विपरीतबुद्धिं निःसंशयं राक्षस लक्षयामि । यो मां हितं तथ्यमपिब्रुवन्तं नमन्यसेराक्षस वीरमध्ये ॥ ३६८ ॥

सूत्र । अथचरणहतो दशाननेन प्रकृतिविपर्य्यय मस्यलक्षयित्वा । सपदिच परिहृत्य तं समन्त्री परिकुपितो नभसा जगाम रामं ॥ ३६९ ॥

गमनसमये पुनर्विभीषणः सानुनयं ।

प्रगृह्य रत्नानि विभूषणानि वासांसि दिव्यानि मणींश्चमुख्यान् । सीताञ्च रामाय निवेद्य देवीं वसाव लङ्कामपयातु शङ्का ॥ ३७० ॥

रावणः। आगामिसीता जनकप्रसूता आगामिरामो मधुसूदनश्च। अहञ्च जानामि हि तेनवध्य स्तथापिसीतां न समर्पयामि॥ २७१।

सूत्र। ततश्चतुर्भिः सहमंत्रि पुत्रैरुपेत्यरक्षः कुलधूमकेतुः। लङ्कामहातङ्क-दशाम्बरेण विभीषणोराघव मन्दिराय॥ २७२॥ निष्क्रान्तो विभीषणः।

पुनर्लङ्का समुद्रयोः कल्पनं।

सूत्र। विभीषणे समायाते सूर्य्यकोटि समप्रभे। तदादौ रावणभ्रान्त्या भङ्गःकपिकुलेऽभवत्॥ २७३॥

हनूमतायं निर्णीतो रावणो न विभीषणः। रामचन्द्र पदद्वन्द कामसेभ्रमरायते॥ २७४॥

दौवारिकस्यागमनं।

देव द्वारि नभः पथेषु मिलिताः पञ्चनिशाचाचरा एकस्तत्रविभीषणो दशमुखभ्राता परे मंत्रिणः। यान्तोशरणं भयापहरणं किं तन्नजानीमहे ज्ञात्वाज्ञात्य विचारणैकनिपुण स्तत्र प्रमाणं प्रभुः॥ २७५॥

अथ रामचन्द्रंप्रति हनूमान्निवेदयति।

सत्यंदाशरथे विभीषण इति भ्रातास्ति लङ्कापतेर्निद्रासिन्धुतिमिङ्गिल-स्यचरमः श्रीकुम्भकर्णस्यच। दाक्षिण्याभ्युपलक्षितः पितृकुलापेक्षावशच्छा-ग्रयोरक्षोलोक विलक्षणं कलयति प्रव्यक्त लक्ष्मीमयं॥ २७६॥

अथ रामलक्ष्मणयोरुक्ति प्रत्युक्ती।

धर्म्मात्मा दशकन्धराद्वहिरभूत्कस्मादयं रावणात् संभ्रान्तो भिनयेन किं नकुरुते सुग्रीवतदासिनः॥

रक्षोराज सहोदरस्य निभृतारम्भोपि सम्भाव्यते किंकुर्म्मः शरणागतं रिपुमपि द्रुह्यन्ति नेक्ष्वाकवः ॥ १७७ ॥

समागत्य श्रीरामंप्रति प्रति विभीषणः ।

भ्रान्त्वा दिग्वलयं दशास्यदमन त्वत्कीर्त्ति हंसीदिवं यातान्ब्रह्ममरालकङ्कम वशात्तत्रैव गर्भिण्यभूत् । यस्य स्वर्गतरङ्गिणी परिसरे कुन्दावदातं तयामुक्तंभा-ति विश्राणमखण्डमिदं शीतत्विषो र्मण्डलं ॥ १७८ ॥

वीर क्षीर समुद्रसान्द्रलहरीलावण्यलक्ष्मीमुष स्वत्कीर्त्तौ तुलनांकलङ्क-मलिनो धत्ते कथं चन्द्रमा । स्यादेवं त्वदरातिसौधनिकरप्रोद्भूत धूम्याङ्कया-सक्तप्रमनाः पतेद्यदि पुनस्तस्याङ्कच्छायायां मृगः ॥ १७९ ॥

कोदण्डमण्डलविनिःसृतचण्डबाणतुण्डाग्रखण्डित दशाननबाहुदण्डः । आ-खण्डलादिगण खण्डनचण्डहासः श्रीजानकी परिवृढः सुदृढप्रतिज्ञः ॥ १८० ॥

पातुं त्रीणिजगन्ति सन्ततमकूपारात्समभ्युद्धरन् धात्रीं कोलकलेवरो हरि रभूद्यस्यैकदंष्ट्राङ्कुरात् । कूर्म्मः क्रन्दति नालति द्विरसनः पतन्ति दिग्दन्तिनो मेरुः क्रोशति मेदिनी जलजति व्योमापि रोलम्बति ॥ १८१ ॥

कूर्म्मः पादोस्य यष्टि र्भुजगपति रसौभाजनं भूतधात्री तैलोत्पूराः समुद्राः कनकगिरिरयं दीप्त वर्त्ति प्ररोहः । अर्च्चि श्चण्डांशुरोचि र्गगनमलिनता कज्जलं दह्यमाना शत्रुश्रेणीपतङ्गा ज्वलति रघुपते त्वत्प्रतापप्रदीपः ॥ १८२ ॥

कूर्म्मं कुपयितुं दिशःस्थगयितुं भेत्तुं च पृथ्वीधरानब्धीन्पङ्कयितुं तथादिन मणिं प्रच्छादितुं रेणुभिः । सद्वीरेषु पुनःपुनस्तवबलक्षोणाहताडम्बरान्धत्सुं वीरवर्द्धयिनी तवपराजेतुं परान्धावति ॥ १८३ ॥

गुणाधारो धातावहति वसुधा भूर्पपदवीं मणीन्द्रः स्यात्स्तम्भं कनकशिखरीमा

नपत्तिका । तुलादण्डः सत्यं यदि भवति दामोदरगदा तदाप्येषोऽध्यक्ष स्तवगुणसमूहं तुलयितुं ॥ १८४ ॥

अत्युक्तौ यदि नैव कुप्यसि मृषावाचं न चेन्मन्यसे त्वद्रूपोद्भुतवस्तु वर्णनविधौ-व्यग्राः कवीनां गिरः । देव त्वत्तरुणप्रतापदहनज्वालावली शोषिताः सर्वे वारिधयस्तद्वारिवनिता नेत्राम्बुभिः पूरिताः ॥ १८५ ॥

हनूमच्चरितं स्तौति ।

रथः क्षोणी लोकोधनुरगपतिर्ज्या फणिपतिः शरोन्माथी योधः सरसिज-भवः सारथिरपि । शरः शौरि र्दैवत्रिपुरपुरदाहे परिकरो ज्वलज्ज्वाले लङ्का वतभसितभूता हनूमता ॥ १८६ ॥

विभीषणं दृष्ट्वा सुग्रीवो लक्ष्मणमाह ।

यस्य न स्वजने प्रीतिः का प्रीति रितरे जने । शङ्कितव्योऽस्मि सौमित्रे दूर-स्थोऽपि विभीषणः ॥ १८७ ॥

तदन्ते विभीषणावस्था ।

दृष्ट्वा वानरवाहिनी मणिभूतान् हर्षार ऊर्ध्वरिणीं शङ्कावान् विभीषणः क्षणमभूद् वीरदोर्विक्रमः । पश्यन्दाशरथिं प्रमोदलहरी गम्भीरमुज्जृम्भित स्तम्भः सम्भृतविक्रमोऽपि चलितुं स्थातुं नचायंक्षमः ॥ १८८ ॥

तं दृष्ट्वा रामः । द्विशरं नैवसंधत्ते द्विः स्थापयति नाश्रितान् । द्विर्ददाति न चार्थिभ्यो रामो द्विर्नैवभाषते ॥ १८९ ॥

विभीषणस्य हृदयं हनूमान् कथयति ।

सुग्रीवस्य श्रियं दृष्ट्वा लक्ष्मणस्य च सेवनं । विभीषणस्य दोलेव मतिरायाति याति च ॥ १९० ॥

ततः श्रीरामंप्रति सुग्रीवः ।

ज्येष्ठत्वं त्वधिकं तत्र लङ्कानाथे विभीषणात् । हनूमतास्य राजेन्द्र कथितः प्रचुरो गुणः ॥ १९२ ॥

श्रीराम विभीषणयोरुक्ति प्रत्युक्ती ।

अये रक्षोराजानुज कुशलमद्यैव कुशलं यतो योष्माकीनं चरणकमलं दृष्टमधुना । किमुद्देश्यं युष्मात्पदकमलसेवैव विदितं भवानद्यैवाभून्निज नगर लङ्कापरिवृढः ॥ १९३ ॥

तस्याति भक्तिमधिगम्य विभीषणस्य सौमित्रिणा रजनिचारगणश्च राज्ये । प्रत्तोऽभ्यषेचयदमुं प्रवरो रघूणां प्रायः प्रपन्नकरुणावशगा महान्तः ॥ १९४ ॥

परस्परं वानराः ।

अद्यैवास्य विभीषणस्य शरणापन्नस्य मूर्द्धानते हर्षादत्र ददात्ययं रघुपति र्लङ्काधिपस्यश्रियं । एतस्यैव भुजाविह प्रतिभुवौ सुग्रीवराज्यार्पणे अत्रास्य प्रथमानसत्यचरिते सर्वेवयं साक्षिणः ॥ १९५ ॥

समुद्रं प्रति रामः ।

त्वमसिकुलगुरुर्मे मुञ्च वर्मानुरागे शिरसि विनिहितोऽयं भक्तिपूतोञ्जलिस्ते । दशवदनहृता मे सा वधूर्मेऽभ्युपेयाद्दशमुखनिधनेन क्षीयतां सेकलङ्कः ॥ १९६ ॥

अथप्रायोपविष्टे रामे मार्गमत्यजति समुद्रे लक्ष्मणंप्रति रामः ।

अचिरादैन्यपराभवप्रणयणी नेक्ष्वाकुभिः शिक्षिता सेवासम्वलितः कदा रघुकुले

मौलौनिबद्धोऽञ्जलिः । तत्सर्वं विहितं तथाप्युदधिना नैवोपरोध कृतः पाणिस्ते प्रतिसंप्रति प्रतिपदं प्रष्टुं धनुर्वाञ्छति ॥ ३९७ ॥

अथ सूर्य्योदये सूर्य्यसमुद्रयोरुक्ति प्रत्युक्ती ।

भोःसिन्धोभगवन्नमस्खलसिकिं श्रीरामभद्रानुगोदष्ट्वा रिभयेन किं तव-भयं त्वत्स्नवस्त्व द्रुमाः । तस्येन्दुर्वदनेरमाचसदने पीयूषमाभाषणे बाहोकल्प-तरु निंशातविशिखश्रेणीषु हालाहलं ॥ ३९८ ॥

श्रीरामः सरोषं ।

चापमानय सौमित्रे शरान् कालानलोपमान् । समुद्रं शोषयिष्यामि पद्भ्यांयान्तुप्लवङ्गमाः ॥ ३९९ ॥

दम्भोलितीव्रै र्विशिखैरनेकैरम्भोनिधिं पांशुनिधिं करिष्ये । स्थलीकरिष्ये मरुभूमयिष्ये भस्मीकरिष्ये मृग तृष्णयिष्ये ॥ ४०० ॥

सूत्र । श्रीरामचन्द्रे दशवक्त्र पुर्य्यामादाय पाथोनिधिबद्धकोपे । आग्नेय-मस्त्रंप्रतिसंदधाने वेलागिरीन्द्राश्चकितावभूतां ॥ ४४१ ॥

अनन्तरञ्च । दिशोधूमायन्ते ज्वलितमभवत्सागरजलं परित्रेसुर्नक्राः स्फुटनमगमन् शङ्खमणयः । परित्यक्तोमाशो रघुपरिवृढे नाथ सहसा दधन्मूर्त्तिं सिन्धुर्ज्वलनमलिनां प्रादुरभवत् ॥ ४०२ ॥

अथ समुद्रः सानुनयं ।

शमयदहनतीव्रं क्षामितं ते शरौजः क्षम मितसलिलोऽहंदेवकोपंजहीहि । नरककरतलास्त्रैर्वानरानीतशैलैर्विरचयमयिसेतुं सुखुपारं प्रयाहि ॥ ४०३ ॥

सेतुबद्धारम्भे रामं स्तौति नलः ।

रामरत्नमहं वन्दे चित्रकूटकपेटके । कौशल्याशुक्तिसंभूतं जानकी कण्ठभूषणं ॥ ४०४ ॥

सूत्र । उत्पाट्योत्पाट्य शैलानतिबहलतलग्रामपाताल मूलानुत्तुङ्गान् शृङ्गानति कलितनभो मण्डलान् दिग्विकीर्णान् । दुर्धार्य्यानाञ्जनेय प्रभृतिकपिभटा क्षेसमानिन्युरन्तः सिन्धोसन्धायदोष्णा विरचयतिनलोनिर्भरं सेतुबन्धं ॥४०५॥

सेतुबन्ध समये श्रीरामं प्रति सुग्रीवः स्तौति ।

श्रमचतुर कपीन्द्रैर्नीय मानेनगेन्द्रे गिरिकुहर निवासा राघवत्प्रसादात् । सुरकरि परिपेयां प्राप्यमन्दाकिनीं खेसवलितकरदण्डाः कुम्भिनोन्तःपिबन्ति ॥ ४०६ ॥

पयसि पाषाणेषु स्थितेषु विभीषणः ।

येमज्जन्तिजले कियत्यपिचिरं ते प्रस्तरादुस्तरे सिन्धौ हन्ततरन्ति राक्षस भयं सम्पादयन्तो भृशं । नैतेग्रावगुणा नवारिधिगुणानो वानराणांगुणाः श्रीम द्दाशरथेरियं स्फि सत्त्वजाशक्तिः समुन्मीलति ॥ ४०७ ॥

अथ समुद्रं प्रति सुग्रीवः ।

दुर्वृत्तसंगति रनर्थ परम्परायाहेतुः सतां भवतिकिं वचनीयमत्र । लङ्के-श्वरोहरति दाशरथेः कलत्रं प्राप्नोति बन्धनमसौकि लसिन्धुराजः ॥ ४०८ ॥

खलः करोति दुर्वृत्तं नूनंफलति साधुषु । दशाननो हरेत्सीतां बन्धनं स्यान्महोदधौ ॥ ४०९ ॥

ततः प्रविशति प्रहस्तः ।

समुद्रबन्धनं श्रुत्वा प्रहस्तः ।

विरमजलधिमध्ये सेतुबन्धं विधाय निशितशरनिपातै राक्षसेन्द्रं निहत्य।
यदि नयति ससीतां रामनामा तपस्वी मशककगजकारंध्रे हस्तियूथं प्रविष्टं ॥४१०॥

अत्रावसरे रावणचेष्टा ।

सूत्र । आदौ राजहास बद्धविस्मयमाप मध्येसेतोः समाप्तिसमये सनिशाचरेन्द्रः ।
उद्धूतवन्मघम निर्भरसेव्यमान उत्पातवातहतपर्वतवच्चकम्पे ॥४११॥

रावणः । पाषाणाः पयसि प्रसन्नवपुषः तिष्ठन्ति सेतुं गताः श्रुत्वैवं वदतां दशाननधरः क्रुद्धः समुद्रं प्रति । धिक्त्वां नामतवाम्बुधिः सलिलधिः पानीयधिस्तोय-धिः पाथोधिर्जलधिः पयोधिरुदधिर्वारां निधिर्वारिधिः ॥४१२॥

श्रुत्वा सागर बन्धनं दशशिराः सर्वैर्मुखैरेकदा तूर्णं पृच्छति वार्त्तिकान् सचकितो भीत्याकुलः सम्भ्रमात् । बद्धः सत्यमपांनिधिः सलिलधिः कीलालधिस्तोय-धिः पाथोधिर्जलधिः पयोधिरुदधिर्वारां निधिर्वारिधिः ॥४१३॥

अपिच । पीतस्त्वं कलशोद्भवेन मुनिना ध्वस्तोऽसि देवासुरैराबद्धोसिच रामनामहरिणा शाखामृगैर्लङ्घितः । नाम्नामारभटी तथैवभवतो लोकैरियं घुष्यते पाथोधिर्जलधिः पयोधिरुदधिर्वारां निधिर्वारिधिः ॥४१४॥

सेतुबन्धं दृष्ट्वा लङ्कापुर्यां वृत्तान्तः ।

सूत्र । महत्पुत्रस्त्वेकः कपिकटकरक्षामणिरसौ समुद्रं लाङ्गूलध्वज इव समाश्लिष्टगगनः । पुनः प्रत्यायास्यत्यहह कपिनाथे प्रचलिते वचः प्रोचुर्नैवैर्भयचकितलङ्कापुरजनाः ॥४१५॥

अष्टादशमहापद्मसेनाध्यक्षाधिपालिता । साराघववचमूस्तेन सेतुमागन्तुमुद्यैया ॥४१६॥

लङ्कायामधिगर्व्विता पलभुजामाकर्ण्य कोलाहलानुत्फालान् विदधुः प्लवङ्गमभटा युद्धोद्भटाटोपिनः । भोभोकुम्भनिकुम्भशारणशुकाः सज्जाभव-ध्वाभृशं निर्गच्छन्त्विति निर्भरं समभवल्लङ्केश्वरस्योक्तयः ॥ ४१७ ॥

कृतकलकलशब्दं भर्त्सिताशेषलोकं प्लवगनृपतिसैन्यं सेतुनातेननीत्वा । मुदितविपिनदुर्गे पर्वतेऽसौ सुवेले शिबिरमकृत लङ्कानाथनाशाय रामः॥४१८॥

सूत्र । आयातौशुकसारणौ दशमुखप्रस्थापितौ हौचरौ देहं वानरमाश्रितौ चकटकं संख्यातुमभ्युद्यतौ । विज्ञायाथ विभीषणेन यमितौ मुक्तौ चतौतत्क्षणं रामेण प्रभुना विलोक्य कटकं रामाज्ञयातौगतौ ॥ ४१९ ॥

अथ लङ्कायां परावृत्यगतौ शुकसारणौ रावणाय निवेदयतः ।

आकाशे दिशिकानने जलनिधौ शैलेतटे गह्वरे नस्थानं तिलधारणेपि-कलितं संख्याकथं कथ्यतां । भ्रातातेयमितौ कपीन्द्र कटकं तद्दर्शयित्वोज्झितौ श्रीरामेण महात्मना कुरु यथायोग्यं द्रुतं रावण ॥ ४२० ॥

ततः प्रासादमारुह्य वानरसैन्यं पश्यतारावणेन कतमोरामइति पृष्टौ शु-कसारणौ श्रीरामचन्द्रं दर्शयतः ।

यत्रव्योम्नोपतति च मधुस्यन्दमन्दारवर्षं यत्रातोद्यध्वनिरुपचितो यत्र च स्तोत्रघोषः । रामःश्यामः कमल नयनस्तत्रलक्ष्मी सरोषंलङ्कां पश्यन् भ्रमयति शरंपाणिना दक्षिणेन ॥ ४२१ ॥

अङ्केकृत्वोत्तमाङ्गं प्लवगबलपतेः पादमक्षस्य हन्तुस्तारापुत्रस्य हस्तं त्वचि कनकमृगस्याङ्गशेषं निधाय । बाणंरक्षःकुलघ्नं प्रगुणितमनुजेनादरादीक्षमा-णस्त्वत्तुः कोणेनलङ्कां त्वदनुजवचनेदत्तकर्णोयमास्ते ॥ ४२२ ॥

अत्रावसरे रावण वाक्यं ।

एते ते ममबाहवः सुरपतेर्दोदण्डकण्डूहराः सोऽहं सर्वजगत्त्रयाभयकरो स-

ह्वेश्वरोरावणः । सेतुं बद्धमहं श्रृणोमिकपिभिः पश्यामिलङ्कां हतां जीवद्भिर्मम दृश्यते किमथवाकिंवा मनश्रूयते ॥ ४२३ ॥

अपिच । आश्चर्यं तापसोसौ गिरिकुहर चरान् वानरान् मेलयित्वा वाञ्छत्यागत्यनेतुं किलजनकसुतां मद्गृहीतां दुरात्मा । दंष्ट्राः आस्तां हरेःकःखर नखर मुखोत्खात मातङ्गकुम्भभ्रश्यद्दन्ताग्रमुक्ताफलनिकर रसास्वादसक्ताश्च शक्ताः ॥ ४२४ ॥

अपिच । मत्तश्चन्द्रादित्यौ शतमखमुखाश्चेन्द्रभुजः पुरद्वारेयस्याः सभयमुपसर्पन्त्यनुदिनं । प्रकोपव्याकम्पन् खरनख पुटैर्वानरभटैः समाक्रान्ता सेयं हरिहरिदशग्रीवनगरी ॥ ४२५ ॥ इत्युक्त्वा ।

शुकशारणौ तिरस्कृत्यरामं प्रतिदूतप्रस्थापना । ततः प्रविशतिनिकुम्भः ।

सूत्र । आदायलेखं दशकन्धरस्य गत्वानिकुम्भोऽखिलरूपधारी । ददौरघूणां पतयेपुरस्तादुपेत्यगाढा रभटी पटीयान् ॥ ४२६ ॥

स्वस्तिश्री दशकन्धरस्त्रिभुवनव्यापि प्रतापानलो व्यामुग्धं लिखतीन्द्रवज्र-भिदुरोरामं वनावासिनं । आनीताजनकात्मजा खलुमया सुग्रीवसेनान्वितो नेतुं वाञ्छसि मूढतापसकथं प्राज्ञैःपरिक्रीडसे ॥ ४२७ ॥

वाचिकं । इन्द्राद्यास्त्रिदशा विलोक्यसमरे यं विद्रवन्तिद्रुतं तं त्वं तापसरावणं क्षयमहोयोद्धुं किमुत्सार्द्धसे । अज्ञस्त्वं प्रतिपक्षराक्षसमुखेमोक्षात्परं मा-ऽस्याः सीतायाविनिवृत्य याहिभवनं गत्वेति शीघ्रं वद ॥ ४२८ ॥

अहमपिब्रवीमि । रेरेतापसमूढ रावणहृतामुद्धर्तुकामः प्रियां किं लङ्काभिमुखं प्रयासिकपिभिः प्रोत्साहितः कातरैः । कोयत्नं कुरुतेच पन्नगपतेर्रत्नं फणामण्डला दाक्रष्टुं सहसा सचेतनमतिः स्वश्रेयसं चिन्तयन् ॥ ४२९ ॥

अपि च । यच्छित्त्वा मुदितः शिरांसि कृतवानर्घ्यां भवानीपतेर्यस्याज्ञावशवर्त्तिनोऽमरगणा यः सर्वमायानिधिः । यः कैलासगिरिं भुजैस्तुलितवान्यः काल दर्पापहस्तं त्वं तापस दुर्बलैर्जलनिधिं बद्ध्वा कथं जेष्यसि ॥ ४३० ॥

अन्यच्च । यावन्नायाति रुष्टः प्रलयघनघटाघोरनादैर्विचित्रैः संग्रामं कुम्भकर्णस्त्यज समररसं रामसीतां विहाय । आयाते कुम्भकर्णे तव कपिसहितस्यापि सेनाविदूरान्नस्थातुं शक्यते तत्प्रलयजपवनश्वासवातावधूता ॥ ४३१ ॥

अत्रावसरे मन्दोदरी समागत्य स्वगतं ।

कैलासशैलोद्धरणप्रवीणो वीरः कुबेरानुज एक एषः । तथापि रामाजितबालिवीर्य्यः शङ्कास्पदं संप्रति राक्षसानां ॥ ४३२ ॥

अपि च । यद्दूतो हरिपुङ्गवः समतरद्दुर्लंघ्यमम्भोनिधिं दुर्भेद्यां प्रविवेश दैत्यनिवहैः संप्रेक्ष्य लङ्कापुरीं । हत्वा तान्वनरक्षिणो जनकजां दृष्ट्वा च भंक्त्वा वनं हत्वाक्षं प्रदहन्पुरीं गत इतो रामः कथं वर्ण्यते ॥ ४३३ ॥

प्रकाशं । रामोऽयं रविवंशजो दशरथक्ष्मापालचूडामणेः पुत्रः सर्वमहीश्वरैर्नरगणैः संपूजितो रक्षणात् । सीताहारिहतान्तको निजभुजप्रौढप्रतापानलस्त्रैलोक्यस्य हितार्थसाधनविधौ जानासि नैनं कथं ॥ ४३४ ॥

समागत्यारविन्दमंत्रिब्रूते । देव त्वां प्रति संप्रति प्रतिभट क्षोभं न कर्म्मेऽवयं दैवायप्रतिपद्यते हितमिदं यस्मादयं मंत्रिणः । सीतारक्षणलक्षणाहतधनुर्लीलापिनोलङ्घितो हेलोल्लङ्घितवारिधिः कपिबलैः सार्द्धं स रामो महान् ॥ ४३५ ॥

यत्सन्देशहरेण मारुतसुतेनातारि वारांनिधिः क्षिप्रं गोष्पदवन्निजालय इव प्राविशि लङ्कापुरी । सीता दर्शि समभ्यभावि निखिलं चाभञ्जि रक्षःपतेरण्यं त्वत्पुरतो व्यदाहि च पुरी रामः कथं मानवः ॥ ४३६ ॥

अथ पुनर्मन्दोदरी ।

एकःसुग्रीवभृत्यः कपिरखिलबलं पत्तनश्चाप्युदध्वा यातस्तूर्णीं तदानीं दशमुखभवनं किंकृतं वीरवर्गैः । संप्राप्तोराघवोसौ सकलकपिबलैः सार्द्धमुल्लं घ्यचाब्धिं सीतांतां मुञ्चमुञ्चेत्यनिशमकथयत्प्रेयसी रावणस्य ॥ ४३७ ॥

इतिसर्वे निष्क्रान्ताः ॥ ॥ इति षष्ठोऽङ्कः ॥

अथ सप्तमोऽङ्कः ॥

ततः सीतामत्यजति युद्धेमनसिकृतेरावणे मन्दोदरी चेष्टा ।

दृष्ट्वाराघवमेवराक्षसकुलस्वच्छन्ददावानलं जानक्यां निजवल्लभस्य परमं प्रेमाग्रमालोक्यच । काङ्क्षन्तीमुभरात्मपक्ष विजयं भङ्गञ्च मुग्धामुहुर्ध्यायन्तीद्वय मन्तरालपतिता मन्दोदरी वर्त्तते ॥ ४३८ ॥

ततःप्रविशतो रामसुग्रीवौ ।

अथ रामः सुग्रीवंप्रति ।

लङ्काप्रस्थापनायोग्यः कोऽस्तिवीरोमहाबलः । राजवंशोद्भवोविद्वान्सम्मतेयः कपीश्वर ॥ ४३९ ॥

सुग्रीवो रामंप्रति ।

*राजवंश्योमशूरश्चकश्चित्शूरोनभूमिभुक् । राजपुत्रोगुणैर्युक्तःश्रान्तो भ्रातृसुतोऽस्तिमे ॥ ४४० ॥

सूत्र । रामःसुबेलाद्रितटेनिषस्मः समुद्रमुल्लंघ्य विकीर्णसैन्यः । लङ्काधिनाथस्य गृहाय दूतं सुरेन्द्रनप्तारमथादिदेश ॥ ४४१ ॥

अथ दौत्येन प्रस्थापितो लङ्कांप्रविश्याङ्गदः ।

गत्वा ताराकुमारः प्रथममभिनवं सौधमुल्लंघ्यभित्तिं पादाघाताद्बभंज प्रलयजलधरध्वानगम्भीरघोषः । एतत्कस्मादकस्मादिति चकितदशग्रीवमुद्भाव-यन्त्राकुर्वन् दूतानपूर्वान् बहिरभवदथ द्वारगः किञ्चिदूचे ॥ ४४२ ॥

रे राक्षसाः कथयत क्वसरावणाख्योरलं रघुप्रवरयोरपहृत्य नष्टः । त्रैलो-क्यदीपन शरोग्रशिखाकराले कोरामदावदहने भविता पतङ्गः ॥ ४४३ ॥

राक्षसाः । मागास्तिष्ठ बहिर्व्रज त्वमपिस्थित्वा पुनर्गम्यतां यत्रास्तेभुज विक्रमाखिलजगद्विद्रावणोरावणः । अस्यैवाङ्गदवाऊपाश पतितोमूढः किमाक्र-न्दसे सिंहस्याग्रमुपागतं मृगमिव त्वां कः परित्रायते ॥ ४४४ ॥

अथावलेपादङ्गदे राक्षसश्रेणिधूमकेतौ रावणसिंहासनमधिरूढे । राव-णाङ्गदयोरुक्ति प्रत्युक्ती ॥

कस्त्वंवालितनूद्भवो रघुपतेर्दूतोऽस्मि वालीतिकः कोवा वानरराघवः समु-चितं ते वालिनोविस्मृतिः । यद्बाहून्तनितान्तबद्धवपुषः संमूर्च्छितस्य ध्रुवं मा-सादर्पमिवक्षमुर्विरहयन्नामःकथं विस्मृतः ॥ ४४५ ॥

श्रुतमप्यर्थंक्रोधातिशयात् विस्मृत्यसरावणः ।

कस्त्वंवालितनूद्भवः कुतइहश्रीराम संप्रेषितावार्त्तां ब्रूहि हनूमतः सचक दाराद्यो भयान्निरस्तनः । तद्ब्रीतेर्वद कारणं दशमुखं साङ्कं सपुत्रानुगं हत्वाचेन्नगतो निग्रन्थवनं चित्रार्पितारावसाः ॥ ४४६ ॥

रावणः । रेरे वाम्यासि कोसिवा पुनरिहगतः कस्यदूतः किमर्थं विस्पष्टं विश्वपामांविजयिनमपिमां मन्यसेत्रंतृणाय । अङ्गदः । रुद्रैपौलस्त्यसूनो तव

बलमथनसुतात्मजोऽहं सुवेलात्प्राप्तो रामदूतो विरुद्ध मदमते जानकीं वाप्यशून्या ॥ ४४७ ॥

पुनरङ्गदः । येनैकेनशरेण सप्तनिहताःतालाः धनुस्त्रुटितं बद्धोवारिधिरेष तातमपिमे यः प्रापयत्पञ्चतां । तद्भृत्यं खलुविद्धि राक्षसपते तत्पादपद्मद्वरजूषो पीनपरागरेणुकलिका जाताङ्गदश्चाङ्गदं ॥ ४४८ ॥

तयोःपुनरुक्ति प्रत्युक्ती ।

रामः कोनामजेता जयति भृगुपतेः कस्ततादृक्भृगूणां यज्जन्मख्यातिपन्नं प्रभवतिविदितस्तस्य यादृक प्रभावः । योहन्ताहैहयेन्द्रप्रभृतिनरपतेः कस्तदाहैहयोवा व्यक्तं जानीहि यस्त्वां सुचिरमगमयत्क्रूरकारं निकारं ॥ ४४९ ॥

रावणः । कस्त्वं वन्यपतेः सुतोवनपतिः किन्नाममामाग्रे वदे देवाःश्रवणरोग मामम गृहेनित्यं स्वदास्येस्थिताः । रामः किंकुरुते कपीन्द्रपृथुकैः संलंघ्यरत्नाकरं चेदायाति मदीयदर्पदहने सस्यात्पतङ्गोपमः ॥ ४५० ॥

अङ्गदः । रेरे रावण रावणानपिबहूनेतान्वयंशुश्रुमस्तत्रैकः किल कार्त्तवीर्य्यनृपतेर्दोर्दण्ड पिण्डीकृतः । एकोनर्त्तनलम्भिताङ्गकवलोदैत्येन्द्र दासीभृतैरन्योमत्पितृबाहुमूलगलितस्त्वं तेषु कोन्योऽथवा ॥ ४५१ ॥

रावणः । दोर्दण्डास्तइमे त्रिलोचनगिरेरुत्तम्भसम्भाविताःतान्येतानि दशाननानिदशभिर्दिग्भिस्तथाविश्रुतिः । यस्याद्यापि सएव वीर्य्यमहिमा तस्मिन् पुनस्तापसे श्रोच्यःसोऽपिरिपुः सचापिकुपित स्तस्यापिदूतःकपिः ॥ ४५२ ॥

अङ्गदः । दोर्दण्डातिप्रचण्डत्र्यम्बकधनुर्भञ्जनविधौ प्रौढदोष्णां सहस्रच्छेदक्रीडाप्रवीर स्थिरपरशुमहागर्वनिर्वापकस्य । दूतोऽहं राघवस्य त्वदपघनचिरावासकष्टायशोभः पुत्रःसुनामसूनोः प्लवगबलपतेर्नामतश्चाङ्गदोऽहं ॥ ४५३ ॥

रावणः । भ्राता मे कुम्भकर्णः सकलरिपुबलप्रायसंहार हेतुः पुत्रो मे मेघनादः प्रहसितवदनो येनबद्धः सुरेन्द्रः । लङ्का मे चन्द्रहासो रणमुखचपला राक्षसा मे सहायाः सोहंगीर्वाण शत्रुस्त्रिभुवन विजयी रावणो नामराजा ॥ ४५४ ॥

अङ्गदः । रे रे रावण कार्त्तवीर्य्यदलिताहङ्कार गत्वा स्वयं सीतामर्पय पाशयखतनयान् यावन्नरामःशराम् । कोपान्मुञ्चति हैहयाधिपभुजश्रेणीमहाकाननच्छेतुर्यस्यकुठारधारणपटो रामस्यजेता रणे ॥ ४५५ ॥

तयोःपुनरुक्ति प्रत्युक्ती ।

रामः किं कुरुते प्रतीपविजयं कोसौप्रतीपोजितो वाली सोपिचकोनवेत्सि किमम्ं कोवेत्ति शाखामृगं । श्रावत्नापि तथापि विस्मृतिरहो मोहो महाभीरुणः पर्य्यङ्के निज बालकेलिकृतये बद्धोसियेनोरसि ॥ ४५६ ॥

किंकार्य्यंवदराघवस्य सतथाबद्धः किमम्भोनिधिः क्रीडार्थं कपिपोतकरिह गते जीमात्ययंमांनहि । लङ्कालोक निकायनाथवचसावेत्त्येव किं किं कथेको लङ्काधिपति र्विभीषणइति प्रख्यातकीर्त्तिर्भुवि ॥ ४५७ ॥

रावणः । प्रवीरगणणासुरे तवपितेव कोगंण्यतेपतिः सहिवनौकसां त्वमपि कोवराकोर्भकः । चकारकिलराघवः किमपिकर्मलोकोत्तरं तरङ्गयसियन्मुखं र्ममपुरस्त्वदीयं यशः ॥ ४५८ ॥

अङ्गदः । रामोनाम स एष येनभगिनीनासावसायश्रिलः हङ्कस्वरदूषणत्रिशिरसांधौतः शिरःशोणितैः । बद्धात्वांचतुरम्बुराशिषु परिभ्राम्यन्मुहूर्त्तेन यः संध्यामर्चयतिस्म निस्त्रपकथं तातस्त्वयाविस्मृतः ॥ ४५९ ॥

रावणः । यस्तातं तव निर्व्वलीकमवधी त्तत्रापि निर्म्मत्सरस्तस्य प्रेष्यतयाभ्रमन्कपिशिशो निर्लज्जकिंगर्ज्जसि । त्वत्पित्रेपुनरेकदा किलमया मैत्रीप्रसादःकृतस्तत्पुत्रेत्वयि तावदेवमुचितोदण्डः कथंधीयतां ॥ ४६० ॥

अङ्गदः। प्रपन्नः पन्थानं नयमयमितोन्योपि नियतं निषेव्यःसाधूनां न पुनरपिनीतिः सुहृदपि। तथाह्येनं हित्वा सहजमपिनक्ताञ्च रघमूविरामं श्रीरामं भवदनुज एवैषभजते॥ ४६१॥

रावणः। श्रुतमस्तिविभीषणाख्यकः सहजः सम्प्रतिराममाश्रितः। कतिसन्ति न रामनामकाः कतमस्तेषुसयस्त्वयोच्यते॥ ४६२॥

अङ्गदः। जघान युधिताडकादि कमसीमरक्षः कुलंबभञ्जधनुरैश्वरं परिबभूव तं भार्गवं। स तालतरुसप्तकंसपदि लङ्घवानम्बुधिं बबन्ध न तथापि तेपरिसाङ्गिमितोरघूणाम्पतिः॥ ४६३॥

रावणः। भग्नं भग्नमुमापतेरजगवं वालीहतोऽसौहत स्तालासप्तहताहताश्च जलधिर्बद्धश्वबद्धश्वसः। आः किं तेनसशैलसागर धराधारोरगेन्द्राकुलं ब्रह्मुदस्यतो निजभुजान् जानात्ययंरावणः॥ ४६४॥

अङ्गदः। एकस्त्वया सशिखरी स्वभुजैरुदूढः शम्भोःप्रसाधन विधौदशकन्धरेण। पूर्वंवराहवपुषाम्बुधि मध्यमग्नातेनोद्धृतागिरि सहस्रधराधरित्री॥४६५॥

रावणः। कुतोहन्तारण्ये कनकमृगमात्रं तृणचरं कुतोवृक्षाद्गूढप्लवगिपुण वाली विनिहतः। कुतोवक्रिञ्चालाजटिल शरसन्धान सुदृढंत्वहं युद्धोद्योगी समरमवतस्थेऽन्तकजयी॥ ४६६॥

अङ्गदः सगर्वं। अवेहिमां रावण रामदूतं बाणास्तदीयाः खरदूषणाद्यान्। भुक्त्वातृषार्त्ताइव शोणिताम्भः पास्यन्तिते कण्ठघटैः सरन्ध्रैः॥ ४६७॥

अरे कटुप्रलापिनःपश्य।

मृत्युःपादान्तभृत्यस्तपतिदिनकरोमन्दमन्दं ममाग्रेचाप्यष्टौलोकपाला मम भयचकिताः पादरेणुं चरन्ति। दृष्ट्वामच्चन्द्रहासं पततिसुरवधूपन्नगीनाञ्च गर्भो निर्लज्जोतापसोऽयं कथमिहसमितो धानरम्भेलयित्वा॥ ४६८॥

अपिच । अरे त्वामहं धर्म्मशीलतयाकटुक प्रलापिनमपि नहन्मि । यथो-क्तावादीदूतः स्यान्नसवध्यो महीभुजां । भूरं तदीय कोपेन क्वचिदेहप्यमर्दति ॥ ४६९ ॥

अङ्गदः सवैदग्ध्यं ।

परदारापहरणे नश्रुता यादृशानन । हत्वादूत परित्यागे साधोस्ते धर्म्म शीलता ॥ ४७० ॥

रावणः । बद्धःसेतुर्यदिजलनिधौ वानरैस्तावकैः किं नोवल्मीकाः क्षिति धरनिभाः किं क्रियन्तेपिपीलैः । लङ्कादग्धायदपि कपिनासप्रभावः किलाग्नेः शौर्य्याख्यथं निजभुजबलैः किं कृतंरामनाम्ना ॥ ४७१ ॥

अङ्गदः । रे रे रावण शम्भुशैलमथने प्रख्यातकीर्त्तिर्भवान् रामेणुद्धमिहे च्छतीदमुचितं मन्यामहे केवलं । रामस्तिष्ठतु लक्ष्मणस्य धनुषोरेखापिनोलङ्घिता सप्तारेणच लङ्घितो जलनिधिर्दग्धाच लङ्कापुरी ॥ ४७२ ॥

रावणः । यच्छिन्नाःकिल बाल तालतरवो रामेण सार्द्रत्वचोभग्नं यच्च पुरा-तनंशिवधनुस्तद्वीर्य्यं मुत्तीर्य्यते । नासीदेतदनागतं श्रुतिपथे स्वर्लोकधूमध्वजः पौलस्त्यःकरकन्दुकीकृतहरक्रीडाचलो रावणः ॥ ४७३ ॥

अपिच । अलमप्रस्तुतालापैः श्रुत्वापि ममविक्रमं । इदानीं रघुडिम्भेन वद किं कर्त्तुं मिष्यते ॥ ४७४ ॥

अङ्गदः । स्वसुर्मांसावसानन्न पश्चिमामसिवल्लरीं । कदुष्णैरवच्छिरोरक्तै रामःक्षालितुमिच्छति ॥ ४७५ ॥

रावणः । श्रावः कश्चित्तिरश्चां त्वमसि नविदितास्तेपि कीदृक्प्रभावास्ते

किं मां नोविदन्ति त्रिभुवनजयिनं रामसुग्रीवमुख्याः । तथा किं केनतावन्निज परबलयोस्तारतम्यं विदित्वा सन्दिष्टं दुष्टदूतचरितमवितथं तत्सदावेदयस्व॥४७६॥

अङ्गदः । प्रथमतः श्रीरामपादास्त्वामादिशन्ति ।

अज्ञानादथवाधिपत्यलभनादस्मत्परोक्षेहृता सीतेयं परिमुच्यतामिति वचो गत्वा दशास्यं वद । नोचेल्लक्ष्मणमुक्त मार्गणगणच्छेदोच्छलच्छोणित च्छत्रच्छन्नदिगन्तमन्तकपुरं पुत्रैर्वृतोयास्यसि ॥ ४७७ ॥

कुमारो लक्ष्मणस्त्वामाह ।

सीतांमुञ्च भजस्व रामचरणौ राज्यंचिरंभुज्यतां देवाःसन्तुहविर्भुजः परिभवंमायातु लङ्कापुरी । नोचेद्वानरवाहिनीपतिमहाचण्ड चपेटान्तरैस्तत्सन्मुष्टिभिरेव संगरगतस्तत्तत्फलं प्राप्स्यसि ॥ ४७८ ॥

सुग्रीवस्त्वामाह ।

दृष्टःश्रीरघुनन्दनोमनु बलैर्वीर्य्यैर्मदादपित लङ्केश्वर मुञ्च मानमखिलं श्रुत्वा वधं वालिनः । सीतामर्पय रक्ष राक्षसकुलानिन्द्राधिकंसंपदं तस्माद्रुच्छ्रयास्य रामचरणेदासत्वमंगीकुरु ॥ ४७९ ॥

अन्यच्च प्रधान सेनापतिभिरादिष्टं ।

रेरेरावण राक्षसाधम पयोमग्नोसिशोकार्णवे प्रभुरूपमुपागत स्तमिह किं नोबुध्यसेकेवलं । रामश्चापि कराबलम्बित धनुर्दीप्तोज्ज्वलत्सायकः साक्षादिन्द्रइवा परस्तवपुरद्वारे स्थितःसानुजः ॥ ४८० ॥

अपृष्टोपि त्वामहं पितृबन्धुबुध्या ब्रवीमि ।

रे रे रावण सर्वलोकविदितः श्रीरामनामानृपस्त्वांहन्तुं समुपैति वानर चमूमादाय बद्धोदधिं । तेनाहं प्रहितस्त्वदीयनिकटं मद्वाक्यमाकर्ण्यतां सीतां देहि भजस्व रामचरणौ राज्यं चिरंभुज्यतां ॥ ४८१ ॥

रावणः । मिथ्योत्तम्भितताल विक्रमकथा विस्फारनिस्फारणं तस्यक्षत्रिय डिम्भकस्यचरितैस्खिद्यीयते त्वादृशः । यद्यातस्य मुकुर्महेश्वर धनुर्भङ्गादिकं गायसि प्रायस्त्वविचारतो नमहिमप्रागभावमारोहति ॥ ४८२ ॥

तयोःपुनरुक्ति प्रत्युक्ती ।

भग्नं प्रम्भुधनुर्गुणौरपहृतं संताडिताडका सापिस्त्रीजरिता खरप्रभृतयो व्यापादितास्तेऽर्भकाः । तालाःसप्तहतास्तृणानि किलतेवालीहतो ऽसौकपिर्बद्धो वारिनिधिर्निशाचर इतिश्रुत्वा भवद्रावणः ॥ ४८३ ॥

रावणं निरुत्तरीभवन्तं दृष्ट्वा तदाच्छादनाय प्रविशति प्रहस्तः ।

ब्रह्मन्नध्ययनाय नैषसमयस्तूष्णींबहिः स्थीयतां स्वल्पंजल्प बृहस्पतेजड-मते नैषासभा वज्रिणः । वीणांसंवृणु नारदस्तुतिकथालापैरलं तुम्बरोसीताग्रस्त कभल्लभग्नहृदयः सुस्थोनलङ्केश्वरः ॥ ४८४ ॥

सुस्थोनलङ्केश्वर इति प्रच्छादयितुं पुनः सएवाह ।

प्रतापंसंसोढुं रविरपिदशास्यस्यचकितो निमज्जत्युन्मज्जत्यपरजलधौ नव सहसा । हरिःक्षीरोदान्तर्वसति च हिमाद्रौस्मरहरः सुरज्येष्ठो धाता नहि सरसिजंमुञ्चतितरां ॥ ४८५ ॥

अङ्गदः । रे रे राक्षसराज मुञ्च सहसा देवीमिमां मैथिलीं मिथ्याकिं निजपौरुषप्रकटनप्रागल्भ्यमभ्यस्यसे । एनांपश्यसि किं न किन्नरगणाद्गीत दोर्विक्रमांसेनां वानरभर्त्तुरङ्गद भुजस्तम्भैर्गभीरां पुरः ॥ ४८६ ॥

रावणस्यपुनरुक्तिः । एतेतेममबाहवः सुरपते र्दोर्दण्डकण्डूहराः सोहं सर्व्वजगत्पराभवकरोलङ्केश्वरो रावणः । सेतुं बद्धमहं शृणोमिकपिभिः पश्यामि लङ्कांवृतां जीवद्भिर्नघटिष्यते किमथवाकिन्नामनश्रूयते ॥ ४८७ ॥

अङ्गदः । रे रे रावण दीनहीनविमते रामोपिकिं मानुषः किंरम्भाप्यबला कृतं किमुयुगं कामोपिधन्वी किमु । किं गङ्गापनदीगजः सुरगजोप्युच्चैःश्रवाः किं हयस्त्रैलोक्यप्रकटप्रताप विभवः किंरे हनूमान्कपिः ॥ ४८८ ॥

उपेक्षितस्मृत हनुमच्चरितोरावणः ।

ये नादाह्यिममाग्रतः पुरमिदं यातोवलीलीलया येना मारिच पर्व्वतस्य कुहरं याभार्यैवराक्षसैः । येना भाञ्जिमहावनं कपिवरेणातारिवारांनिधि कागुण्यो भवतां नृपस्य कटकेवीरोऽस्ति किमङ्गद ॥ ४८९ ॥

अङ्गदः । योयुष्माकमदीदहत्पुरमिदं योऽदीदलत्काननं योऽघ्नं वीरममीमरद्विरिदरीं योवीभरत्राक्षसैः । सोस्माकं कटककदाचिदपिनोवीरेषु सम्भाव्यते दूत वेनइतस्ततः प्रतिदिनंसंप्रेष्यते प्रेष्यवत् ॥ ४९० ॥

रावणः । ज्ञातंरामस्यवैदग्ध्यं येनदूतःकृतोभवान् । त्वयिदूतगुणाः कोवातं ब्रावद्धववनेचर ॥ ४९१ ॥

अङ्गदः । सन्धौवावि ग्रहेवापि मयिदूते दशानन । अक्षतोवाक्षतोवापि क्षितिपृष्ठे लुठिष्यसि ॥ ४९२ ॥

रावणः । रेरे पवनकपे सुवेलकटकात्तौ तापसौ वारयप्राणैर्वा विनियोज-यन्निजतनुं गच्छेति शीघ्रं वद । उन्निद्रः समदः समुद्रनिकटे वीरोऽस्तिकुम्भः स्वयं लङ्कालङ्कृतकः सुरेन्द्रभवनाक्राक्षीकृतो रावणः ॥ ४९३ ॥

सूत्र । अयमयमतिदुष्टो हन्यतां हन्यतामित्यभिहितवति को पात्रावण वालिसूनुः । धृतभुज मयरत्नो वृन्द मुद्भूयसौधं चरणतलनिपाते चूर्णयित्वोत्प-पात ॥ ४९४ ॥

अथाङ्गदो रामसन्निधौ कथयति ।

गणयति हितवाक्यं रावणो नैव दर्पात्तव भुज बलवक्रो प्राप्तकालः पतङ्गः । तमयमुदित सेनाचक्र संपूर्णयुद्धं रघुकुलनृपवीर त्वं सुग्रीवैर्विधेहि ॥ ४९५ ॥

इति सर्वे निष्क्रान्ताः । इति सप्तमोऽङ्कः ॥

अथाष्टमोऽङ्कः ॥

पूर्वोक्ताश्चैव चित्रं ।

सूत्र । काकुत्स्थः सविग्रहमङ्गदमुखादाकर्ण्य लङ्कापतेर्वृत्तं सम्यगलंकुलव विभत्रं चक्रे विमर्षं मुहुः । श्लाघ्योऽयं दशकन्धरो मम रिपुर्दुःश्लाघ्य महिक्रमं वदे-द्योन समर्पिता यदमुना मुक्ताचनाङ्कृतिः ॥ ४९६ ॥

रावणागमनं ।

ततो लङ्कायां निजराजमन्दिर शिखामारुह्य रावणः ।

लङ्कायाः शतवानयं हिविक्षतिं दग्धाग्रपुच्छः पुरा सोऽप्येष प्रतिभाति काष सद्दशो नूनं नभस्वसुतः । श्यामः कामसमाकृतिः शरधनुर्धत्ते ससीताप्रियः प्रत्येकं रिपुमेत्यतेति निगदन्पश्यस्थितो रावणः ॥ ४९७ ॥

प्रविशति मन्दोदरी ।

अत्रान्तरेऽश्रुवर्षिं मक्त्वा मन्दोदरी वैरिविक्रावम्बं विज्ञापयति ।

मन्दोदरी । त्वं चाक्षकृत चन्द्रशेखरगिरि भ्रं ताजागच्छन्कः शुनःशक्तजयी रिपुः सरलधीर्नूनं बलीवालिजित् । तत्राजन्नबला बलादपहृता देयास्य सा जानकीलङ्कायां वसतीत्युवाच वचनंमन्दोदरी मन्दिरे ॥ ४९८ ॥
इत्युक्त्वा मन्दोदरीगमनोन्मुखीजाता ।

ततो रावणोनिजभुजाडम्बरं नाटयन् ।

रावणः । किन्तेभीरुभिया निशाचरपतेर्नासौरिपुर्ममहान् यस्याग्रेसमरो-द्यतस्य नसुराश्तिष्ठन्तिशक्रादयः । मद्दोर्दण्डकामण्डलोद्यतधनुः च्छिन्नाःक्षणा-न्मार्गणाःप्राणानस्यतपस्विनः सतिरणे नेष्यन्ति पश्याधुना ॥ ४९९ ॥
निष्क्रान्तामन्दोदरी ।

अत्रान्तरे विरूपाक्षनामामंत्री प्रविश्य ।

जयति जयति देदश्चिदशाधिपमौलि मुकुटरत्ननीराजित पादपीठा-रावणः ।

राजन्मुखसुखावाचोमधुराः बहवनप्रियाः । ताश्चोदयमाः किन्नु नेता-स्य समसङ्गमे ॥ ५०० ॥

प्रियावामधुरावातु खाम्येश्वेवविराजते । शौरश्चोप्रमाणत्नुवाचः सुनव कर्णश्चाः ॥ ५०१ ॥

विभवेभोजनेदाने तिष्ठन्तिप्रियवादिनः । विपत्तौचागतेऽन्यत्र दृश्यन्ते खलु साधवः ॥ ५०२ ॥

अग्रेप्रस्तुतनाथानां मूकतापरमोगुणः । तथापिप्रभुभक्तानां सेाधर्म्यादेव-मुच्यते ॥ ५०३ ॥

यैरेवस्तुतिभिः स्वामीप्राप्यते व्यसनावटं । यत्नान्मूकत्व मापन्नैरुद्धर्त्तुं नैव शक्यते ॥ ५०४ ॥

यावद्दाशरथेर्नपश्यसिमुखं यावन्नपाथोनिधिं शुष्कं यावदिमां नपाकवशगां लङ्कां निरस्ताशकां । यावन्नैव निजानुजस्यचरितं यावत्कुशाङ्कारतां तावन्नाथ लोकनाथदयिता सीतास्वयंदीयतां ॥ ५०५ ॥

रावणोधैर्य्यमालंब्य । मन्त्रिर्विपश्चितां मंत्रोरस्तिमंत्रो विभासितां । यदा कमैक सारायामस्माकमसिवल्लरी ॥ ५०६ ॥

ततः पुनःप्रविशति मन्दोदरी ।

मन्दोदरी । विभीषणोवैरि वनप्रविष्टो निद्रावशः सीदतिकुम्भकर्णः । राजा-भिमानीपतितः कलङ्के लङ्के निमग्नासि गभीरपङ्के ॥ ५०७ ॥

ततोमायां नाटयति रावणः ।

सूत्र । अथदशवदनोयं रामसौमित्रिमाया विरचितशिरसीतेतरक्षयायाता-वदीर्य्य । गद्गदविरतरक्तेप्रेतपर्य्यस्तनेत्रे जनकदुहितुरग्रेस्थापयामासपापः ॥ ५०८ ॥

तद्दृष्ट्वा जानकीसबाष्पं ।

सूत्र । अथदशजनकपुत्रीफुल्लराजीवनेत्रा नयनसलिलधारा वर्षणिर्भिन्नहारा । रमणमरणभीता मृत्युनाकिं नसीताहृदयदहनजातं सन्देहेनाविप्राणं ॥ ५०९ ॥

रामशिरः समधिगम्य हागनदीयहाजगदेकवीर तर्व्विकरोमीतिसीता बहुशोविलप्य ।

सीता । स्फुरतिमधुरवाणी किं नवस्मारविन्दे नयनकमलयोस्तेकोमदङ्के विलासः । अमरपुरवधूनां वल्लभोऽद्यासिभूतोव्रजति परमहंसं सियमाहिष्णुकैसे ॥ ५१० ॥

इतिरामशिरः समाश्लिष्य प्राणवधावं नाटयति ।

सूत्र । आकाशे । नखलु न खलुसीते रामभूपालमौलिः समरशिरसिवध्यो नप्रियस्ते कदाचित् । स्पृश कथमपि मातर्मामिमायारियस्थं हरिहरविहरभ-क्तस्यैममायावतारः ॥ ५११ ॥

ततः प्रविशति सरमा ।

सरमा । विरमविरम शोकात्कोपमानोऽद्यरामः सतनय यमुबन्धुं रावणं मर्द्दयित्वा । बलिभिदुपवनीलःकोमलः कोमलाङ्गिस्त्वदधर मधुपानं स्वीकरि-ष्यत्यजस्रं ॥ ५१२ ॥

रावणः स्वगतं । पुनरपि मायाधारिणा समागन्तव्यमिति तथाकरोति ।

सूत्र । भेरीनिःस्वान शङ्खध्वनि गज तुरगस्यन्दनस्फीतनादैःसानन्दंराक्षसे-न्द्रःकटकभटभुजास्फाल कोलाहलेन । लङ्कामापूर्य्यकामं स्वयमभवदयो राघ-वोरावणस्य छिन्नामूर्द्धं दधानः शिरसिवहभरेश्चे कतः पद्मपद्म ॥ ५१३ ॥

एवंभूतः पुनरप्यशोकवने सीताभिमुखञ्चलेरावणः ।

सूत्र । साक्षादालोक्यहर्षांञ्झटितिकुचतटीभारनम्रापिरामंसोत्थायोदस्त दोर्भ्यां दरविदलित कुचाभोगपेशोन्नताङ्गी । धन्याहं प्राणनाथत्यजरजनिचर च्छिन्नग्रीवांगिगाढंमामालिङ्गाद्यखेदं जहिविरहमहापावकःशान्तिमेतु ॥ ५१४ ॥

आकाशे। मन्दोदरी रघुराघव राक्षसेन्द्रं चुम्बिष्यति त्वमपिवेत्सितुतत्र रामं। जानीहि राक्षसपतिं नहि रामभद्रो मायामयेन वपुषा विदधच्छिरां-सि ॥ ५९५ ॥

ततो रावणःस्वगतं। भवतु रक्षःस्वीषु तापसवधं निहत्यवैदेहीकेलीकथा कुतूहलमनुभवामीति निष्क्रान्तः ॥ इत्यष्टमोऽङ्कः ॥

अथ नवमोऽङ्कः ॥

ततः पुनः पूर्वोक्तयेव चित्रं।

प्रविशतिविभीषणः।

भोभोवीराङ्गदवानरभटा अद्य रात्रौ खलु सावधानैः स्थातव्यं। रावण प्रस्थापिता प्राभञ्जनी राक्षसी निशि शयानौरामलक्ष्मणौ हनिष्यतीति वि-भीषणोवदति।

ततोनिशिप्रविश्य प्राभञ्जनी स्वगतं ॥

उत्खातदारुण सुतीक्ष्णकृपाणपाणिवीराटवीषु निशिनिर्भयतः शयानं। छायासुदर्शन परिभ्रमणेन गुप्तं रामंनिहन्मिकथमद्यवरंवराकी ॥ ५९६ ॥

तद्गत्वाशङ्केश्वमेव निवेदयामीति। निष्क्रान्ता।

ततोलङ्कायाम्प्रविश्य प्राभञ्जनी।

जयतिजयतिलङ्कानाथःराजन्सुदर्शनचक्र भ्रमणेनरक्षितं रामभद्रंनिशि हन्तुं नशक्यतेतस्माद्रक्षसाः प्रातःसमराङ्गणप्रयायिनः कार्याः ॥

रावणः। सत्यमेतत्तथा करोमि। इतिश्रुत्वा निष्क्रान्ता।

अथयुद्धोद्योगप्रविशं।

रामलक्ष्मणरावणाद्यागमनं।

सूत्र। सुग्रीवोराजलक्ष्मीपरिमिलितवपु र्वालिपुत्रःकुमारःश्रीगम्भीरात्मिका मःप्लवगपरिवृढाः प्रौढिमारूढवन्तः। उल्लंघ्योल्लंघ्य लङ्कांजलनिधि परिखीभूत भूरिप्रभावांसर्वे सर्वामखर्वां पिदधुरथ रखे राक्षसान्क्षोभयित्वा॥ ५१७॥

प्राकारकूटादुपलान् पलाशैर्निपात्यमानान् प्रतिगृह्यदोर्भ्यां। तैरेवतैधा-न्वि बभञ्जुरन्वैः प्लवङ्गमाः कम्पकराः क्षिपन्तः॥ ५१८॥

रावणः। श्रीरामस्यकटकं दृष्ट्वा तदागमनदिनं महोदरं पृच्छतिस्म।

महोदरागमनं।

महोदरः। न्यञ्चत्भूवलयं चलत्क्षितिधरं क्षुभ्यत्समस्तार्णवं नश्यद्वैरि वधूविलोचनजलैः प्रावोक्तवर्षोद्गमं। प्रोद्यत्कपिवाहिनी कपिभटव्याधूतधूली पटच्छन्नादित्यपथं कथंनविदितं तद्रामयात्रादिनं॥ ५१९॥

रावणः। क्व राज्यरहितरामलक्ष्मणावाक्रान्तौ।

महोदरः। भ्रूभङ्गाद्बद्धसिन्धू रघुपतिरवताद्वन्दिनावेदितोसौविरूक्षे मातुलस्यत्वपि पुनरनुजेमं निविप्रप्तकर्म्मा। वालोदत्वाङ्गं दृष्टिस्तवभय पिशुने चञ्चले लक्षितोयः सुग्रीवग्रीवबाहुःक्षतचरणभरः सोङ्कदेवायुपुत्रे॥ ५२०॥

रावणः साभ्यसूयं। आःकिमिति पश्यासे पथ्याथमेवाहुवीर्यमिति संग्रा-मावतरणं नाटयति।

अथयुद्धचित्रं ।

योद्धुं वानरराक्षसाः समराङ्गणं प्रविशन्ति ।

अत्रावसरे विभीषणः । संभूयप्रसभं प्रबोधितहरीपुङ्गवैरिवप्रावृता रुद्धा राक्षसयूथपैःशिखिशिखाभङ्गी पिशङ्गोज्ज्वलैः । वैदेहीविरहव्यथैकविधुरः क्लिष्टो-ऽथलङ्केश्वरःसोयं संप्रति राजपुत्रकटकाटोपःसमुज्जृम्भति ॥ ५२१ ॥

सूत्र । आकण्ठं पिशितवपुर्विशालवक्त्राः प्राकारव्यतिकरआगतैककर्णाः । उद्दामे नभसि यथैवसैंहिकेयस्तेरेकोरजनिचरो न्यतर्कि लोकैः ॥ ५२२ ॥

कुम्भकर्णमहोदरःप्राह ।

अग्रेसरी रघुपतेः परिनद्धपाकबिम्बाकपाटलमुखी कपिवीरसेना ॥ निःशेषमापिबतिराक्षस वीरचक्रं प्रातःप्रभैवतपनस्य तमिस्रजालं ॥ ५२३ ॥

युधिहतेषु राक्षसेषु रावणः । भोभोमंत्रिणःप्रबोध्यतां मयमनयग्रजन्मा कुम्भकर्णः ॥ मंत्रिणः । यदाज्ञापयति देवइति तथाकुर्वन्तः ॥

रावणः स्वगतं । न्यक्कारोह्ययमेव मे यदरयस्तत्राप्यसौतापसःसोप्यत्रैवनि-हन्तिराक्षसकुलं जीवत्यहोरावणः । धिक्धिक्शक्रजितं प्रबोधितवता किं कुम्भकर्णेनवा स्वर्गग्रामटिकाविलुण्ठनवृथोच्छूनैः किमेभिर्भुजैः ॥ ५२४ ॥

सूत्र । दत्वासंततनैलानि कुम्भकर्णस्यकर्णयोः । निद्रादरिद्रितं चक्रुःसाम-मात्यपुरोहिताः ॥ ५२५ ॥

प्रविशति कुम्भकर्णः ।

विनिद्रःकुम्भकर्णो राजसमीपमुपेत्य । जयन्तिजयन्तिप्रणमपिशरणपादाः ।

कुम्भकर्णः । यद्यपिच्छितिपालानामनाख्यासर्वमगालयं । तथापिज्ञातृदीयेन नरत्येवमतिःसतां ॥ ५२६ ॥

रावणः । इतिभ्रातृवचःश्रुत्वा तथेत्याहदशाननः । शास्तिनिःसंशयावाचः- सतां व्यसनदुर्लभाः ॥ ५२७ ॥

उत्क्षिप्तस्फटिकाचलेन्द्रशिखरश्रेणीविमुक्ताङ्गदैरेभिः पीनतरैःसुरासुर जयप्राप्त प्रतिष्ठैर्भुजैः । संग्रामेममकुम्भकर्णविजयः किम्वद्भुताडम्बर भ्रात्याम्रा शिथिलोस्म्यहं व्रज पुनःस्वप्नाय निद्रालयं ॥ ५२८ ॥

कुम्भकर्णः । सीताप्रियस्य दलितेश्वरकार्म्मुकस्य वालिद्रुहस्वरचिताम्बुधि बन्धनस्य । रक्षोघ्नस्य विजिगीषु विभीषणस्य रामं निहत्य चरणौ तव वन्दि- ष्ये ॥ ५२९ ॥

किञ्च । देवत्वं राक्षसेन्द्रपरिहर तृणवद्दिशःशोकशल्यं हत्वावैदेहिवृन्दं कलुषमपि परिक्षालयाम्यस्त्रतोयैः । कोरामो लक्ष्मणःकःकहहहरिपतिःकोङ्गदः को हनूमान् कः कालः कोविधाताचलति मयिरणे रोषणेकुम्भकर्णे ॥ ५३० ॥

रावणः । महाबल पराक्रमैर्राक्षसभटैः परिवृतोभवतुवत्सः कुम्भकर्ण- स्तथाकुर्वेति रणशिरसि ॥ कुम्भकर्णोरणमूर्ध्नि स्थितोवदति ॥

कुम्भकर्णः । नाहंवालीसुबाहु र्नखरत्रिशिरसौ दूषणस्ताडकाहं नाहंसेतुः समुद्रोनचधनुरपि यत्त्र्यम्बकस्यत्वयात्तं । रेरे राम प्रतापानलकवलमहाकाल मूर्त्तिःकिंनाहंवीरागामूलशल्यं समरभुविपुरः संस्थितः कुम्भकर्णः ॥ ५३१ ॥

सूत । विघटितवज्रसेनापारिवीरःकपीन्द्रंपरिघगुरुभुजाभ्यां गाढमापीड्यधृ- त्वा। निरगमदतितूर्णंचूर्णयन्पूर्णदिक्कांकपिकुलमकलङ्कग्रासमुखंकुम्भकर्णः॥५३२॥

तच्छ्रुत्वा रावणः । यदर्पितं प्राग्बलेन वालिना विधाय दोर्युग्मबन्धं दशा-
ननं । तदुद्धृतं प्राप्य मनेनमानिना निवेश्य कण्ठाकुहरे कपीश्वरं ॥ ५२३ ॥

गगनमुपेत्य सूत्र । सुग्रीवं बाहुमूले प्लवगबलपतिं कण्ठदेशे भुजेनक्षिप्ता-
निक्षिप्य गाढं रजनिचरपुरीं सन्दधानो जगाम । सानन्दं कुम्भकर्णस्तदनु कपिभट
स्तस्य तूर्णं सकर्णौ घ्राणं जग्ध्वा जगाम स्वशिबिर मुरसः कूर्परेणाहतस्य ॥ ५२४ ॥

निश्वस्योत्सृज्य बाष्पं नयनकमलयोः रात्मनैवाविदित्वा कस्मालङ्केापगूढं
सकलगमपुनर्भ विनीत्वा त्रिशूलं । क्रोधान्धः कालमूर्त्तिः प्रलयकृतवदाङ्कारने-
नावकीर्णश्छिन्नघ्राणोवतीर्णः पुनरपि समरप्राङ्गणे कुम्भकर्णः ॥ ५२५ ॥

तं दृष्ट्वैव प्रविष्टा गिरिवरकुहरं त्यक्तचित्ताः कपीन्द्राः केचित्पादान्तदन्त
प्रचलितपवनान्दोलिताः खे चलन्ति । केचिद्दोर्दण्डचण्डभ्रमणनिपतिताः शो-
णितान्युद्गिरन्ति प्राणान् केचित्प्रवीराः कथमपि जहतिस्फीतफूत्कारभिन्नाः ॥ ५२६ ॥

सुग्रीवागमनं ।

सूत्र । उत्क्षिप्य शूलमजयं त्रिपुरान्तकस्य संहारकेतुमिव कालितहित्प्रभञ्च ।
घोरं ज्वलन्त मुरसि क्षिपति स्मरन्स्तारापतेस्तदिषु मारभुजानिरस्तं ॥ ५२७ ॥

तातं विलोक्य विषमस्थमथाक्रन्दन्तं गाढमतेन भुवि पातयति स्मभग्नं ।
मुक्तोपि निश्वसति यावदसौ कपीन्द्रस्तावत् बबन्धनरसिंहमदाक्रन्दं सः ॥ ५२८ ॥

दृष्ट्वा नीलस्तदुभयमपि प्रस्तमाक्रन्यरक्षः स्कन्धे मौलौ अवयहृदये मध्यम-
क्षोदरेषु । तीव्राक्षेपैर्दहतिकुपितः खे नक्षेपेषवीरः क्रव्यादोऽभूत्तदनु विक-
लः प्रोत्थितौ वानरेन्द्रौ ॥ ५२९ ॥

दम्भोलिः कुम्भकर्णं गिरिमिव तरसा पातयन्नागुबन्धं कण्ठे गाढं विधृत्य सभुज

मुखमदंशात्सवानुग्ररोषः । निर्मुक्तौतावभूताम भवदथमहत्पुष्पवृष्टिः स्वदङ्के भूखाघातेनरोषाद्गजनिचरभटस्तं निरस्योपतस्थे ॥ ५४० ॥

सुग्रीवस्तमवलोक्य रणोज्ज्वलन्तं कादम्बिनी सहचरोऽमृतवारिधाराः । तूर्णं मुमोच तदुपर्य्यथलक्ष्मसङ्गेभोक्तुं कृतान्तइव नीलनलौसदर्थ्यौ ॥ ५४१ ॥

आलोकितोरघुवरेण सलक्ष्मणेन कालान्तकादिवरिपोः परिघाङ्कितेन । स्थानंजगाम हनुमान्समरेऽवतीर्य्यमाहेन्द्रमुग्रनरसिंहइवारुणाक्षः ॥ ५४२ ॥

कुम्भकर्णोहनूमन्तं निबध्यस्वगणावली । रावणायददौभ्रात्रेउपायनमिवा दरात् ॥ ५४३ ॥

कुम्भकर्णेनानीतं हनूमन्तं गृहीत्वाऽशोकवनेरावणः । सीतेपश्यपश्य ।

रावणः । रामःस्त्रीविरहेणहारितबलस्त्वच्चिन्तयालक्ष्मणःसुग्रीवोऽग्रजसूनु सैन्यभयतो विन्ध्यस्यमूलं गतः । नष्टः क्वापिविभीषणः सचरिपुः कारुण्यदैन्यातिथिर्लङ्काद्वारकपाट पेटमपटुर्बद्धोयमेकःकपिः ॥ ५४४ ॥

अथ रावणसीतयोरुक्तिप्रत्युक्ती ।

भविभीरम्भोरुचिरश्रवदन गुणनिरचिरात् सतेरामः ख्यातानयुधिपुरतो लक्ष्मणसखः । इयंशास्यत्युच्चै र्विपदमधुनावानरचमूर्लघिष्ठेदं सत्याक्षरपरविशेरात्पठपुनः ॥ ५४५ ॥

सूत्र । अथचरणयुगं तदङ्कसंस्थापयित्वा खरनखरकराग्रैर्गाढमुत्पाट्यकर्णौ । क्रकचकठिनदन्तैरस्य संरुध्यनासामुदपतदति वेगादुग्रकर्माकपीन्द्रः ॥ ५४६ ॥

सपदिपरिनिवृत्तः क्रोधनःकुम्भकर्णस्तुमुलमतुलमंभोघेघस्त्रं वाता- नीत् । निशितशरनिपातैर्लीलया तस्यरामोनिरभिनदभिलीनं तत्तदङ्गंक्रमेण ॥ ५४७ ॥

कुम्भकर्णमूर्ध्नि पतति हनूमान् ।

धीरंधारयकूर्मराजधरणींसार्द्धं फणिस्वामिना दिङ्नागाः कुरुतस्थिरान् कुलगिरीन् दन्तैर्दृढैर्धरणीं । यस्मादेतदकाण्डखण्डनगलद्रक्तौघ मत्युन्नतं रामशरोत्करैः पततियत्कौम्भकर्णंशिरः ॥ ५४८ ॥

सूत्र । कबन्धेप्रपतति । देवाःसर्वेविमानान्यपनयतरवेःस्यन्दनोयातुदूरं रे रे शा- खामृगेन्द्राः परिहरतरणप्राङ्गणंराक्षसाश्च । वेगग्रस्ताम्बुनाथ प्रतिनिधिवर- धिः सर्वविस्मापकानां लङ्कातङ्केकहेतुर्निपतति नभसः कौम्भकर्णःकबन्धः ॥ ५४९ ॥

उत्क्रान्तोपिस्वदेहात् प्रवरसुरवधूदोर्भिराकृष्यमाणः प्राणत्राणायभर्तुः पुनरपिसमरापेक्षयानारुरोह । संगीतैर्नारदाद्यैर्मृदुमुरजरवैः स्तूयमानोवि- मानं वीरःसंग्रामधीरः शिवशिवकथं कथ्यतेकुम्भकर्णः ॥ ५५० ॥

प्रविशति मन्दोदरी ।

मन्दोदरी । लङ्कानाथतवानुजो युधिहतोरामेणरत्नाकरं संबध्यप्लवगोत्क- थापरिवृतस्तेद्वारिपूर्वंस्थितः । रामेपिस्मृतिगोचरेसतितथानैव रोषान्विता सीतासंप्रतिसंमता किमुभवेत्तत्रैवतूष्णींस्थितः ॥ ५५१ ॥मन्दोदरीनिष्क्रान्ता ॥

रावणः स्वगतं । अहहहतविधे । मरुच्चन्द्रादित्यौ शतमखमुखास्तेक्रतुभुजः सुरद्वारेयस्याः सभयमुपसर्पन्त्यनुदिनं । प्रकोपव्याकम्पाधरतटपुटैर्वानरभटैः समाक्रान्ता सेयंशिवशिव दशग्रीवनगरी ॥ ५५२ ॥

रावणः । सत्वरमाखण्डल खण्डनदृष्टप्रापञ्चमेघनादं दुष्कारसमरायाह्वया तिस्म । मेघनादोपि समरावतरणं नाटयति । वानराःपलायन्तिस्म ॥

प्रविशति मेघनादः ।

मेघनादः । क्रूराःसंभ्रमसमेतै विजहितहरयोभिन्नभल्लैर्भकुम्भायुधाद्दे-

हेमुखन्यांदधतिपरममीसायकानिष्पतन्तः । सौमित्रेतिष्ठपार्श्वं त्वमसिनहि सुधांगन्धहंमेघनादः किञ्चिद्भ्रूभङ्गलीलानियमितजलधिं राममन्वेषयामि ॥ ५५३ ॥

सूत । मायारथंसमधिरुह्य नभस्यसक्षोभगम्भीर घोरघनघटध्वनिबद्धगर्वं। बाणैरपातयदथोफणिपाशबन्धै तौमेघमन्दरगिरीपरिभूतपक्षः ॥ ५५४ ॥

प्रविशति सरमा ।

अत्रान्तरेसरमाराक्षसीरावणाज्ञया रामलक्ष्मणयोरिमां गतिंसीतायैकथितवती । सीता । हेरामभद्रहावत्स लक्ष्मणमदर्थे युवयोरेताहशीगतिः ॥

सीता । किं भार्गवच्यवनकाश्यपगौतमानां वाचावशिष्ठमुनिसोमपकौशिकानां ।
जातानृताप्यहहयाखपितात्वयास्यान्मन्दभाग्यमिव मेसकलंनिहन्तुं ॥ ५५५॥

सूत । अमरपतिजितौतौ नागपाशेनबद्धौ खगगरुडनिपातोन्मुक्ततत्पाशबन्धौ ।
विदधतुरतियुद्धं तत्ररामानुजन्मासितशरहृतजीवं मेघनादंचकार ॥ ५५६ ॥

जनमुखरवार्त्ता श्रूयतेराक्षसेन्द्र तवतनयसुवेषः पातितोलक्ष्मणेन ।
वदतिचदशवक्त्रेदिष्टचित्तःसभायां महाकागरन्ध्रे पक्षियूथं प्रविष्टं ॥ ५५७॥

पुनःप्रविशति मन्दोदरी ।

हतेषुरावणपुत्रेषु सर्वेषु रावणंप्रतिमन्दोदरी ।

हृष्टुं दैन्यंभगिन्याखिशिरस उतवामातुलस्यापिनाशं ताताग्नोभेदनं त्वपिवरहननं तत्रसुग्रीवसख्यं । कर्म्भौखुद्धामहनूर्जंसनिश्चितरयो धामजात हासींसेयंतस्ते कुलेस्मिन् कथमिहकमितुर्जायतेतेविवेकः ॥ ५५८ ॥

अथतोरावणः। रामायप्रतिपद्य कर्णशिखिनेदास्यामिवामैथिलीं युद्धे रावणसायकैरभिहतः स्वर्गंगमिष्यामिवा। नीतिज्ञेकथय त्वदेचिकतरः पन्थो गृहीतस्त्वयातन्मेब्रूहि यथास्मदीयमभवन्मन्माननीयं कुलं॥ ५५९॥

जानामिसीता जनकप्रसूता जानामिरामोमधुसूदनश्च। वधंचजानामि निजेनवक्षः तथापिसीतां न समर्पयामि॥ ५६०॥

प्रविशति यमः।

अथ रावणः। कालमधिक्षिपन्नाह। रेकालत्वमपिकालं वृद्धविभवःसैरं सङ्ग्रामेभवतश्चनेभूषयतांग्रावल्लिरः श्रेणीभिरकुंस्वलं। तस्माद्राघवमेत्यमां स सहसाक्षोभय त्वत्कृतेसंरुद्धः कारवाणभीषणभुजो युद्धायलङ्केश्वरः॥ ५६१॥

हनू। येषंविभीषणेमुक्ता शक्तिःक्रूरेणरक्षसा। लक्ष्मणेनगृहीतासाप्रियेवनिजवक्षसा॥ ५६२॥

अथ रावणशक्तिविद्धे लक्ष्मणेरामविलापः।

रामः। वत्सोत्तिष्ठ धनुर्गृहाणरिपवःसैन्यं विनिघ्नन्तिनः किंशेषेऽथनिद्रा कथाः किमरयःप्रत्युद्गताकिंप्रिया। भ्रातर्देहिवचोऽभीहिहृदयभ्रान्तिंनृपंविद्धिमांकैकेयिप्रियसाहसे सुतवधान्मातःकृतार्थाभव॥ ५६३॥

तातःस्वर्गमुपागतः प्रियसखीदैवेनदूरीकृता सीतादुष्टनिशाचरेणवशिना पत्नी मनोहारिणी। भ्रातासर्वगुणाकरलनिलयः सन्दिग्धदेहोऽधुनादुःखाद्दुःखपरम्परापरिचयं दैवेन नीतावयं॥ ५६४॥

सुग्रीवः। पातालात्समुद्धृतो वसुमतिर्नीतोनमृत्युःक्षयंनोम्मृष्टंमयलाञ्छनस्य मलिनंनोन्मूलिताव्याधयः। शेषस्यापिधरां विधृत्यनकृताभारावतीर्णं ध्वतां चेतःसत्पुरुषाभिमानपदवी मिथ्यैवकिंखिद्यसे॥ ५६५॥

अथ सुग्रीव प्रबोधितस्य रामस्य वचनं ।

भ्रातुर्बहिस्त्रिभुवनेनहि बन्धुरस्ति प्राणाङ्कभागघटितः परिभूसप्नुः । हा
वत्सयद्यितिभुजो रघुनन्दनस्त्वं यास्यसिकाननदनं किमुमांविहाय ॥ ५६६ ॥

महाप्रयमयाहार्द्रं त्वमरण्यमुपागतः । नगच्छामित्वयासार्द्धं नाकमप्यहम
प्यः ॥ ५६७ ॥

सुषेणागमनं ।

सूष । अद्यैवौषधमानेतुं यावद्धातिनभास्करः । कोपिरामसमर्थश्चेत्तदा
जीवतिलक्ष्मणः ॥ ५६८ ॥

औषधानयनप्रस्तावे नलादीनांवाक्यं ।

गवाक्षिरात्रात्पुनरेतिगत्वा तथात्रमैन्दद्विविदौहिरात्रं । सुग्रीवनीलोपुन
रेकरात्रं वीराङ्गदोयामचतुष्टयेन ॥ ५६९ ॥

अथ महौषधिमानेतुं गते हनूमतिरामवाक्यं ।

मातर्निशीथिनिचिरंभव दीर्घयामातातान्धकार वपुषागगनं पिधेहि ।
नाथप्रभाकरवचो नकुरुप्रचारं यावन्नदृष्टि पथमेतिसमीरसूनुः ॥ ५७० ॥

शुकसारणयोरागमनं ।

हनूमतानीतौषधिविशल्ये नसुत्थिते सौमित्रौरावणंप्रतिशुकसारणयोर्वाक्यं ।

हत्वामायामयीं तांरजनीचरवधूंभीमरूपंद्रुदस्थं ग्राहंप्रोन्मथ्यवीर्यात्प्रथ-

मथनंरक्षसां मर्दयित्वा । जित्वागन्धर्वकोटिर्झटिति ततमखिला समाराध्य श्रेयप्राप्तः श्रीमद्धनूमान् पुनरपिभविता लक्ष्मणस्येपुरस्तात् ॥ ५७१ ॥

अथतदाकर्ण्य समरमवरति रावणोरक्षसां कर्णैनाद्यवचः ।

अयमनुक्तवल्ली फुल्लतापिञ्छगुच्छोरगा भुवमवतीर्णः कार्मुकीरामभद्रः । अयमपिदशकण्ठःकुण्ठिताम्भोदशोभः परिकालयतिरामं भ्रान्तकोदण्डदण्डः ॥ ५७२ ॥

रावणः । रेरेवीरप्रवीराः कुशलरणमितः किंपलायध्वमेतैः सन्नद्धीभूयशस्त्रैर्भजतरिपुगणान् कोवकाशोभयस्य । हत्वाद्याहंहनूमद्रणा विजयबलंजाम्बवन्तंचनीलं तान्वाप्रौढाङ्गदादीन् करकलितधनूराम मन्वेषयामि ॥ ५७३ ॥

श्रीरामः । भोलङ्केश्वरदीयतां जनकारामः स्वयंयाचते कोयं तेमतिविभ्रमः स्मरनयं नाद्यापिकिञ्चिद्गतं । नैवञ्चेतात्खरदूषण त्रिशिरसां कण्ठासृजापङ्किलः पत्त्रीनैवसहिष्यते ममधनुर्ज्यावन्धबन्धूकृतः ॥ ५७४ ॥

अथान्तरे रावणहनुमतोरुक्तिप्रत्युक्ती ।

साधुवानरगच्छत्वंश्लाघ्यो जीवसिभूतले । धिगस्तुममजीवत्वंयस्त्वंजीवसिसवण ॥ ५७५ ॥

रामस्यदिव्यास्त्रोपक्रमे रावणवाक्यं ।

आग्नेयास्त्रं हृदयदवथूर्वारुणाः शस्त्रमुख्यैर्धाराबाष्पः पवनपरतां यान्तिनिश्वासदण्डाः । तज्जानक्याकिमपिनकृतंरक्षसां स्वामिनोमेदिव्यैरस्त्रैर्यदयमपरंतापसःकर्तुकामः ॥ ५७६ ॥

श्रीरामः । रेरे निशाचरपतेत्वरितं गृहाणवाणा सनंत्रिदशदर्पहरं शरघ्नं । निर्वापयामिविरहाग्निमहं प्रियाया मन्दोदरीनयनजलप्रवाहैः ॥ ५७७ ॥

रावणः । स्त्रीमाथं ननुताडका भृगुसुतोवृद्धस्तपस्वी द्विजो मारीचोमृगएव भीतिभवनंवालीपुनर्वानरः । भोकाकुत्स्थविकत्थसेकिमधुनावीरोजितःकस्त्वया दोर्दण्डस्तवकथ्यते यदिपुनःकोदण्डमारोपय ॥ ५७८ ॥

अपिच । जातस्त्वंचण्डांशुवंशे त्वमसिपुनरहंपद्मयोनेः प्रपौत्रोराजः क्रूराज्ञाति मेंस्फुरति दशमुखोत्वंकिलैकाननेन्दुः । बाहूनांविंशतिर्मेविफलितकुलिशादोर्युगं निर्जितं तेस्पर्द्धांबध्नासिमोघां रघुतनयमयापौरुषेवाकुलेवा ॥ ५७९ ॥

रामः । सत्यंतेपद्मयोनिः प्रथमकुलगुरुः किन्तुतज्जन्मभूमेः पद्मं सैवोपजी-व्योममतुविजयतेवंशबीजंविवस्वान् । धिक्तेवक्त्राणितानि प्रकटयसिपुरायानि जीवन्मृतानिस्पष्टंव्याचष्टवाली ममयुधिपुरतोबाहुबाहुस्थवीर्य्यं ॥ ५८० ॥

अपिच । छित्वामूर्ध्नः किमितिसवृतोधूर्जटिर्यद्यमीषां दोस्तम्भानांत्रिभु-वनविजय श्रीरियंवाक्तवीति । मूर्द्धानोवा नखलुभवतोदुर्लभाःसंभवेयुर्यद्वेवस्य त्वमसिभवतांश्चिपिनोपिप्रयोगः ॥ ५८१ ॥

अथ श्रीरामदशास्ययोरुक्ति प्रत्युक्ती ।

रेरेदशशिरस्क साधुसमयेभोक्तुं भवानग्रवीर्युद्धेमां पुरतोनिधायभव-तांकिंपृष्ठतोगम्यते । नैवंरामदयानिधेरघुपते रागत्यकर्णान्तिकं पृष्ठान्नेकम-संशयंदशमुखःकिंवध्यएवेत्यसौ ॥ ५८२ ॥

अथ रामेणछिद्यमाने रावणशिरसितं प्रशंसन्जनोप्याह ।

सूत । एतन्नूनंदशमुखशिरः ध्वंसतेकण्ठपीठाच्चक्षुर्धत्ते धनुषिचशरेचैतद्-ग्राह्यहासं । एतद्रामंप्रतिचकुरुतेविक्रमं क्रोधवाचामैतच्चक्रामभिपरतिपुन स्त्री जनान्वाजनाय ॥ ५८३ ॥

तेभूमौपतिताः पुनर्नवनवानालोक्य मूर्द्धोपरान्प्रोच्छिद्यन्त इमेनहीत्यपि परं प्रत्याहृत्य हासंदधुः । येद्यंपूर्विकयाप्रहार मभजन्मांछिन्धिमां छिन्धिमांछिन्धी त्युक्तिपराःपुरारिपुरतोलङ्कापतेर्मौलयः ॥ ५८४ ॥

रामः । हत्वातेदशमंशिरो दशमुखप्रायो नभोमण्डलं दृष्टो देवगणैः समं सुरपतिस्त्रातस्त्वयस्मान्मया । तस्मात्त्वां पुनरन्यजन्मनिरिपुं वाञ्छाम्यहं वाणपन् रामस्तुष्यतिरावणस्यवदनं सीतावियोगातुरः ॥ ५८५ ॥

सूत्र । छिन्नाच्छिन्नानवीना भवदथवक्त्रोराक्षसाधीश शीर्षश्रेणीत्यालोक्य मुग्धे सकलकपिकुलेमातलेर्वाक्यजातैः । बुद्ध्वातंमर्मवध्यं ज्वलित शिखिशिभं ब्रह्मबाणं गृहीत्वा भित्वावक्षःस्थले तंक्षयमनय दथोरावणं रामचन्द्रः ॥ ५८६ ॥

इति रावणवधः ।

रणशिरसिसुरस्त्री मुक्तमन्दारमालं स्वयमथमवतीर्णोलब्धमान्यत्तहस्तः । विरचितजयशब्दोवन्दिभिःस्यन्दनाद्वादिनकरकुलचक्रीसत्कृतोरामभद्रः ॥ ५८७ ॥

नेपथ्ये । सर्वांगीर्वाणवन्द्याः व्रजतनिजगृहान् रम्भमाधोरणाग्राक्स्वर्गेभर्त्त-स्तृष्णासां नयसुरकरिणां यामिकायातदेवाः । भूयादेवद्रुमाणां मनुभवतुवनेमन्द-ने सन्निवेशोदारे छिन्नंयदेतद्दश वदनशिरः किङ्करैरन्तकस्य । ५८८ ।

अथ मन्दोदरी विलापः ।

असुराधिपमयतनया दशमुखपत्नी सुरेन्द्रजिज्जननी । अथमनुकंप्याकपि-भिर्धिग्दैवंविसदृशारम्भं ॥ ५८९ ॥

नाम्भोधिःक्वचसेतुबन्धनविधिःक्वावस्थितिर्भूभृतांक्वप्लेच्छः क्वचराघवोजल-

निधिःपारं कथाद्दुःसहाः। किष्किन्धानगरासिनोऽपिकपयः कैतेनिमग्नाः पारिकाः कार्य्याणां गतयोविधेरपि मनसांवाचांचनागोचरं ॥ ५९० ॥

भुजाग्रजाग्रत्करवालजाल कोलीकृतां खण्डितपन्नगारां। संहारकं हन्त तथाविधन्तुं कोरामभाण्डादपरःप्रवीरः ॥ ५९१ ॥

छिन्नशिरसि शिरांसि यानि रेजुः छिन्नछिन्नतानि लुठन्ति गृध्रपादे। अपि खलुविषमः पुराकृतानां प्रभवतिजन्तुषु कर्म्मणां विपाकः ॥ ५९२ ॥

राक्षसाः। रावणस्यरक्षोभङ्गः पुष्पकस्यपराभवः। कपिभिर्विजिता लङ्का जीवद्भिः किं नदृश्यते ॥ ५९३ ॥

जातोब्रह्मकुलेऽग्रजोधनपतिर्यः कुम्भकर्णोऽनुजः सूनुर्वासवजित्स्वयं दशशिरादेहे सहकाविंशति। अक्षंकामगमं विमानमजयं मध्येसमुद्रंपुरीसर्वं निष्फल मेतदेवनियतं दैवंपरंदुर्जयं ॥ ५९४ ॥

यस्यैषानगरी समुद्रपरिखाकामप्रदंकाननं आज्ञाशक्रशिरोमणिप्रणयिनी त्रैलोक्यराज्यंपरं। छित्वायेन शिरांसितीव्रतपसासंसेवितःशङ्करस्तस्यैषामतिरीदृशी किमपरंसर्वं विनष्टं हठात् ॥ ५९५ ॥

अथ लङ्कार्पणं।

प्रविशति विभीषणः मन्दोदरीच।

अथ मन्दोदरी प्रणामेरामंप्रति विभीषणस्य वाक्यं।

इयमियं मयदानवनन्दिनी त्रिदशनाथजितः प्रसवस्थली। किमपरंदश-कन्धरगेहिनी त्वयिकरोति करद्वययोजनां ॥ ५९६ ॥

रामः । मन्दोदरीवत्सविभीषणपट्टराज्ञी भूयादिमाञ्च परिपालय वीरलङ्कां ।
आज्ञाप्यतं तदिति दत्तसमस्तराज्यं सीतां समीपनयनाय दिदेश रामः ॥ ५९७॥

अथ सतीत्वपरीक्षार्थं अग्निप्रवेशे सीतावाक्यं ।

सीता ।अयंरामःस्वामी तदनुजवरो लक्ष्मणस्त्वयं वायोःसूनुर्धृ तिकरमु-
खावानरगणाः । ममाकारोज्ञातोयदि दशमुखेभाववशगस्तदाहं भक्षीस्यामिति
बिभ्रतिवह्नौरघुवधूः ॥ ५९८ ॥

वचसिमनसिकाये जागरेस्वप्नभावे यदिममपतिभावो राघवादन्यपुंसि ।
तदिहदहममाङ्गं पावनंपावकेदं सुकृतदुरितभाजां त्वंहिकर्मैकसाक्षी ॥५९९॥

वह्नौप्रविष्टायां सीतायां ।

सूत । यदेयासीयाच्चालसनमिव कौसुम्भरजसं कटीदेशे तस्याभवदजवचि
कुङ्कुमकुसुमं।हरिद्रामुक्ताक्षेपणकुचवटे कण्ठनिकटेक्षणानुवैदेह्याःप्रथमपरमये
भूषणमभूत् ॥ ६०० ॥

सीतामुदीक्ष्य सुमुखीं शिखिनः प्रवेशेमुक्तास्तदा सुमनसःसुरसुन्दरीभिः ।
शुभ्रश्रियः सकलखेचरमानिकानां जातोयथाचिरतरं त्रिदिवेमहार्घः ॥६०१॥

वह्नेःशुद्धिविधौतदा भगवतस्तेजोभिरभ्युक्षितैरङ्गानामनसूयया विरचितां
माणिक्यमंविभ्रती । पादाङ्गुष्ठ नखाग्रदत्तनयनामालीवो विनिन्यासमः कोकाको
कमुखीक्षणानु वचसाशाकृनिर्गता जानकी ॥ ६०२ ॥

अत्रावसरे अदुष्टायां सीतायां ।

भग्नं यत्कगुरीश्वरस्य त्रिपुरा यत्नामदग्न्योजितत्त्यक्ता येनगुरोर्गिरा वस-

मतीबद्धोयमम्भोनिधिः । एकैकं दशकन्धरक्षयकृतो रामस्य किंवर्ण्यतेदैवं निर्वय येन सोपिसहसासीता वियुक्तःकृतः ॥ ६०३ ॥

अदग्धायांसीतायां दशरथसमेतानां आकाशेदेवानांवाक्यं ।

विरमविरम रामत्वत्कृतं पवित्रंवयमधिगतवन्तःसाक्षिणोलोकपालाः । किमपरमनलेऽस्मिन् हेमवल्ली वशुद्धाकुल विपुलविभूषां जानकीतेतनोति ॥ ॥ ६०४ ॥

देवाः। विजेतव्या लङ्काचरणतरणीयोजलनिधि र्विपक्षःपौलस्त्योरणभुवि सहायाश्चकपयः । तथाप्येकोरामः सकलमजयद्राक्षसकुलंक्रियासिद्धिः सत्त्वेभवति महतांनोपकरणे ॥ ६०५ ॥

रामोमूर्धिनिधाय काननमगान्मालामिवाज्ञां गुरोस्तद्भक्त्याभरतेन राज्यमखिलंमात्रासहैवोज्झितं । तौसुग्रीवविभीषणावनुगतौनीतौपरां संपदंप्रोद्वृत्तादशकन्धर प्रभृतयोध्वस्ताःसमस्ताद्विषः ॥ ६०६ ॥

त्रैलोक्यविदितस्त्वैतन्नामोच्चारयतिध्रुवं । मैथिलीरामरामेति रामोजानकि जानकि ॥ ६०७ ॥

प्रविशन्ति लङ्कास्थलोकपालाः ।

लोका।अथात्रीमालङ्का मयमियमुदन्वन्त मतरदिवशल्यं सौमित्रेरयमुपनिनायौषधिवरं । इतिस्मारंस्मारं त्वदरिनगरीभित्तिलिखितं हनूमत्संदर्भैर्दशतिकुपितोराक्षसगणः ॥ ६०८ ॥

अयोध्यागमनोद्योगचित्रं ।

सूत्र।हत्वातंरावणंवीरं सीतामादायराघवः । अयोध्यांगन्तुकामोऽभि मुमुदेसहसीतया ॥ ६०९ ॥

सीतांप्रतिरामः ।

यस्यांमणिर्ज्झरित पञ्चिमामर्क्यपादैःक्लासाग्निमाम्बरपतेश्च वसिष्ठ्यासि ।
ख्यावर्त्तवक्त्रकमलं कमलाधिप पश्य लङ्केति तां नवविभीषणराजधानीं ॥ ९१० ॥

अत्रासीत्फणिपाश बन्धनविधिः शक्त्याभवद्देवरे गाढं वक्षसि ताडिते हनुमता द्रोणाद्रिरत्राहृतः । दिव्यैरिन्द्रजिदत्र लक्ष्मणशरैर्लोकान्तरं प्रापितःकेनाप्यत्रमृगाक्षि राक्षसपतेः कृत्ता च कण्ठाटवी ॥ ९११ ॥

सूत्र। वैदेहींसमवाप्यदाशरथिनारक्षःप्रयाणेऽस्यतोहृष्टात्पुष्पकसंस्थितेन रभसादाकाशमारोहता । लङ्कासागर जानकीवनरयश्चोच्चाटी चमत्कारिता जम्बूवल्लम बिन्दुवज्जल जवज्जम्बालवज्जालवत् ॥ ९१२ ॥

अथदहनविशुद्धांतां समादाय सीतांरजनिचरकपीन्द्रैर्वन्दितःपुष्पकेन ।
पुरमगमदयोध्यां मन्त्रियूथैर्मिलित्वा सपदिभरतदत्तां राज्यलक्ष्मींसभेजे॥९१३॥
सर्वे निष्क्रान्ताः ॥ इतिनवमोऽङ्कः ॥

॥ समाप्तोऽयंग्रन्थः ॥

महानाटक शुद्धिपत्रिका ॥

अशुद्ध	शुद्ध	पृष्ठ	पंक्ति
कुमुद	कुमुद	२	४
साम्राज्य	साम्राज्य	२	९
देवासुर	देवासुर	२	१०
बन्ध	बन्ध	२	१२
वाल्मीके	वाल्मीके	२	१५
वाल्मीकिव्यपदेशतः	वाल्मीकिव्यपदेशतः	२	१८
महो:	महो	२	१८
कुवत	कुवत	२	२०
क्षिबो	क्षिबो	३	५
सिद्धौ	सिद्धे	३	११
सम्हितः	सम्हित	३	१५
यौता:	यौताः	४	१
वयं	वयं	४	१
वव	वव	४	१६
कुण्ठिता	कुण्ठिता	५	४
रुचिः	रुचिः	५	९
दारुणः	दारुणः	५	१५
वज्र	वज्र	५	१७
कुर्वन्तितवे	कुवततक्षितवे	६	७
बिभृत्	बिभृत्	६	८
यत्नतो	यत्नतो	६	१८
बभूव	बभूव	७	१५
प्रमद	प्रमुद	७	१७
माम्बा	मौम्बा	८	११
कुम्भान्	कुम्भान्	९	११

अशुद्ध	शुद्ध	पृष्ठ	पंक्ति
कार्ष्णेव	कार्ष्णेंव	१०	१
निह्वपम	निरुपम	१०	८
निह्नन्तं	निहन्तुं	१०	१०
दाशरथिः	दाशरथिः	१०	१२
युष्माकं	युष्माकं	१०	१४
क्षितिभजां	क्षितिभुजां	१०	१८
वद्धो	बद्धो	१०	१८
वाक्य	वाक्य	११	६
साक्षात्मकरध्वज	साक्षान्मकरध्वज	११	७
वृक्षम	वृक्षम	१२	४
कमयी	कैमयी	१३	१२
विम्भागो	विग्भागो	१५	७
विम्बला	विद्रुषा	१५	१७
पातं	विपातं	१९	९
किंभ्रमो	किं भ्रमो	२०	१७
क्षतो	क्षतो	२०	१८
राघवेन	राघवेण	२३	७
बुद्धा	बुध्वा	२४	२
वाक्येन	वाक्येन	२४	४
पश्चाता	पर्यश्चाता	२४	१६
नपस	तपस	२६	२०
वुद्धि	बुद्धि	३०	१६
यया	यता	३१	१
वर्हिर्व	बर्हिर्वं	३१	१२
गमना	गमना	३१	१८
कुट्टनैः	कुट्मलैः	३२	२
वत्ति	वर्ति	३३	१३
जोवितु	जीवितुं	३३	१७
मन्त्यचन्द्र	मन्तंचन्द्र	३४	१४

अशुद्ध	शुद्ध	पृष्ठ	पंक्ति
हाहा	हा	३५	१
सार्ध	सार्धं	३५	६
मान्यक्रागा	मान्याक्रना	३७	१०
सामित्रे	सैामित्रे	३८	१२
रामचन्द्र	रामचन्द्रः	३९	६
वेलाबलाका	वेलाद्बलाका	४०	८
किष्किन्धा	किष्किन्धां	४१	१०
भीयम	भीषय	४१	१४
वृच्या	पृष्ट्वा	४२	१६
बोत्कर्ष्यं	स्रोत्कर्षं	४३	८
भुवन्तं	ब्रुवन्तं	४३	११
आम्बुवतो	जाम्बवतो	४४	२
मभत्	मभवत्	४६	२२
रघूत्तमन	रघूत्तमेन	४७	१८
मासाद्य	मासाद्य	४८	७
आम्रोद्यान	आम्रोद्यान	४९	८
सत्तिरण्य	सत्तेरण्यं	४९	१५
गर्व	गर्वं	५२	३
यारत्	यावत्	५२	६
धूंव	ध्रुव	५३	११
याटिक	स्फाटिक	५३	२४
ताचिः	तार्चिः	५३	१७
बः	बोः	५४	१२
पाले	पालेः	५५	३
कबिः	ऋषिः	५६	४
यथा	हया	५७	१०
प्रासान्दास्य	प्रासान्दास्या	५८	१८
तुष्काब	तुष्कोष	६३	१०
विभीषवं	विभीषयां	६४	१०

अशुद्ध	शुद्ध	पृष्ठ	पंक्ति
——	सुग्रीव	६४	१४
शुष्कात्पद	शुष्कात्पद	६५	६
मद्दन्तः	मदान्तः	६५	९
मधोक्ष	मैधोक्ष	६५	१२
भ्राति	भ्रांति	६७	१
उदूत	उद्भूत	६८	७
बच्छवा	बच्छिता	७१	१
रामा	रामो	७१	८
ध्रूव	ध्रुव	७२	१०
प्रेषिता	प्रेषितो	७३	१६
पोतक	पोतके	७५	२२
बन्ध	सन्धिबन्ध	७६	११
तथारेव	तथारेव	७७	१२
प्रभुकी	प्रभु को	७८	१६
कटक	कटके	८०	१५
कोपाग्रावक	कोपाग्रावके	८१	४
तमय	समय	८१	९
युद्धं	युद्धे	८१	९
वदेही	वैदेही	८१	१४
पीठा	पीठो	८२	१३
पुत्र	पुत्रे	८७	३
क्ते	के	८७	७
यत्नमक	कथमाक	८८	१७
काटि	कोटि	८९	१३
वाक्यं	वाक्यं	९४	९
पीठायधु	पीठायधु	९६	१८
रामपुष्पति	रामपुष्पति	९७	६
वऊझो	वऊझो	९७	७
भब्दो	भब्दो	९७	१२

अशुद्ध	शुद्ध	पृष्ठ	पंक्ति
सुरेन्द	सुरेन्द्र	९७	१७
भाद्रा	भद्रा	९८	४
देवं	दैवं	९८	११
मालि	मौलि	९९	१६
मूर्धि	मूर्ध्नि	१००	१०
स्तद्भक्त्या	स्तद्भक्त्या	१००	१०
रत्वे	रत्ने	१०१	७
	अनुक्रमणिकापत्रे।		
स्तोत्रि	स्तोत्रिय	——	७